A GRAMMAR OF THE LANGUAGE OF BURMAH

A GRAMMAR OF THE LANGUAGE OF BURMAH

THOMAS LATTER

GYAN

Published by

Gyan Publishing House
5, Ansari Road
Daryaganj, New Delhi-110002
Phone: 011-47034999, 9811692060
E-mail: books@gyanbooks.com

Distribution Network
gyanbooks.com
India, USA, Canada, UK, Australia, France

ISBN : 978-81-212-4395-7 (PB)
First Published, 1845

2nd Impression 2020

Printed at: Gyan Press, Delhi.

A Grammar of the Language of Burmah
Author: Thomas Latter

A

GRAMMAR

OF THE

LANGUAGE OF BURMAH,

BY

THOMAS LATTER,

LIEUTENANT, BENGAL ARMY.

῞Εχω καλά τε φράσαι, τόλμα τέ μοι
Εὐθεῖα γλῶσσαν ὀρνύει λέγειν.

Olymp. *Carm.* xiii.

῎Εστι δὲ φῦλον ἐν ἀν-
θρώποισι ματαιότατον,
῞Οστις, αἰσχύνων ἐπιχώ-
ρια, παπταίνει τὰ πόρσω,
Μεταμώνια θη-
ρεύων ἀκράντοις ἐλπίσιν.

Pyth. *Carm.* iii.—PINDAR.

CALCUTTA:

SOLD BY MESSRS. THACKER AND CO. AND MESSRS. OSTELL, LEPAGE AND CO.

LONDON:

MESSRS. SMITH, ELDER AND CO. AND OSTELL, LEPAGE AND CO.

TO THE

RIGHT HON'BLE LIEUT. GENERAL SIR HENRY HARDINGE,

G. C. B. &c. &c.

GOVERNOR GENERAL

OF

INDIA

THIS ENDEAVOR

TO PROMOTE THE ACQUIREMENT OF THE VERNACULAR DIALECT

OF ONE OF THE NUMEROUS PROVINCES

UNDER HIS SWAY,

AND THEREBY TO BENEFIT A LARGE PORTION

OF

BRITISH SUBJECTS,

IS,

BY PERMISSION, INSCRIBED

BY HIS OBEDIENT SERVANT,

THE AUTHOR.

PREFACE.

" What ought to have been the course pursued by the British Rulers? Certainly it was their duty, first, to have ordained that the language, and character of the country, should be that of the courts of Justice."—*Shore's Notes on Indian Affairs.*

It would perhaps have been more adviseable that this work should have gone before the public without the accompaniment of a Preface; but this will be the more readily excused, when it is borne in mind that through its medium may be brought to public notice, and perhaps to that of those persons in whose hands lie the remedial powers, the existence of a system as liable to the perversion of justice, as it is discreditable to the present era of British rule in India; and that is, the circumstance, that though the provinces on our South Eastern Frontier, conquered from the Burmese, have been for twenty years under our sway; their Courts of Law are conducted in a language foreign to that of the Inhabitants. If this system was found so objectionable as to call for its abolition in the Courts of Law of Hindoostan, where the Omlah or Native officials were of the same religion as the Plaintiff and Defendant; it becomes a glaring evil and a crying injustice in the case of our Burman fellow-subjects, who, as untrammelled as ourselves by caste, have not, like us, the vantage ground of place or the prestige of a ruling name to shield them from the religious prejudices of the Hindoos and Musalmans who compose the Omlah of the Courts at whose bar they are obliged to sue for justice, and by whom any complexion may be given to their case.

In the numerous discourses handed down to his followers by that great Reformer of his age, Gaudama, though dwelling upon the various moral and social duties incumbent upon mankind, as parent and child, in language too as forcible and beautiful, at times also in words almost identical with those found on the same subject in the scriptures of the Christian; he still urges more particularly the necessity of rulers dealing justice, with impartiality and the greatest care, to their subjects. Among the various circumstances which he declares are likely to pervert justice, he instances the four states of mind. "Listen well," he says, "to both parties in a suit, and then let your decision be in conformity to truth and justice. Avoid the four states of mind; the state of covetousness, and the state of malice, the state of fear, and the state of ignorance;" on this last he lays a peculiar stress and adds, "For as a beautiful and wooded landscape, otherwise gladdening and cheering to the eye, is rendered dreary and miserable by the continued mist and sleet of a November sky; so is the uniform and beautiful system of justice rendered vile by the incapacity of a fool, and the want of ability, to grasp the case, of one who is placed in the judgment seat, when deficient in the necessary acquirements."

To make the subject more striking, let us give a general sketch of what the search after justice appears to a Burman peasant, when a British subject. He usually first makes his complaint to the Magistrate, when the latter is engaged in hearing the morning reports of the Police,—if it be a case that does not admit of summary adjudication, he is directed to proceed to the Thannah or Police station, and make his deposition. When there, he finds his story taken from him and recorded in an unknown tongue; finally placed in Court before the Magistrate, he finds every question given, and every answer made known, through the medium of an unknown tongue. And when at last he hears the decision given, whatever may have been his fate, he hastens back to his village with feelings widely different from those with which he left it: in the one instance he endeavoured, as he sped his way, to store his mind with those phrases, which he hoped might most essentially urge his plea; to him, then, the pursuit of justice was identified with the choicest reminiscences of his faith; in the other, it appears a confused and dizzy jargon utterly unintelligible, and carefully to be avoided. And this, then, is all that we, in the full conceit of self-arrogated superiority, have been enabled to give him in return for the sacred "Yoon" of the Buddhist sway.

It was therefore to obviate in a measure the mischief of such a system as at present obtains, and to mitigate the estrangement caused by the thraldom of a foreign tongue, by facilitating the acquirement of the Burmese language, that the author has been induced to draw up the following work; ever bearing in mind those peculiarities and difficulties, which, however naturalised by custom, were found almost insurmountable to him as a beginner; and it is sent forth with a knowledge that it is required and with every hope and confidence that it will be of use to those who require it.

INTRODUCTION.

The physiognomy, character, and traditions of the Burmese people all join in pointing them out as of Tartar origin; but, at what period they were indebted to their Pali neighbours of Hindostan, for an alphabet, we are unable to decide. It is generally supposed that this took place on the expulsion of Boodhism from Hindostan Proper; but, though they may not have earlier received their alphabetical system, many circumstances join in inducing one to consider that the worship of a Boodh existed from the earliest ages in Trans-Gangetic India,* and it is to these

* As the opinion here advanced may appear at variance with that of a most distinguished Burmese scholar, Capt. Phayre, Assistant Commissioner of Arrakan, (as recorded in his notes on the History of Arrakan, published in the Transactions of the Asiatic Society of Bengal;) a few remarks in elucidation may not be considered out of place. Though there is but little doubt that the Boodhism of Gaudama, the last Boodh, was not introduced into the countries beyond the Ganges, till at a comparatively modern period, on the final expulsion of Boodhism from Hindostan, and posterior perhaps to the Christian Era; yet there is every probability that the Boodhism of former Boodhs, existed long previous to that date. A detail of the historical grounds on which this opinion is founded, would be inadmissible in the "Introduction" to a grammatical work; we must confine ourselves, therefore, to the testimony afforded by the language itself. Boodhism acknowledges that there were three Boodhs who lived and died previous to Gaudama; that he, the fourth, revived the antient faith, reformed and purified it of the errors and perversions, that time and negligence had gathered round it, and rendered it more abstruse in its psychology. A fifth and last Boodh, it is believed, will arise,

provinces, through the means of their sacred literature, that we may look forward for much information, not only upon the history of Boodhism as a religion, which has there remained in a great measure free from the extraneous matter with which it is generally found mixed, as with the Demonolatry of Ceylon, the Hero worship of Nepal, and the Fetichism of Hindostan; but also for many occasional lights upon the early history of the Peninsula of India Proper; as the rule of the Brahmin has not penetrated into the provinces beyond the Ganges, and their records have been therefore neither destroyed nor altered.

It is not in the sphere of this Introduction to give a detailed analysis, or a historical sketch, of the language and literature of Burmah. But it is proposed to be confined to a rapid summary of some of its structural peculiarities.

---

who will in like manner revive and reform the faith now fast hastening into decay. In page 89 of the following work it has been noticed that the names of certain numbers in the Burmese language had attributive significations, which could only be accounted for by their allusion to certain tenets of the Boodhist faith, tenets inherent in, and appertaining to, Boodhism *per se*. Although there is not the slightest doubt that the Pali language was introduced into Burmah and India beyond the Ganges, with the Boodhism of Gaudama, yet the Burmese language existed there as a vernacular long previous, for it is not in the slightest or most remote degree connected in structure, idiom, or system with any of the languages of Hindostan. As these roots then are Boodhistical in their allusion, and as they express certain qualities, and ideas, which (especially in the case of the name of the number *nine)* would be required for use in any language, the inference that fairly may be drawn is, that the name of the roots, and the allusion to the religion were coeval. Let us exemplify this in the case of the Pali, an essentially Boodhistical, language: the name of the number "five" *(pegnyatsa)* in the Pali language is composed of the root *pegnya*, which implies "Wisdom, Understanding;" the final *tsa*, is an expletive in very common use in

The distinguishing feature of the Burmese language is, that its roots, and whole system are *monosyllabic;* this at once separates it most markedly from all connection with any of the languages of the West, such as Pali and Sanscrit, which are *polysyllabic* in structure. On the introduction however of the Pali alphabet and literature from Hindostan, a numerous admixture of terms from that dialect took place; but they remain as distinctly extraneous at the present time, as they were at that of their first admission. They are made use of in Burman works for the expression of those metaphysical ideas appertaining to the abstruse psychology of present Boodhism, (that of Gaudama) which neither the Burmese, nor any dialect of modern nations is capable of conveying. Except in

---

the Pali language. It has been shewn (p. 90) that, in the eye of the modern Boodhist, the number 5 typifies the five commandments, in fact the Law. It will be self-evident to the intelligent mind, how naturally that the fulfilment of the Law, was identified with "Wisdom," and "Understanding." Examples might be multiplied to show that it was so, in the minds of the early races of mankind; "Behold the fear of the Lord that is Wisdom, and to depart from evil, that is Understanding." Job c. 28. v. 28. "Give me Understanding, and I shall keep thy Law; yea I shall observe it with my whole heart." Psalm cxix. 34. The same connection between "knowledge, wisdom, understanding," and the precepts of the Law, exist in the Burmese language. The pure Burman term for these five commandments is သိတင်း *thiedengs,* which implies "news, information, &c." and is composed of the root သိ *thie,* "to know, perceive, understand," and တင် *teng,* (with or without the points,) "to contain, hold," &c. whence အတင်း *adengs,* "a measure of capacity, a basket." We shall in the analysis of the root "*Boodh,*" have again occasion to notice the connection between "wisdom, and understanding" as the attribute of, and identified with, a "GOD," and the number "five." The appreciation of that argument of mind which thus gives to numbers a typical value, is one that will greatly assist in raising the veil which now shrouds the mysteries of Boodhism.

comparatively a few isolated cases, these Pali words are never made use of in common conversation; thus စကြ *tsĕkră*, and ဌါန *hṭană*, would not be employed to express severally "a wheel," and "a place;" but their Burman equivalents ဘီး *bhee*, and အရပ် *ărăt*. When brought into use, however, they generally undergo a slight modification in their finals; thus ကာလ *kală*, and စက် *tsĕt*, are Burmanized Pali for ကာလော *kalăŭ*, and စကြာ *tsĕkra*, or in some cases the final syllables are omitted; as ရတ် *răt*, for ရတနာ *rătănă*, "a jewel;" စိတ် *tsiet*, from စေတန် *tsétăn*, "mind, heart;" လင် *lĕng*, "a husband," from လိင်ဂ် *lienggăn*, "penis."

The Alphabet of this language is a circular variety of the antient Nagri or Pali, divided like it into the several classes of Gutturals, Palatals, Labials, Dentals, &c. expressing in the same manner the combination of its vowels with consonants by the use of symbols, and conforming in every way to the *earlier* alphabetical system of Hindostan: but, though the alphabet of Burmah presents all the arrangement of that of a finished tongue, such as the Pali—its dialect offers to our view a language in an early stage of formation, in fact one, which on that account, is difficult of acquisition by a person accustomed only to the grammatical and finished structure of the languages of modern nations; and it affords very many interesting and instructive examples of the various mental reasonings and processes required by man to express his ideas.

All words, taking them generally, may in the Burmese, as in other languages, be divided into two classes, Apellatives and Attributives. The apellatives are noun substantives, including proper names; as လူ *lōō*, "man," ရခိုင် *răkhŏing*, "Arracan," a proper name. The attributives are a class which form the great staple of a language. It must be borne strictly in mind, that, in their radical forms, in this language they express an abstract idea, that is, one without any of its relations or modifications expressed; but an idea of some attribute, that is some quality, fact, deed, act, principle, or peculiarity abstractedly considered; thus ကောင်း *koungs*, implies "good," abstractedly considered; neither substantive, adjective, nor verb. By the use of certain affixes, and, in one or two cases, of prefixes, we are enabled to express the modifications of this abstract quality "good;" as အကောင်း *ăkoungs*, or ကောင်းခြင်း *koungs khyĕngs* "goodness;" ကောင်းသော *koungs thău*, adjective "good:" by the addition of certain other affixes, again, we express the various relations of these modifications of "good;" as ကောင်းခြင်းသဖြင့် *koungs khyĕngs thăhpyĕngs*, "by means of goodness," and so on with the rest.

Again, by taking such a root as ချား *khyas*, and bearing in mind that it implies the active principle of "separation," (the corresponding neuter of which is ကျား *kyas*, or as it is often written ကြား *kras*,) the following instances of its meaning will be the more readily appreciated. ချား *khyas*, when formed into a substantive by the prefix အ *ă*, as အချား *ăkhyas*, implies "an interval," whether of time, or space, as any thing intervening has necessarily the power of causing separation, or separating; exemplifying therefore the substantive fact of the active principle of separation. ချား *khyas*, compounded with တ *tă*, "one," forms တချား *tăkhyas*, "another," because the fact, or principle of being "another," implies "separation," not being one and the same. ချာ *khya*, (without the points of intonation,) implies "alternation, leaving one and taking one, causing intervals," &c., in all of which the idea of the active principle of "separation," or want of uniformity and homogeneousness may be traced; and by a perversity of meaning it implies, "the point where several lines cross each other but preserve their individuality, that portion common to several roads crossing each other," also "a person under whom several others are equally subordinate;" hence, metaphorically, "a rule, or regulation conducive to sociability and good fellowship." ကျား *kyat,* the intransitive form, implies "variegated with alternate bars, chequered, striped," &c. hence "a Tiger," in all of which the inference of want of uniformity, &c. is conveyed. ကြား *krat,* another form of the intransitive, with the heavy intonation, formed into a substantive by the prefix အ *ă,* forms အကြား *ăkrat,* "between, betwixt, a crack, narrow road, gully, fissure," &c. &c. through all of which the intelligent mind may in the same way trace the same idea. ကြာ *kra,* the simple form of the intransitive, implies "separation in time," whether past, or future. Its application in the word ကြား *krat,* "to hear," is not so evident, unless it imply that a thing to be "heard," necessarily implies "separated" from its original source. Though all the roots of the Burmese language by no means admit of so ample an illustration as the foregoing, yet many of its compounds will be the more easily understood, by bearing in mind the force of the original roots. Having digressed thus far to give an idea of the power of these attributives in their pure radical form, we will revert to a further analysis.

We have now before us two words လူ *lōō,* "man," abstractedly considered, and ကောင်း *koungt,* "good," abstractedly considered. It is evident that both these have many relations independent of, and still more in connection with, each other; now the host of these relations that arise, and which are powerfully styled by the Greek Grammarians σύνδεσμοι, and by the Latins *convinctiones*, "binding link or co-fetterings," are expressed in most languages by prepositions, adverbs, &c. or by an inflection of the radical, *(Conf. Blair's Lectures on Elocution.)* but in the Burmese language by certain affixes: a Grammar therefore of this language is nothing but a "Catalogue Raisonné" of these affixes. But, it is singular that many of these *convinctiones*, which are thus used with appellatives and attributives, are themselves nothing but attributives, (and it is probable that all originally were so, though, from the lapse of time, we are unable to trace the word or the metaphysical reasoning that gave rise to the idea.) This fact might be exemplified more or less from all languages; but many affixes in the Burmese language eminently shew it; thus "*to* man," is လူအား *lōō aas;* the word အား *aas,* implying the attribute "force, power, possession." Again လူဖြင့် *lōō hpyĕng,* implies "*by means of, through the instrumentality of* man," ဖြင့် *hpyĕng,* implying "strength, power, force." The past tense of a verb is rendered by the use of the attributive ပြီး *byees,* "done, finished;" as သွား *thwas,* "to go," သွားပြီး *thwas byees,* "gone."* One of the affixes of the future tense is မည် pronounced, and often found written မယ် *may,* and which there is no

* All our ideas may be said to be identified with the Past, the Present, or the Future; even the cases of nouns, as will be shewn hereafter, have in them an inherent idea of time. The *Past* has been to us a possession, and by its reminiscences in a measure now is; the *Present* we possess, but the *Future* we are deficient in.

doubt is a dialéctic variety of မဲ့ *mąi,* (pronounced with a light intonation) "to be without, be deficient in ;" as it is evident that if an attributive be future when used in connection with an appellative, such appellative must at that same time be deficient in the attribute implied by such attributive; as a boy that *will* be good, or is *going to* be good, is evidently not a good boy.

To develope this idea more fully, if we trace the progress of written language, we perceive in its earliest stage, when the sketch of an object represented it *ideographically,* a *hand* was drawn to convey the idea of "hand." But when it was found necessary to convey the idea of attributes, which have no external form of their own, certain objects were considered as imbued with certain attributes; thus a *lion* was sketched to represent "valor;" a *lamb,* "meekness:" in this second, or *symbolic* stage, a *hand* would aptly represent "force," "power," "instrumentality." The third process was the *phonetic* stage, where certain marks represented certain sounds: generally external objects were made to represent the initial sounds of their names; thus we find a *lion* representing the letter "L." *(Champollion Gram. Egypt.)* In this third stage to continue our example a *hand* would be drawn to represent an "H." So in the case of the Burmese language, although adapted to a comparatively modern alphabet, its antique structure shews it as of a most early date; though the instrumental case is not *symbolically* represented by the word "hand," its *symbolic* character is *phonetically* preserved in the word ဖြင့် *hpyĕ̜ng,* as shewn in the example above quoted. Many words in this language may be said to be a translation of symbols, as the term used to convey the idea of "truth," "exactness," is မှန် *hmăn,* "a looking glass, a mirror." A curious instance of mental reasoning that occurs in this language, and the resolution of which I leave to my readers, is, that although perhaps there may seem to be no two ideas more distinct than "similarity," and "dissimilarity," the "being similar" and the "being dissimilar;" yet they are rendered in Burmese by the same root, with this only difference, that in the one case the root is in its *active*, in the other in its *neuter* or *intransitive* form; when active ထူ *htōō,** implies to be "dissimilar;" when neuter တူ *tōō,* implies "to be similar." From whence we may infer that in their metaphysics "dissimilarity" is considered a *positive*, "similarity," a *negative* quality; or to continue the idea, it requires *action* to procure ourselves the attribute of "dissimilarity," and *inaction* to remain possessed of "similarity."

It has been truly remarked by all writers on the subject, how unphilosophically the term "Noun" has been applied to an adjective, and that the adjective and the verb are identically the same. With this difference, however, that the attribute expressed by an adjective is always present in time, and present, that is indicative, in mood or manner; whereas that of a verb varies from past, present, and future, with their various modifications. This is admitted in the Burmese language, ကောင်းသည့်လူ *koungː thee lōō,* and ကောင်းသောလူ *koungː thăŭ lōō,* imply a "good man," a "man possessing the attribute of present goodness." To conform as

* The presence of the mark of heavy intonation does not in any way affect the derivative radix of this word. The nature of these marks, and the misapplication of the term "accents" to them will be pointed out below.

much as the subject will allow to the phraseology of English grammar these affixes သည် *thee,* and သော *thău,* when in such positions, are styled "relative increments," or "connective affixes," but they will likewise be found mentioned (what they in reality are, and nothing more) as affixes of the *present* time: in the same way they are used with attributives of action; as လာသည်လူ *la thee lōō,* or လာသောလူ *la thău lōō,* "the coming man," or if the same words are transposed လူလာသည် *lōō la thee,* "the man is coming." We see this idea in the same way carried out in the use of the affix ၏ *ee,* which is at the same time an affix of the *possessive case,* and of the *present tense;* thus ငါသည်ဥစ္စာ *gna thee ŏŏtstsa,* or ငါသောဥစ္စာ *gna thău ŏŏtstsa,* imply ဥစ္စာ *ŏŏtstsa,* "goods," affected with the *present* attribute of ငါ *gna,* "the first person singular:" ငါသည်ဥစ္စာ *gna thee ŏŏtstsa,* implies then the "goods which are mine;" ငါ၏ဥစ္စာ *gna ee ŏŏtstsa,* implies again, the "goods of me," both synonymous; for it is evident that possession implies an idea of some thing present, in hand.

We will now enter into detail on the various parts of speech, and point out how they, or their relations, are expressed in the Burmese language.

Articles.—Like the Latins, the Burmese have none. When "*a*" is used to imply *one,* the numeral is employed; and when "*the*" is used with emphasis, the demonstrative pronoun is made to supply its place. But when the appellative လူ *lōō* is found by itself, the context only can shew whether it implies "*a* man," or "*the* man."

Number.—The next point connected with appellatives is number. The Burmese, like most other nations, acknowledge but two numbers—the singular and the plural. The noun by itself implies the singular, but, in the formation of the plural, we find one of the many instances of peculiarity that enable us to decide with precision the comparative age, or perhaps, to speak more correctly, the metaphysical age of this language. The *singular* number was ideographically represented among the early nations of the world by a *single* representation of the object, the *plural* was in the same manner implied by a *repeated* representation of the object, *twice* for the dual, and *three times* for the plural.—*(Champol. Gram. Hieroglyph. passim.)* In the Burmese language the plural of a noun is often to be expressed by reduplicating the root. And the only affix of number which it has, for appellatives, and which may be applied in all cases, is the attributive ဒို့ *dō̤*, which is the same root as ဒိုး *dōs*, "to increase, multiply." It may not be out of place here to remark, that almost every step in our analysis of this dialect admits of being illustrated by the method used by the antient Egyptians in representing their ideas, as handed down to us in the sculptured reliques of their country.

Gender.—Gender is strictly confined to those appellatives, which imply objects distinguished by sex, and is usually expressed by affixes referring to the sexual difference; such nouns as *virtue, house,* are not held to be of the neuter gender, but are considered of no gender at all. We find, according to Champolion, *(Gram. Egypt,)* that the masculine of an animal was often found expressed by the addition of a "phallus" to the representation of such animal; thus a donkey with a phallus painted over it implied a male donkey. In the Burmese language likewise, the word သို *thō*, "penis," is often affixed to the names of animals to express the masculine of such animal.

Cases.—The cases of appellatives are expressed by the use of certain affixes, the attributive signification of which, may, in some instances, be traced, whilst in others they are lost. These affixes, which correspond to the prepositions of case, in other languages, have a peculiar application in this, and one which demands a somewhat detailed analysis. That is, that these *causal* affixes, or affixes of *case*, are used to express the *times* of attributives. This peculiarity of application depends upon the fact that those relations of appellatives styled their cases, and which are expressed by prepositions, imply "direction in *space*;" either direction *from*, or *to*, or position *in*, which is nothing but a point in a direction: in the same way the corresponding relations of attributives imply "direction in *time*;" either *from*, or *to*, or position *in* "time;" and both so perfectly correspond as mutually to express one another.* Thus the pre-

* We see here a novel, and curious illustration of one of the least understood portions of the physics of the human mind. Every thing to be truly viewed must be viewed in two lights: 1st, *per se*; 2dly, *per aliis*. A piece of ice for instance, viewed in the first light, would be nothing more than a mass composed of certain elementary substances, and occupying a certain space. In this point of view certain functions of the mind being exercised on it, its relations of *space*, or in the phraseology of Grammar, its *cases* are eliminated. It is then a substance, substantive; and may be said to be negative, and quiescent. When however it is viewed as an antecedent, or a consequent, or in other words in reference to the varied changes of which it is the agent, or the object; it is then that its energies are awakened, and its qualities elicited; the mass of ice becomes cold, heavy, transparent, fusible, &c. &c. In this state, the same functions of the mind being brought to bear on it, its relations of *time* are eliminated. It is then an attribute, attributive. But in both the object is *one*, and the mental functions the *same*. In this latter state the effects of comparison are evident, but they exist just as certainly, although perhaps not as evidently, in the other; for no appreciation of the idea of a substance, or of an attribute can exist without causality,

positions "from," "in," "to," may be said to be severally "past," "present," and "future:" or to place them categorically; We come *from* the *past*, we are *in* the *present*, and we go *to* the *future*. We find therefore in the Burmese language many instances of this; the causal affix မှ *hmă*, "from," is applied to a verbal root to express the past participle; thus ပြော *pyău*, "to speak," ပြောမှ *pyău hmă*, "having spoke;" with မှာ *hma*, "in," ပြောမှာ *pyău hma*, "speaking," "while speaking." In the same way the prepositions "with," "together with," express the *present*; "by," "by means of," express the *past*. Though the English language affords no direct instance of the use of prepositions, in connection with verbals, to express *time*, yet the preposition "to" is employed to convey the future signification inherent in the infinitive mood, and which, in many languages, the Burmese among the rest, can only be rendered by the future tense. The Burmese generally add the prepositions "to," "in order to," "for," &c. with the future tense to express the infinitive mood. We find, however, instances in the English language, in which

---

which is nothing but a phase of comparison; and as has been remarked by an eminent philosopher (*Brown, Phil. of Human Mind*) "form, and power if considered "separately from the number of elementary corpuscules, and from the changes "that arise successively, are equally abstractions of the mind, and nothing more." The analysis of the curious questions that must arise is foreign to the purpose to which we are confined. But it may be asked will the knowledge of either of these two states enable us to ratiocinate the other, or do they point to a third, an original, of which we have no means of appreciating the existence. Would the possession of another sense gift us with the perception of the identicalness of the rich ideality and gorgeous imagery by which the poet builds his rhyme,—with the common place realities of those material substances which surround our every day path through life; in fact the point of identity of the contrary, and the impossible.

time is expressed entirely by a preposition; as, for instance, the word "time" conveys in itself no definite idea of either *past, present,* or *future;* if however we say "*from* time, *to* time," we immediately give the idea of *past,* and *future;* in the same way "*from* everlasting, *to* everlasting." We may perceive, therefore, some incorrectness in the following definition given by Blair of the power of the infinitive mood; "the Infinitive Mood may be called the name of the verb; it carries neither time, nor affirmation, but simply expresses that attribute, action, or state of things, which is to be the subject of the other moods and tenses." That author has drawn some of the most powerful illustrations of his subject from holy writ—on this, likewise, might he have found one, in Hebrews, c. 13. v. 14. "For here we have no abiding city, but seek one *to* come," i. e., that shall come.

It will be observed also how the tropical use of prepositions, is made, in the English language to vary so as to adapt them to their relative ideas of time; thus "*from* fear, *through* fear, and *for* fear," all imply the "*instrumentality* of fear"—but they are correctly used thus; I *ran* (past) *from* fear of being late: I *run* (present) *through* fear of being late; and I *shall* run (future) *for* fear of being late.

The following definition of the various cases (as it bears on the subject) is copied from *Zumpt's Latin Grammar,* a work of some authority; the part between inverted commas is the quotation, the remainder are remarks in illustration.

"The Nominative case has been defined to be the subject of a proposition"—hence it implies something proposed, indicated, and placed before us and therefore *present* in its nature; as is shewn by the use of the nominative affixes သည် *thee,* and ကား *gas,* to express the *present.*

"The Accusative is the object *to* which the action tends, and *in* which it terminates; as the cause to the effect, the agent to that acted on"—hence it implies both progression "*to*" and arrival "*at*" or "*in*;" being both *present,* and *future* in its signification; both of which are shewn in the use of the locative causal affix မှာ *hma,* "in," to express the *present,** and သို့ *thō,* "towards," to express the *future.*

"The Dative denotes the remoter object to which the action of the subject refers, not immediately, but *to* which the action is directed, and *for* "(i. e. in order to arrive at) which something is done"—hence it is *future* in its signification, as is shewn in the use of the causal affixes ငှါ *gnha,* "for," and ကြောင့် *gyoung,* "on account of," to express the *future.*

"The Ablative" (here alluded to as the instrumental case) "denotes the instrument by which the subject of the verb operates,"—hence it implies something *done, past, perfect,* as the active power of the instrument must be complete, before the subject of the verb can operate. This is shewn by the use of the causal affixes မှ *hmă,* "from," က *gă,* "from," and သဖြင့် *thăhpyĕng,* "by means of," to express the *past.*

Pronouns.—The three personal pronouns ငါ *gna,* သင် *thĕng,* and သူ *thōō,*

* It may be here noticed, as it has been accidentally overlooked in the body of the work, that the locative affix ၌ *hnŏit,* "in" is likewise found expressing *present* time, but chiefly in negative clauses, such as မစားဘဲ၌သွားသည် *mă tsa: bhai hnŏit thwa: thee,* "(he) goes without eating."

corresponding to the first, second, and third persons, have no gender in this language. As the two first refer to persons in the presence of, or otherwise in communication with each other, the distinction of gender is not necessary: as the third is never used except in connection with, or allusion to, some appellative that has preceded it—its gender is satisfactorily settled by such allusion. In this, however, as is the case in most other eastern dialects, so many appellatives are used in the place of pronouns, that such words, as "your slave," "my Lord," &c. have been classed, when so used, as pronouns; and these of course are subject to the accidents of gender.

Adjectives.—As these express, as has been before remarked, only the *present* attribute of an appellative, they are confined in the Burmese language entirely to that use. All the accidents of case, gender, number, &c. belonging exclusively, to the noun substantive, the adjective does not express them; thus the adjective attribute ကောင်းသော *koungsthăŭ*, would be equally applicable to a *masculine*, *feminine*, *singular*, or *plural* noun. The degrees of comparison, and other peculiarities of this part of speech are fully detailed in their proper places in the following pages. But it will be necessary to remark, as it exemplifies the philosophical structure of this language, that, correctly speaking, there are only two absolute degrees of comparison. For instance, to take the case of such an adjective, as "good," 1st, there is the assertion of the *positive* attribute or quality "good;" 2dly, the assertion of the *comparative* quantity, "more," or "less." The first is what is called in the general parlance of grammars, the *positive* degree of comparison, (a term which in itself is a contradiction). The second, if the comparison be "one" against "one" or in other words between "two," is what is in the same way styled the *comparative* degree of comparison; but if the comparison be "one" against "many," it becomes according to the same phraseology the *superlative* degree of comparison. If however, this idea be philosophically analysed, it will be found that "comparativeness" exists as evidently in the one, as "superlativeness" does in the other: for if this man is *better* than that man, he is the *best* man; and if that man is *best* he is "de facto" the *better* man. The Burmese language appreciates this; for the way in which it expresses, what we term the superlative degree of comparison, is by the use of what is styled by us the comparative degree, but placing the noun, against which the comparison is asserted, in the plural number, and using in connection with it the preposition "in," "among," or some such similar one;—thus for the comparative degree, ဤလူသည်ထိုလူထက်သာ၍ကောင်းသည် *ee lōō thee htō lōō htĕt tha rwẹ́ koungः thee,* "this man above that man excels and is good;" for the superlative degree, ဤလူတို့တွင်ထိုလူသာ၍ကောင်းသည် *ee lōō dọ̄ dwĕng htō lōō tha rwẹ́ koungः thee,* "this man, among those men, excels and is good." It must be remembered that we are now speaking of the superlative as (what is called) a degree of *comparison,* in fact of the "*best* man;" not as a mere *positive* assertion of quality, a "*very good* man."*

Numerals.—In combining a numeral with a noun, a peculiarity ob-

* These remarks, should be borne in mind, whilst perusing p. 86. et seq.; as also that the sentence (4th line from bottom in that page) beginning with "When the superlative comparison, &c." ought to have commenced a new paragraph.

tains in this language,* which cannot be thoroughly appreciated unless we bear in mind, the mental process gone through in forming a language. Man, in a first attempt at naming all the objects around him, would find it utterly beyond his power to give to each individual object its proper term at once; his power of memory alone would be insufficient. But he would be led, (in order to reduce the number of names required) to group them as it were in classes; thus all animals would have a term in common, all liquids one to themselves, and the same with all solids, &c. The next process would be subdividing these larger classes, by bringing together those that had any similarity to each other; thus among solids he would remark that there were some of a round shape, some long and narrow, &c.; among animals he would observe that there was a large class which were quadrupeds, and others which were distinguished by the possession of wings. At length as his memory strengthened by familiarity with these objects, and his mental powers became enlarged, he would be enabled to give to each object its proper individual appellative name.† The Burmese language may be said to

* This peculiarity exists likewise in the other Indo-Chinese languages, as the Malay, and Siamese.

† This is exactly what Blair *(Lectures on Elocution)* and some of the more antient philologers, have theorised would take place, and it is singular that their views should be borne out by the corroboration of an existing tongue. Some writers on the subject, however, have reversed the order, and speculate that first arose the knowledge of the individual instance in the Species; that the accumulation of these formed the Genus; then followed in succession the Order; Sub-class; and Class. But the fact is that the one is the process gone through by man possessing knowledge, the other by man without it. In the instance before us, viz. the formation of language

be in a transition between these two last processes. In combining a numeral with an appellative, the term implying its genus is likewise superadded; as "two horses," would be expressed "horse, two animals;"* "two dollars" would be rendered "dollar, two flat things:" and even when the appellative is used without a numeral, the term implying its class, is often superadded; as စာငှက် *tsa gnhĕt*, "a sparrow," from စာ *tsa*, "sparrow," and ငှက် *gnhĕt*, "bird;" နှစ်လုံး *hneet lŏŏns*, "the

---

by man in an early age, the process is that of the ignorant, for to him, then, objects and ideas are introduced for the first time. The second was the inductive mode pursued by Linnæus in his classification of Nature. And even now in the search after knowledge and in discoveries in natural history, the process is that of the ignorant, the attainment of an individual name. In the case of any new plant that may come to hand, first we determine the class, then the sub-class, the order, genus, and finally close with the specific instance of the individual, giving it, should it be an unknown species, a proper name. The strange torturing of sound that any work on natural science exhibits in its nomenclature, bears witness to the process that is urging us on in our destiny, that of the ignorant, the search after a specific name. The curious similarity that exists between the nature of man in the mass and man in the individual, has been the subject of frequent remark; the infancy of the one seems but an exemplification of the earli-hood of the other. But in no particular is this more striking, than in their attempts at conveying their ideas; the dialect of the one being as crude and unformed, and leaving as many chasms to be filled up by induction, as does the prattle of the other. One among the many instances is the predilection in archaic dialects for onomatopœia. In the same way how frequent are the examples that fall from the lips of a child, of such compounds as moo cow; baa lamb; dickey bird, &c. &c.—the latter member of the compound it is aware of from instruction and it becomes the generic determinative, whilst the former is identified to its infant mind, as the distinguishing appellative of the individual.

* It may perhaps be said, in support of the other view of the question, that in the example before us in the text of "horse two animals," the individual name "horse" was known first,—and the generic term "animal" was the after-thought. But this

heart," from နှစ် *hneet*, "heart," and လုံး *lŏŏns*, "rotundity." These affixes, to which the name of Generic Affixes has been given, are identical with what Champollion styles the "déterminatif générique," which he considers was in use among the antient Egyptians; (*Conf. Gram. Egypt. p.* 82, *et seq*) although it does not appear to have been used by them in connection with numerals, but merely to point out the genus, and thus assist in determining a phonetically expressed appellative. Another instance of how, in an early stage of language, the names of objects were assigned to them in connection with some assimilation of form, is in such compounds as လက်သီး *lĕt thees*, "a fist," (which abound in the Burmese language) compounded of လက် *lĕt*, "the hand," and အသီး *ăthees* "a fruit," from the similarity of shape.

It may be here the proper place to remark whilst on the topic of generic affixes, that a system of a kindred nature exists, in this language, in the case of attributives. The Burmese seldom, it may be said never, especially in writing, make use of a simple verbal root to convey the idea of an attribute, but add one, or more cognate ones to complete and determine the signification. One example will be sufficient to explain this peculiarity. The simple verb "to choose" would be rendered by ရွေးကောက် *rwésgouk*, compounded of ရွေး *rwés*, "to choose," and ကောက်

could not be the case; as, if it was only required to convey the idea of "two individuals," the proper terms for which were already perfectly familiar, it would be a work of supererogation and merely conducive to confusion, to instance the genus; whereas in reality being only but partially accustomed to the individual *Nomen*, they hasten, after asseverating it, to fall back, as it were, in reliance upon the old familiar term, which thus becomes the Generic *Cognomen*.

gouk, "to pick, or peck," as a fowl whilst eating; and still further to exemplify the singular kindredness of these two facts,—if in the first instance the names of external objects are often given to them on account of some assimilation of idea in the way of form, so in this is the term of the attributive applied on account of some assimilation of idea in the way of power; for the two roots ရွေး *rwés,* and ကောက် *gouk,* are both taken, severally, from two appellatives signifying "small *(peckable)* grains or seeds." In this case likewise it is singular that, according to Champollion, there seems to have been a similar mode of expression in use amongst the antient Egyptians; *(Conf. Gr. Egypt, pp. 366, et seq.)* where he classes certain representations of external objects as the different determinatives of verbs. In the case before us, of the connection of idea between "picking and choosing," and "rice grains and small seeds;" the one is what he would call the "détérminatif tropique," tropic determinative, (determinative by means of trope) of the other; thus in page 373 of his work, the tropic determinative of the phonetically expressed verb "to labor," he declares to be "a plough."* And it is to be doubted whether

* Whilst every enquiring mind cannot but feel gratified at finding the opinions of Champollion, which have by many been looked upon as visionary, thus corroborated by existing instances which no one can gainsay; it becomes lost in admiration at the transcendent acumen and surpassing intuition of that wonderful man. For though, in the case of appellatives, he might have arrived at the conclusion of "Generic determinatives," by means of the ratiocinating process, we have gone through in the paragraph headed *Numerals;* yet in this instance, of attributives, the case is in nowise similar, for mere reason is at fault. How simple and easy is our analytical path in comparison to that trod by Champollion! It would not be consistent with our subject, but yet a most instructive and interesting occupation, to go systematically

there is a single instance of verbs, in the Burmese language, for which a parallel case might not be made out by means of homonyms.

Before dismissing the subject of Numerals, it will be necessary to mention that the mode of forming Ordinals from Cardinals, in the Burmese language, tallies singularly with that obtaining in the Coptic, and of which a parallel according to Champollion existed among the antient Egyptians; with this difference, that according to the genius of the several languages, the one was prefixed, the other affixed. In Coptic a cardinal number was rendered Ordinal by having the root ⲙⲁϩ *mah,* "to fill up," prefixed; in the Burmese language it is done by affixing a root of a cognate signification, viz. မြောက် *myouk,* "to raise." A further identity and connection in the way of meaning of these two roots is shewn by the circumstance, that when combined severally with the words ϩⲏⲧ *hēt,* and ဝမ်း *wŏns,* both implying "belly," they express "a happy, contented and benevolent state of mind;" thus ⲙⲁϩⲧⲛϩⲏⲧ *mahtnhēt,* "to be merciful," and ဝမ်းမြောက် *wŏns myouk,* "to be pleased, gentle."*

through the two languages, and draw a continued parallel between them; as has been in a measure done above. The identities of ideas and system that exists, especially in the case of these "determinatives," would be remarkable, and the one would corroborate the other. The French hierogrammate seems to have looked upon these "determinatives," as merely placed in connection with phonetically expressed appellatives, and attributives for the purpose of assisting in determining their names; whereas it is probable, from what has been shewn above, that the cause of their connection arises from a deeper source, and originated in the structure of the language and the similarity of their sounds.

* The stomach, and bowels seem to have been considered by the antients as the seat of the affections, as evinced by the frequent use of the Hebrew רחם and the

Verbs.—We have already remarked that all the relations of our ideas are imbued with, or have in them, the inherent feeling or idea of time. There are only two simple ideas which go towards the making a sentence complete; viz. the idea of the thing, which is the *Noun,*—and the idea of the attribute, which is the *Verb.* The relations of a noun are its cases; these have been already shewn to express in themselves the idea of "time," either Past, Present, or Future. The relations of a verb are its tenses, moods, and voices. The Tenses of a verb speak of "time" for themselves. With reference to its Moods: the Indicative indicates or places the mode of its state or action before us, and is therefore *present* in its nature; thus သည် *thee,* is the assertive affix of the indicative mood, (p. 136,) and is likewise the affix of the present tense (p. 134). The Imperative mood is *future* in its signification; thus in the clause "go to the ant thou sluggard," it neither implies that the state of "going" *has been gone,* (past,) or that it is in the *act of going,* (present,) but that it *is to be gone,* (future;) thus we find the future tense forming an imperative in the Burmese language *(vide* p. 137). The Potential mood "could" or "can" is *future,* for, if the "going" *had been gone* (past) or was in the *act of going* (present), it would be unnecessary to asseverate that it *could be gone* (future). The Subjunctive mood "should," and

---

Greek σπλαγχνον, and γαστηρ. But the instance in point is interesting, as it introduces us to the style of reasoning adopted in the formation of a rude and imperfect tongue; for the idea is evidently taken from the soothing effects that the sense of repletion has upon the nervous system, inducing a desire for rest and a dislike of exertion either in mind or body.

the Optative mood "would," at once express the *futurity* of their time, being tenses of the future verbs "shall" and "will." The times of the voices of a verb are exemplified in its participles, the active participle "loving" being a *present* participle, and the passive participle "loved" being a *past* participle.

We have already had occasion to notice the philosophical principles on which are based the structure of this language, and in no point is it more strikingly the case, than in the mode in which it expresses the various relations of its verbs. The first thing that is evidently requisite is to asseverate the action or state, the idea of which we wish to convey; for instance "going." The mind having appreciated this, next enquires whether this "state of going," is one of "singular going," or "plural going." Having then satisfied itself, that it is an act of "plural going;" the next in the category of requisites is to know, whether there is any peculiarity or modification in this state of "plural going." Suppose then, that its mode is Optative; having realised the idea of its being a "plural state of would be going;" the next enquiry is concerning its time, whether past, present, or future. This point having been satisfactorily settled; every condition to a perfect and systematic appreciation of the idea becomes fulfilled. But supposing that, after stating the fact of the "going," the speaker were to declare that it was a "*modal* state of going;" the hearer might justly enquire, whether it was a "modal state of *singular* going," or a "modal state of *plural* going." Again, if the mere fact of its being a "*future* state of going" were to be asserted; the question might be asked, is it a "future state of *singular* going," or a "future state of *plural* going?" and if a "future state of plural going," is it a "*modified* state of such plural going," or not? Thus then, we perceive that true philosophy requires, that after stating the *verb*, we should mention its *number*, then its *mood*, and finally its *time*. This is strictly followed out in the Burmese language; the affix of number being always attached to the root, the affix of the mood coming next, and lastly the affix of the tense; as in the clause သွားကြနိုင်ပြီး *thwas kyă hnŏing byees*, "(they) could have gone." How much more force do we give, to these identical words, if we accord them the order above stated; "gone (they) could have."

Accents.—These have been so styled, at page 20 of the following work, in order to conform, as much as the subject would allow, to the phraseology of European grammar; but they by no means perform the duties of accents in the usual acceptation of that term; being nothing more than what their name imports in the language, မြိတ် *myeet*, "stops;" affecting in no wise the sound of the vowel, but merely regulating the length of time on which it is to be dwelt on. They appear to be nothing but diacritical marks or points brought into use, at comparatively speaking a modern period, (after the adaptation of the language to an Alphabet); and apparently for the purpose of giving some definite distinction to the numerous homonyms that occur in it. In the following pages the same system of punctuation, in reference to these marks, has been, with few exceptions, followed as that adopted by preceding writers on the language.

Having in the detailed analysis (given in the preceding pages) of the peculiarities of this language, as they obtain in its parts of speech, had occasion, although a modern dialect, to exemplify the antiqueness of its structure by drawing a parallel between it, and the mode in which the antient Egyptians expressed their ideas;—the question must naturally arise to the mind of the intelligent reader; Whether any roots in the Burmese language are either derivable from that of antient Egypt, or exhibit any probability of having originated from the same source? To resolve this question we must class our knowledge of the dialect spoken by the antient Egyptians under two heads. 1st, that which is afforded us through the medium of the modern Coptic; and 2ndly, those rare terms which we find dispersed, few and far between, in the pages of antient authors.

With reference to the first, there appears to be no particular similarity either in sound or meaning, between the roots of the Coptic and those of the Burmese language; at least none that might not accidentally have existed between any two dialects quite unconnected with one another.

But in the case of the second, viz. those few Egyptian terms, that have come down to us, scattered through the pages of autient authors, a most surprising identity exists in some of them. Their counterparts may be traced in the Pali and Sanscrit language, but less like the original than when found in the Burmese dialect. They are—

ဘုရား *bhŏŏras*, pronounced *Phra.* This is the usual term of compellation by which the Burmese address superiors; and implies any object of reverence or respect. The similarity between this term, and that given by the Egyptians to the Sun, viz. ⲡⲓⲣⲏ and ⲫⲣⲏ was remarked by the late Doctor Leyden. This word consists of two separate roots; ⲡⲓ *pi*, or ⲫ *phă*, being the masculine article,* and ⲣⲉ or ⲣⲏ *rhe*, or *rha*, implying "Sun." It may be doubted, however, whether the expression that, "this was the name by which the Egyptians worshipped the Sun," conveys the correct idea of the light in which they, at all events originally, held that luminary. It was probably, like the rest of their deified ideas viewed as the symbol of "royalty" and "kingliness;" and thus it became, like the Burmese ဘုရား *bhŏŏrai*, *phŏra*, or *phra*, the cognomen of their kings; פרעה *phrah*, "Pharoah." This interpretation of the power of the root ⲣⲉ ⲣⲏ seems warranted, not only from its being the predominant root running through the words ⲉⲣⲣⲁ *erra*, and ⲟⲩⲣⲟ *ouro*, implying "king," in Coptic; but likewise that the syllables *re*, *ra*, &c., form the staple of the terms implying "king," "royal," &c. in almost all the eastern and western dialects; as *rahe*, *rajah*, *rex*, *roi*, *rey*, *ra*, &c.†

* Omnia nomina masculina uno ex his quatuor signantur articulis; ⲡ, ⲡⲓ, ⲫ, ⲫⲓ, Kircher. Prodr. Copt. p. 294.

† Another corroboration of this view of the question is that the *coiffure*, or cognisance peculiar to Phra, was, 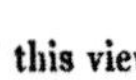 being a solar disc, with a uraeus, aspic, basilisk, or king-snake twined round it; the latter being the acknowledged type or symbol of "royalty," among the ancient Egyptians. A still further corroboration is offered in the analysis of the group 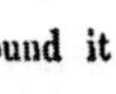 which is found over the *cartouches* containing the names of certain kings; and which has hitherto been rendered "son of the Sun:" the first, "a goose" being the acknowledged *symbol* of the idea "offspring," the other "a solar disc," being held as the *figure* of the idea "Sun;" thus one is translated *symbolically*, the other *figuratively*. Whereas, if *both* were translated symbolically, and the "solar disc" was considered *symbolic* of the idea "king;" the group, according to us, would be rendered "son of a king;" which seems the more probable, as it appears that

ဗုဒ္ဓ *bŏŏddhă.* This is the Burmese mode of writing the term Bood, or Boodh. But previous to entering on its analysis, the reader's attention is drawn to the following extract from the "Essay on the Literature, &c. of the Burmas," by Dr. Buchanan.—*Asiatic Researches, vol.* 6, *p.* 260. As it gives a summary of the dialectic variations of this root.

"In the Pali language, and among the Cingalese, a common name for this divinity" "(i. e., Gaudama)" is Bouddha. This Mr. Chambers writes Buddou; Paulinus, Budha; and from these two authors I have collected the following corruptions of this name. Budda or Butta, of *Beausobre*, and *Bochart*, Bod, of the *Arabians*, Bodda of *Edrisi*, βουττα of *Clemens Alexandrinus*, and Baouth of *M. Gentil.* This name is said to be an appellation expressive of wisdom. I can readily agree with these two learned men, that the Pout, of the *Siamese*, Pout, Pott, Poti, Pot of the natives of Thibet, and the *Chochin Chinese*, may also be corruptions of Bouddha.* The Siamese painter told me that the most common name for Godama, among his countrymen is Pouttee Sat, which he interpreted into Bura Loun, a common appellation among the *Burmas*. Among these indeed I very rarely heard Bouddha

---

this title is only found in connection with the names of those princes, who *inherited* their thrones, and not those who founded dynasties of their own. We have entered at some detail into the analysis of the word *Phŏra* or *Phra;* as we shall have occasion again to revert to the connection in the mind of early nations between the idea of "king," and that of "sun."

* Although there might have been some doubts on this point at the time when the above was written, seeing that *then* next to nothing was known of the Booddhist religion or of the nations professing it, the fact of their identity is *now* placed beyond the shadow of a doubt, thanks to our closer intercourse with Booddhist countries, consequent upon the extension of the British rule in Ceylon and India beyond the Ganges. For not only are the identically same acts, facts, sayings, doings, fables, histories, and anecdotes current among them all of this same "divinity," but likewise there is infinitely less difference in the religion of his votaries, than in that of the God of the *Christians.* For Boodhism may almost be said to know no sectarianism.

used, probably because BURALOUN has the same meaning.* Mr. Chambers following M. Gentil, and followed by Paulinus, conceived the Fo or FOHI, of the *Chinese*, to be a corruption of BOUDDHA. The etymology is here so forced that I do not think it merits attention. Yet I allow it to be a probable opinion, although not completely established, that Fo, and BOUDDHA, are the same God.† .... I must entirely dissent even from the rational Mr. Chambers, when he supposes BOUDDHA to be the same with the WODEN of the *Scandinavians*.‡ No two religions

* BURALOUN, or as it is written in Burmese ဘုရားလောင်း *bhŏŏra: loung:*, implies, a being who is destined to become a *Phŏra*, "an object of reverence and adoration," by attaining to နိဗ္ဗာန် *niebhan*, "the not to be, annihilation." The word is composed of two roots; ဘုရား *bhŏŏra:*, as above discussed, and အလောင်း *ăloung:*, "an embryo;" (thus ဖား *hpa:*, "a frog," ဖားလောင်း *hpa: loung:*, "an embryo frog," ergo "a tadpole.") Gaudama attained နိဗ္ဗာန် *niebhan*, B. C. 543, and thus became a ဘုရား *bhŏŏra:*; so that whenever he is called ဘုရားလောင်း *bhŏŏra: loung:*, it alludes to him when a living being. But before he became man, he underwent *Metamsomatosis*, in the bodies of various objects of the animal creation, in all of which he was still a ဘုရားလောင်း *bhŏŏra: loung:*. Thus we repeatedly find, in Burmese sacred works, such clauses as the following: ဘုရားအလောင်းယုန် *bhŏŏra: ăloung: yŏŏn*, "a *bhŏŏra: loung:* hare," which may be translated, "once upon a time when Gaudama was undergoing transmigration in the body of a hare, &c."

† This is likewise now placed beyond a doubt, consequent on our more intimate acquaintance with Chinese literature. Thanks to the labors of those eminent Sinologists Klaproth, Remusat, Landresse and others, some of the most important lights which have been thrown on the religion of Boodha, have been through the medium of Chinese authors. We there find Chinese Bhoodhist priests travelling to India to visit *Boodhist* spots rendered sacred to them by being the birth place and haunts of their divinity Fo. We shall have occasion in a note a little lower down, to notice the justifiability of the permutation of the initial letter.

‡ Without discussing whether BOODH-a and WOD-en, were or were not the same *divinity*, although a very curious parallel might be drawn between some parts of the religious system of the two; yet this by no means makes them out not to be the same *name*.

surely can be more totally different, nor can I conceive it to be a sufficient proof of a common origin, that the same day of the week is called after the two Gods."

The above has been quoted, not so much for any light it throws on the subject; as the progress of our intercourse with Boodhist nations has enabled us to arrive at conclusions which the learned Buchanan could not reach; but because it gives a succinct idea of the different dialectic variations to which this root is obnoxious. The radix from which the name BOODH is derived is *Păt, Pŏŏt, Pătie, Wătie,** &c. It is thus found in almost every language; as in the Burmese ကြာသပတေး *Kyathăbădé*; in Pali, VRISHPATIE, "the Lord of Taurus," (the name of the planet Jupiter;) the Hebrew יפת *Japhăt,* "the Lord of JA," the Earth,† which has been emphatically declared to be the inheritance of Japhet. It, and the preceding root are found united in the word פוטיפרע *Pŏŏtie Phrah,* "Potipherah."‡ It is likewise the *expressive* part of the word δεσ-πότης. The original and real power of the word is found in the

* A person at all acquainted with languages will not require to be reminded that W. B. P. and F., being all labials, undergo mutual permutation, thus we find *Danuvius* for *Danubius*; Ἰουερνία for *Hibernia*, (Ptolemy, lib. 2. c. 2.) Another exemplification may be met with every day in Calcutta; where, on the ferry boats of its suburbs, their destination may be seen written, on some *Hawrah*, on others *Habrah*.

† This is the interpretation which has been given it by Wilford.

‡ It is generally considered that the meaning of this name is given in the words that follow it; viz., כהןאן "the Prince, or priest of ON—the Sun." But if our interpretation of the root *Phra*—be correct, viz. "King," as also that we shall give to the root *Pătie*, viz. "supporter, maintainer," likewise "wisdom." Then the two might be translated *Pătie*, "a Supporter, Councillor, Minister, Lord, &c." *Phra*, of Pharoah's, "the king's;" and which is the more probable, for, although this Poti-phera, (Gen. ch. xli. v. 45.) was a priest of On; the other Potiphar, (ch. xxxix. v. 1.) interpreted in conformity with our view "an officer of Pharoah," was the Captain of his guard.

epithet စကြဝတိ *tsĕkyă wătie*, or *tsĕkyă pătie*, "the *supporter* of a Sekya system, or Universe." The meaning of this root is very powerful. 1st, It implies the high attribute of the Demi-urge, the upholder, supporter, and sustainer of the Universe. This enables us to arrive at the next step of our analysis which asserts it to be identical with the Egyptian term ⲫϯ *Phtah.* This Deity was falsely considered by the Greeks as corresponding to their Hephaistos, or Vulcan. This idea probably arose from some fancied resemblance in the name. Whereas "*Phtah*" was in reality the impersonification of the highest attribute of the Omnipotent, the *Agathodæmon;* and the only term by which in Coptic is rendered the "Supreme God." This root, however, divides itself into two parts, the ⲫ being the article, the ϯ being the expressive part;* and in discussing this latter character we shall see how admirably it conveys the idea of "support, supporter." In alluding to its hieroglyphic prototype and equivalent ϯ the Champollionist Gliddon sums up the view that his school takes of it, in the following words. "ϯ the sacred Tau, the symbol of "eternal life," which in the Alphabet is an *A*."† Setting aside that it is rather singular that what is a "sacred *T*," in one place, should become an "alphabetical *A*," in another; we will state the principal grounds on which it is considered the "symbol of eternal life." Suidas informs us that, "in the reign of Theodosius the

* Cum articulo ⲫ nunquam scribitur suis litteris, sed sic ⲫϯ et alquando ϯ *Tattam. Copt. Lex.* voce ⲛⲟⲩϯ

† "Antient Egypt" by G. R. Gliddon in Nos. 68, 69 of the "New World," page 15. New York, April, 1843.

Great, when the temples of the Pagans were destroyed, there were found, in the temple of Serapis, certain hieroglyphs having the form of a cross; which, certain Christian Greeks having observed, they declared that the cross was the symbol, among those who understood hieroglyphics, of a future life;"* Sozomen asserts the same. The historians Rufinus and Socrates, declare that this cross referred to the cross of Christ.† But though we might concede that, to the mind of a Christianising Gentile, the cross aptly was the symbol of redemption, an emblem of salvation, of a coming and an eternal life; the very grounds on which we make such concession, viz. the Dominical Passion, induce us to search for some other import in this symbol, in use ages before that event. The most simple solution would be from its form, which is nothing more than a "stand or bracket" ⊤ *supporting* an object ● the shape of which is varied from the angular straightness of the other, to show that it is a distinct and extraneous object. We see then how appropriately it is a sacred emblem, implying (κυριολόγικη κατὰ μίμησιν) the "supporter."

Having thus determined this character and root to imply that Supreme Being, the Supporter and Sustainer of the Universe, we find that its next acceptation, of being, as stated above by Buchanan, an appellation

* Επὶ Θεοδοσίου τοῦ μεγάλου βασιλέως καθαιρουμένων τῶν ἐθνικῶν ἱερῶν, εὑρέθησαν ἐν τῷ Σεράπιδος νεῷ ἱερογλυφικὰ γράμματα σταυροῦ ἔχοντα τύπους. ἅπερ θεασάμενοι οἱ ἐξ Ἑλλήνων χριστιανίσαντες, ἔφασαν, σημαίνειν τὸν σταυρὸν, παρὰ τοῖς ἱερογλυφικὰ γινώσκουσι γράμματα, τὴν ζωὴν ἐπερχομένην. Suidas in Theod.

† Conf. Rufinus Eccles. Hist. L. 2. cap. 29. Sozomen L. 7. cap. 15. Socrates Hist. tripartite. L 9. Item Kircher Prodr. Copt. p. 165. Where these authorities are quoted; and the same view supported.

expressive of "Wisdom,"* is a necessary consequence; for it was peculiarly by the attribute of Wisdom, that the antients believed the Deity upheld his works.† We have had cause to see above, (v. note, p. i.) how that in Boodhism, (wisdom) the Law and its fulfilment, was typified by the number 5; and now we see the idea continued in this root or character ✝ expressive, as we have shewn above, of the High Deity in the mind of the antient Egyptians; for not only is it the character for the number 5;‡ but likewise Hor-Apollo points out the same connection, and declares, that among them "a star represented the number five, also the Mundane God, likewise destiny."§ This is to be accounted for by the circumstance that the Egyptian or Hieroglyphic star, was five-rayed, and from what we have seen above it probably in reality typified the "Law." After having so fully discussed this root, we should not be justified in dismissing it without alluding to the expressive part of the name "God-*ămă*," (the three final letters being a declensional termination:) and which, in reality, is a dialectic variety of the northern type, Wod, of the root under discussion.‖ Thus is explained the true meaning of

* Thus بودھ and बोध understanding, knowledge. Shakespear's Hindust. Dict.

† This may abundantly be proved from the most antient, as it is the most authentic authority on many points of archaiology, viz. the Bible. Thus Ps. civ. 24; cxxxvi. 5. Prov. iii. 19. Jer. x. 12.

‡ Et "quinque." Tattam Copt. Lex. in voce.

§ Θεὸν δὲ ἐγκόσμιον σημαίνοντες, ἢ εἱμαρμένην, ἢ τὸν πέντε ἀριθμὸν, ἀστέρα ζωγραφοῦσι. Hor-Apollo, Lib. 1. c. 13.

‖ This permutation of G. and W. between two dialects is too well known to philologers, to require to be insisted on; witness "William," and "Guillaume;" "Ward," "Garde;" "Wehr," German, "Guerre," French; Latin, "Vadum," French, "Gué."

the name, as mentioned by Buchanan in the above quoted paper, viz., "It has, however, been mentioned to me, on the authority of a Pundit, belonging to our Supreme native court of Bengal, that the meaning of Godama, is *eminently wise, a sage*." We will conclude by remarking that this "sacred dental" forms a component part of the name of the Deity in every language, whether initial, as in the Greek θεος, the Latin "Deus," the French "Dieu"—Or medial as in the Persian خدا *khöŏda,* the Pali and Burmese "Bŏŏddhă" and "Godămă," the Teutonic "Woden"—Or final as in the Saxon Ᵹod the German "Gott," and the English "God." It composes likewise the term တော် *dāū,* the sacred attributive or honorific increment, used in so peculiar a way by the Burmese.

ရွှေ Is a term that is applied to every thing connected with royalty and royal persons. In the general acceptation of the word it implies "golden." It is composed of the following letters H. W. R. E. The W. being a vocal, that is, not employed in the character of a consonant, but appended by symbol after the manner of a vowel, and is pronounced *oo;* thus the word might be written H. O. O. R. E, or H. O. R. E.* Its connection then with the Egyptian ϩⲱⲣ *Hōr,* "Horus," or "Sun,"† becomes at once evident; which was not only a type of royalty, but was itself sym-

* The Burmese not being able to pronounce, an "*r*," but as a "*y*," give a sound somewhat approaching to, "*Shooe*," to this root. But the Arracanese proper being in the habit of pronouncing the "*r*," give it a sound approaching the one in the text.

† ἐν δὲ ταῖς Ἑρμοῦ λεγομέναις βίβλοις ἱστοροῦσι γεγράφθαι περὶ τῶν ἱερῶν ὀνομάτων, ὅτι τὴν μὲν ἐπὶ τῆς τοῦ Ἡλίου περιφορᾶς τεταγμένην δύναμιν, Ὧρον, Ἕλληνες δὲ Ἀπόλλωνα καλοῦσι. Plutarch de Isid, et Osirid ξα. Ἥλιος δὲ ὁ Ὧρος ἀπὸ τοῦ τῶν ὡρῶν κρατεῖν. Hor-Apollo, Lib. 1, c. 17.

bolised by "gold,"* and is the root from which in a very extensive class of languages the term for Gold is derived: as the Hebrew אור *aur,* "light, splendor," the Latin *aurum,* the French *or.* It may be traced, composed of almost the same letters as in Burmese, in the Pali and Sanscrit languages. It composes the words ⲟⲩⲣⲟ "a king,"—and ⲁϭⲱⲣⲓ "a uræus, asp, or king-snake." We thus find the Burmese redeemed from the charge of debased servility in styling every thing royal,—"Golden:" the two terms being synonymous from the highest antiquity.

It will form an interesting conclusion to our subject, if we speculate what would have resulted, if the Burmese language, instead of coming into contact with, and adapting itself to, a finished alphabetical system as that of the Pali, and been thereby enabled to at once express itself phonetically, had been obliged to have had recourse to, what we may call, the hieroglyphic mode of expression. Not only will it be a guide in investigations of a kindred nature; but it will stand a living record of the truthfulness of the position first advanced by that lamented scholar Salvolini;† and supported by Portal;‡ and it will at the same time afford

* Couleurs symboliques. par. F. Portal, p. 71.

† "Comme toute image hiéroglyphique a son terme correspondant dans la lange parlée, il en est un certain nombre qui ont été prises comme signes des sons auxquels elles répondaient, abstraction faite de leur signification primitive. Les caractères hiéroglyphiques appartenant à cette singulière methode d' expression, de même que tous les autres signes *tropiques* qu' emploie l'écriture égyptienne, ont éte employés, soit isolément, soit à la suite des mots." Salv. Analyse Gram. des textes Egypt. p. 225. ad 233. ap. Portal.

‡ Portal symboles des Egyptiens, &c. passim.

an answer to a question put by the latter; "Les symboles avant de se traduire dans la langue écrite, existaient-ils dans la langue parlée? La parole primitive fut elle la source des symboles."* And in perusing the accompanying list, one would almost suspect, that a further acquaintance with the Burmese Empire, will bring to light sculptures analogous to those to which we have alluded.

In the first place, after expressing external objects by their representations, it would, on account of the great number of homonyms with which it, in common with all early dialects, abounds, be enabled to make these representations convey the idea of many attributes. This process must be kept distinct from that which endows certain animals and objects of the creation, with certain attributes, and then sketches their figures to convey the idea of such attributes; for in the case before us the coincidence is only in name. Still, although *we* may not be enabled to trace the slightest connection in idea between the two; we are not justified in asserting that such a connection did not exist in the minds of that primitive race, who were the first employers of this tongue. Among other instances, our improved acquaintance with natural history renders to us ridiculous what to them might have been subjects of implicit credence; thus it would be scarcely out of place, even in the present day, to sketch a "pelican," as the emblem of a mother's love; but how preposterous would it appear to our descendants, if told that the reason

* "Did these symbols, previous to their translation into the written, exist in the spoken tongue? Was the primitive dialect, itself, the source of these symbols." Portal Symb. Egypt. p. 1.

was, because that bird was believed to nourish her young on the life drops of her own bosom!*

Oo, "an egg," might be made to represent "a beginning, chief, first, head, to polish."

O, "a pot," might be made to express, "to be old, homely, useless on account of age."

Kĕng, "a scorpion," .... "to be free, exempt, formed as fruit from the flower; a sentry-box, watch-house."

Kŏŏk, "a lever," .... "to scratch, to exert one's self, to copulate as birds, to subtract as in arithmetic."

Kŏŏn, "the back of an animal," .... "convex, round, merchandise, to be finished, come to an end, to stoop, all, entirely."

Kyăn, "the sugar-cane," .... "to besmear, anoint, to consider, meditate."

Kyăn, "a rhinoceros," .... "to be firm, stable, resolute, strong."

Kouk, "rice grains," .... "to peck, pick up, choose, be crooked, custom-dues."

Kyien, "a ratan vine," .... "to daunt, to threaten, to boast, to brag, to meet with, find."

Kywĕt, "a leech," .... "to be obstinate, perverse, rebellious, to be emancipated, freed from."

Khō "a large species of dove," .... "to hide, avoid, take refuge in or under, to steal."

Khyă, "an ant," .... "to settle, dispose, put in its proper place, to throw down, cause to happen, to teach, give instruction."

Khyĕng, "a gnat, a basket," .... "to desire, wish for, to penetrate, bore, to pierce, to measure the capacity of, to fight, to be in conjunction as heavenly bodies, to compute, reckon, fellow, companion."

* The following list can give but a small idea of the number of homonyms afforded by this language; it is entirely confined to *words composed of the same letters,* and even of these a very great many are omitted; but if all those which are strictly speaking homonyms, viz. that had a similarity of sound, were to be admitted, the catalogue might be indefinitely enlarged; thus တိ *tie,* တီ *tee,* တည် *tee,* တယ် *tay,* တဲ့ *tăi,* ထိ *htie,* ထီ *htee,* ထည် *htee,* ထယ် *htay,* ထဲ့ *htăi,* are all not only not easily distinguished by an unpractised ear, but likewise often interchangeably written.

Khyĕt, "the navel, scale of a fish," .... "to write, make marks, to insert, introduce, to flatten, to scratch, to cook."

Khyé, "the hog-deer," .... "to retaliate, refute, do a thing in return, to please, conciliate, oblige, to pound, erase, to be gentle, to borrow, lend, hire, excrement, rust, particles, to widen."

Khyoung, "the neck," .... "a brook, gutter, to cough, hawk up as phlegm, to peep, pry into, to be sweet, pleasant, lean, poor, break or snap in two, to wash, be deficient, incomplete."

Khwé, "a dog, a hoop," .... "to curve, coil, split, push, divide in two lengthwise, to levy, assess as taxes, to distribute, to checkmate."

Tsŏŏk, "a reed pen," .... "to be torn, rent, disordered, frizzled, to suck, churn."

Tshĕng, "an elephant," .... "to accumulate, cleanse, stretch out, to descend, put in order, adonise."

Tee, "an earthworm," .... "to clear, weed away, to beat the breast, a chirping sound, a great great grandson, to winnow."

Toung, "hill, a cubit," .... "to desire, lust after, to ask, entreat, beg, the south."

Htee, "an umbrella, (an insignia of Royalty,)" .... "to fear, reverence, solitary, alone, deserted."

Htouk, "a crutch," .... "to support, assist, maintain, consider, have regard for, deliberate on."

Na, "the ear," .... "to hear, understand, to alight or perch as a bird, the being beyond, along side of, a side, edge, a shore, disease, ill, unhappy."

Né, "the sun," .... "a day, (in contradistinction to a night,) to remain, continue, be permanent."

Hneet, "the heart," .... "to be pleased with, love, esteem, rejoice, to immerse, a year, the number 2."

Hnăn, "a grasshopper, an ear of grain," .... "to commit, deliver into charge, to pervade, diffuse over all parts, be silly, foolish, be speckled."

Hnŏŏk, "the mouth," .... "to extract, pull out, refute, utter."

Péng, "a tree or plant," .... "to be fatigued, to help, aid, to obstruct, to invite, raise, exult."

Păn, "a flower," .... "to adorn, decorate, to receive an order, to pant, be fatigued, to beg, petition."

Pō, "an insect (that can utter no sound,)" .... "to fix, fasten, suspend by tying, to carry, bring, teach, instruct, throw into."

Pyō, "a plant," .... "to set, to plant, to sow as seed, to be young, prime."

Hpyōō, "a porcupine," .... "to be white, pleasant, pleased, to be taper, slender, to sprinkle, scatter, hiss as a serpent."

Hpwĕt, "a species of lizard," .... "to hide, secrete, make clean."

Hpwai, "husk of grain," .... "to be small, fine, white, to seek, look after to be inadhesive, fit, proper, comely."

Mă, "a female," .... "a mother, chief, principal, to help, assist, relieve, support, bear up."

Mien, "a screech owl," .... "to be confused, absent in mind, astonished, to long for, to speak (honorific.)"

Mé, "the chin," .... "to enquire, investigate, forget, be careless," likewise "the indigo plant, to be dark blue, to threaten, terrify, be dark in mind, ignorant, be dissatisfied, deficient in."

Moung, "the arm," .... "to be of a crimson color, to threaten, daunt, drive away."

Myĕt, "the eye," .... "a gem, grass, to be angry."

Myĕng, "a horse," .... "to see, to hate, to be distant in time, to be high, lofty."

Myŏing, "a forest," .... "to be full, crowded."

Mwé, "hair of the body," .... "to be soft, glossy, smooth, to feed, nourish, cherish, to bring forth, produce, to sleep soundly, to enjoy one's self, a relic, an inheritance."

Hmăn, "a mirror," .... "to be true, exact, to hit the mark, to fit in exactly, to mark, note, remark."

Rĕng, "a fly, gnat," .... "the same, so, if, before, previously, to speak, utter, to be near to, to accumulate, advanced in pregnancy, one's own, as, while."

Lé, "a bow," .... "the wind, to fear, reverence, to be heavy, to exchange, also the number 4."

Gna, "a fish," .... "I, (first pers. pron.) the number 5."

Kyouk, "a rock, or stone," .... "to kick, shove, the back of an animal, the small-pox, to fear, be afraid, the number 6."

Thŏŏn, "a captive," .... "to imprison, to be discouraged, dejected, to be bad, few, inferior, empty, desolate, to use, or spend, to practise good deeds, the number 3."

We have thus endeavoured to point out some of the interesting peculiarities with which this curious language abounds; many others remain, amply to requite the labor and solace the progress of the diligent student. To a mind guided by intelligence, the fragments even of a long extinct tongue may present subjects of the highest interest. They stand, as it were, hoar-worn and time-honoured land-marks, perennial beacons, that guide us over many a wide waste of by-gone days; and if properly analysed they often afford a record as unfailing in its truthfulness, as it is beautiful in its simplicity, of the social and moral condition of the people of whom they may be the only vestige. But this becomes the more striking in the case of a living dialect representing the ideas of a semi-barbarous race. Let one instance, out of many, suffice in the language we have under review. The phrase ရှေးသောဘဝ *shé: thăŭ bhăwă*, implies literally "the time that is *before* (us)," ရှေး *shé:*, meaning "before, in front of:"—but it applies to what we would call "the time that is *behind* us," viz., the "Past." In like manner နောင်သောဘဝ *noung thăŭ bhăwă*, implies "the time that is *behind* (us)," နောင် *noung*, signifying "behind, after;" but it refers to what we would style "the time that is *before* us," viz., the Future. How admirably then do these two idioms illustrate the negative and unhopeful philosophy of Boodhism;* a cold and passionless system of ethics, which

* The whole ethical system of Booddhism, (in reference to its higher and inner grades) as it bears on the moral obligations incumbent upon mankind, may be stated to be an endeavour to avoid sin, by crushing every active principle of the mind, whether for good or evil; to indulge a feeling neither of love nor of anger, of sorrow nor of joy; and to hold the conviction, that as human nature is incapable of doing ought but wrong, the only way to avoid sin is to strive to do nought, and to remain passive and still; thus an in-

teaches its followers to allow themselves to be borne, as it were, along on the tide of time, till engulphed in the abyss of နိဗ္ဗာန် *niebhan,* "Annihilation, Nonentity." To *them* what is "before," has drifted "past." And how strikingly in contrast with the "before" of the philosophy of the Christian, the votary of a creed, that imbues him with an untiring hope, an onward fervor; that instructs him to consider himself but as a probationer in this life; and in the words of one of its great teachers "this one thing to do, forgetting those things which are *behind,* and reaching forth unto those things which are *before,* to press toward the mark, for the prize of a high calling."

---

junction, to those who are aiming at, the higher grades of perfection, as given in the *Wienee,* or book of observances of the priesthood, is, that the commandment never to touch a woman, extends even to one's own mother, and that should she fall into a ditch, her son, if a priest, is allowed to give her his skirt, or a stick to help her out; but he must at the same time bring himself to think, that he is merely pulling out a log of wood. *Conf.* Descript. of Burmese Emp. by the F. Sangermano. p. 91.

In the following pages, wherever an idiom is recorded which has not fallen under the personal observation of the Author; the name of the authority from which it is quoted is superadded. The whole table of Pali Ordinals given from p. 90, to p. 96, has been taken, and in a few instances corrected, from a work by F. Carey, Serampore, 1814. Part V. treating on the Metrology of Burmah, has been compiled with the aid of all previous works on the subject, as of those of Sangermano, Low, Rushton, Carey, Judson, Hough, Crawfurd, Buchanan, &c. &c. as also from personal observation and enquiry; but more especially from a tract drawn up by a learned Native, (now deceased,) of the name of Mengnam, late Mahadan or Religious Superior, and Chief Priest of the Provinces of Arracan; and which was compiled by him from the *Kyăntsa*, or Sacred Books of the country.

ERRATA.

The following Errata require to be corrected. In the first 28 pages of Part II. the short *e*, and *o*, in all such words; as, ခင် ဖြင့် and နှိုင် &c. has been written with a common *e*, and *o*.

Thus *for* ခင် *kheng*, ဖြင့် *hpyeng*, and နှိုင် *hnoing*, &c. *read* ခင် *khĕng*, ဖြင့် *hpyẹng*, and နှိုင် *hnŏing*.

Introduction, p. xv. l. 4, *for* " binding link," *read* " binding links."

In page 2, line 12, *for* ကိ *kei*, *read* ကိ *kie*.

—— 3, — 4, *for* ခါ *khă*, *read* ခါ *kha*.

—— 10, — 3, from bott. *for pietskhăn*:, *read piektshăn*:.

—— 18, — 1, *for* " aside," *read* " a side."

—— 21, — 1, between the words " never" and " admit," insert " by themselves."

—— 41, — 3, *for* အနှိုးရည် *read* အုနှိုးရည်.

—— „ — 9, *for* " passed," *read* " parsed."

—— 45, — 2, from bott. *for* က *ga*, *read* က *gă*.

—— 51, — 9, *for* " contest," *read* " context."

—— 52, — 3, from bott. *for* နှိုတ် *read* နှိုက်.

—— 63, — 6, from bott. *for* လျှာ *lya*, *read* လျှား *lyaः*.

—— 73, — 11, *for* ရှိက and ရှိမှ *read* ဤက and ဤမှ.

—— 78, — 1, *for* သ *tă*, *read* တ *tă*.

—— 99, — 7, *for* " subject", *read* " object."

—— 108, — 4, *for* နါးတသက် *read* နွားတသက်.

—— 117, — 4, from bott. *for* လ *lé*, combined, &c. *read* လေ *lé*. Combined, &c.

—— 120, — 11, *for* နှပ်ဆယ် *read* နှစ်ဆယ်.

In page 128, line 12, *for* မြှစ်ထား *read* မြစ်ထား.

— 130, — 10, *for* ဖြစ် *read* ဖြစ်.

— 134, — 4, from bott. *for* ည်မ *read* မည့်.

— 142, — 4, and 6, from bott. *for* "I have sent," *read* "I have been sent."

— 144, — 3, from bott. *for* ကောက်သည် *read* ကောက်သည်ဖြစ်သည့်.

— 145, — 10, *for* "imitial," *read* "initial."

— *ib.* — 2, from bott. *for* (vide p. 46,) *read* (vide p. 65.)

— 146, — 12, *for* (p. 101,) *read* (p. 153.)

— 160, — 4, *for* ထို and ထိုလည် *read* ထို့ and ထို့လည်.

— 168, — 2, *for* တ်ဂါရ *read* ဂါရတ်.

— 175, — 6, *for* ဓိသာ *read* ဓိသာ.

— 176, — 6, *for* တဝမှိတွဲ *read* တမှိတွဲ.

— 177, — 8, 10 and 11, *for* "*wiemie*," *read* "*wiedhie*."

CONTENTS.

	PAGE.
Preface,	v
Introduction,	ix
Articles,	xviii
Number,	*ib.*
Gender,	xix
Cases,	xx
Adjectives,	xxiv
Numerals,	xxv
Verbs,	xxxi
Accents,	xxxiii
ဘုရာ *bhŏŏra:*, analysed,	xxxiv
ဗုဒ္ဓ *bŏŏddhă*, ditto,	xxxvi
ရွှ *Shooé*, ditto,	xlii
ERRATA,	li

PART I.

Alphabet,	1
On the vowels,	2
The Triphthong,	3
Pronunciation of the Vowels,	4
On the Consonants,	5

	Page.
On the mark called (*thăt,*)	7
Pronunciation of the Consonants,	8
Compound Consonants,	14
Double Consonants,	15
Permutations of the powers of Consonants,	16
——— of final Consonants,	17
Accents,	20
Punctuation,	21
Final Remarks on the Alphabet,	*ib.*
Abbreviations,	23
Numerical mode of writing,	24

PART II.

Nouns,	31
Original Nouns,	*ib.*
Derivative Nouns,	32
Compound Substantives,	37
Number,	41
Gender,	42
Cases,	43
Compound causal affixes,	57
Honorific Affix, or Increment,	65
Pronouns,	66
Pronoun Substantives,	*ib.*
Pronoun Adjectives,	69
Demonstrative and Interrogative Pronouns,	70
Adverbial compounds of Demonstr. Interrog. Pronouns,	73
On rendering the Pron. Adject. "*None,*"	77
The Relative Increment,	78

PAGE.

Adjectives, ... 79
On Comparison of Adjectives, ... 82
The Superlative degree, ... 86

PART III.

Numerical System, ... 89
Table of Numerals, ... 90
Pali Numerals in Burmese Character, ... 97
On compounding a Numeral with a noun, ... 98
Numeral Generic Affixes, ... 102
Combination of the Numeral "*One*," with various roots, ... 114
Numeral Auxiliaries, ... 119

PART IV.

Verbs, ... 125
Number, ... 130
Paradigm of verb, "to go," 131
Verbal Affixes, ... 133
Indicative Mood, ... 136
Imperative, and Precative Mood, ... 137
Subjunctive Mood, ... 138
Potential Mood, ... 140
Optative Mood, ... 141
Infinitive Mood, ... *ib.*
Participles, ... 143
Present participles, ... 144
Past participles, ... *ib.*
Honorific Mood, ... 145

PAGE

Interrogative Mood, ... 147
Negative Mood, ... 149
Auxiliary Affixes, ... 153
Connective Affixes, ... 156
Miscellaneous Affixes, ... 157
Euphonic, and Expletive affixes, ... 162

Adverbs, ... 163
Conjunctions, ... 165
Interjections, ... 166

PART V.

Metrology.

Measures of Distance, ... 167
——— of Weight, ... 169
——— of Capacity, ... 171
——— of Time, ... 172

Era of Burmah, ... 177
Orthography, ... *ib.*
Burmese Index, ... 179
English Index, ... 197

GRAMMAR

OF THE

BURMESE LANGUAGE.

The Burmese Language is written from left to right, and admits of no division between words. The Alphabet consists, correctly speaking, of Forty-four Letters; viz., thirty-four Consonants ဗျည်း *byeens*, and ten Vowels သရ *thără*.

THE VOWELS ARE,

အ *ă*. အာ *a*. ဣ *ie*. ဤ *ee*. ဥ or ဦ *ŏŏ*. ဦ *ōō*. ဧ *é*. ဩ *ey*. ဪ or ဪ *ăŭ*. ဪ် *āū*.

THE CONSONANTS ARE,

က *kă*.	စ *tsă*.	ဋ *ṭă*.	တ *tă*.	ပ *pă*.	ယ *yă*.
ခ *khă*.	ဆ *tshă*.	ဌ *hṭă*.	ထ *htă*.	ဖ *hpă*.	ရ *ră*.
ဂ *gă*.	ဇ *dză*.	ဍ *ḍă*.	ဒ *dă*.	ဗ *bă*.	လ *lă*.
ဃ *ghă*.	ဈ *dzhă*.	ဎ *ḍhă*.	ဓ *dhă*.	ဘ *bhă*.	ဝ *wă*.
င *gnă*.	ည *gnyă*.	ဏ *ṇă*.	န *nă*.	မ *mă*.	သ *thă*.
	ဟ *hă*.	ဠ *llă*.	အ *ă*.	အံ *ăn*.	

These are the most usual forms of the letters now in use, but some scarce variations that occasionally occur will be found below.

On the Vowels, သရ *thără*.

The vowels are written in their original character only when they form the initial syllable of a word of Pali origin; when initial in a pure Burman word they are symbolically combined with the mute consonant အ. When combined with consonants they are represented by symbols.

Table of Vowels with their Characters, Symbols, and Combinations.

Character	Symbol.	Name of Symbol.	Combination with Consonants.
အ	none		က *kă.*
အာ	ာ or ါ	ချ *khiă*, "to place down."	ကာ *ka*, ဂါ *ga.*
ဣ	ိ	လုံးကြီးတင် *lŏŏnȝ gyeeȝ tĕng*, "a large round placed."	ကိ *kei.*
ဤ	ီ	လုံးကြီးတင်ဆံခတ် *lŏŏnȝ gyeeȝ tĕng tshăn-khăt*, "a large round with a little knob placed above."	ကီ *kēē*, or *kee.*
ဥ	ု	တချောင်းငင် *tă khyoungȝ gnăngȝ*, "a reed."	ကု *kŏŏ.*
ဦ	ူ	နှစ်ချောင်းငင် *hneet khyoungȝ gnăngȝ*, "two reeds."	ကူ *kōō.*
ဧ	ေ	သဝေထိုး *thă wéȝ htōȝ* "placed before at a distance."	ကေ *ké.*
အဲ	ဲ	နောက်သို့ပြစ် *nouk thō pyeet*, "projected downwards."	ကဲ *kay.*
ဩ	ေ-ာ or ေ-ါ	သဝေထိုးချ *thă wéȝ htōȝ khyă.*	ကော *kău*, ဂေါ *gău.*
ဪ	ေ-ာ် or ေ-ါ်	သဝေထိုးချရှေ့ထိုး *thă wéȝ htōȝ khyă shé htōȝ.*	ကော် *kău*, or ဂေါ် *găŭ.*

ါ the second symbol of the second vowel အာ *a,* and the final member of the symbols of the 9th and 10th vowels, is used only with the consonants ခ *khă,* ဂ *gă,* င *gnă,* ဒ *dă,* ပ *pă,* and ဝ *wă,* as they would be altered into, or mistaken for other letters by the use of the symbol ာ affixed; thus ခါ *khă,* might be mistaken for ဘ *bhă;* ဂါ *ga,* for က *kă;* ငါ *gna,* for ထ *htă;* ဒါ *da,* for အ *ă;* ပါ *pa,* for ဟ *hă;* and ဝါ *wa,* for တ *tă.*

The Burmese Grammarians style the vowels အ *ă,* အာ *a,* ကဏ္ဍဇ *kăṇhṭădză,* or "guttural;" the vowels ဣ *ie,* and ဤ *ee,* they style တာလုဇ *talöödză,* or "palatal;" the vowels ဥ *öö,* and ဦ *öō,* ဩဋ္ဌဇ *ăüṭhṭădză,* or "labials." The vowels ဧ *é,* and အဲ *ey,* they consider both guttural and palatal; and the vowels ဩ *ăü,* and ဪ *ăū,* both guttural and labial.

The Triphthong ဒို.

The 1st, 3rd and 5th vowels are combined to form the triphthong ဒို *ō,* which has a power intermediate between the "*o*" and "*oo*" in the words "*bone*" and "*moon.*" Its symbol is ို and it may be used with any of the simple consonants, or with those consonants combined with ျ the symbol of the letter ယ *yă;* with ြ the symbol of the letter ရ *ră;* with ွ the symbol of the letter ဝ *wă;* and with ြွ the symbol of the letters ရ *ră,* and ဝ *wă,* combined.

The greater proportion of syllables in which this triphthong occurs end in က် *kă thăt-k,* and င် *gnă thăt-gn,* and it then has the power of a short *ŏi,* or long *ī,* as ကိုက် *kŏik,* တိုင် *tŏing.* In some Romanising systems, its power would be expressed when in this position by the diphthong *ai.*

Pronunciation of the Vowels.

Burm. အ. Deva Nagri अ. Square Pali [illegible].

အ *ă*, has exactly the sound of the first "*a*" in "*papa.*" It is considered as naturally inherent in every consonant, that has not another vowel attached, or the mark ် *thăt*, superadded; as ကနား *kănaः*, "a shed;" ပလင်း *pălăngः*, "a bottle." When inherent in the letter ဝ *wă*, and followed by ဏ် *ṇă thăt-ṇ;* by န် *nă thăt-n;* by မ် *mă thăt-m;* by လ် *lă thăt-l;* or by ံ *ăn*, its power is somewhat more open; as ဝန် *wŏn*, "a bŭrden;" ဝမ်း *wŏnः*, "the stomach," &c. When inherent in a consonant commencing a syllable ending in က် *kă thăt-k*, its power is permuted to *ie;* as ရှက် *shiet*, "to be ashamed." When in the same position in a syllable ending in စ် *tsă thăt-ts*, or ဉ် *gnyă thăt-gny*, its power is permuted to *ee;* စစ် *tseet*, "war," not *tsăt*.

Burm. အာ. Deva Nagri आ. Square Pali [illegible].

အာ *a*, has the sound of the final "*a*," in "*papa;*" as တာရာ *tara*, "a star."

Burm. ဣ. Deva Nagri इ. Square Pali [illegible].

ဣ *ie*, has the power of "*ie*," in "*mien*," pronounced short. မိမိ *miemie*, "self." ဣ, ဣ, are different varieties of this character.

Burm. ဤ. Deva Nagri ई. Square Pali [illegible].

ဤ *ee*, has the power of "*ee*," in "*meet;*" as ထီး *hteeः*, "an umbrella." ဤ, ဤ, ဤ, ဤ, are all varieties of the same character.

Burm. ဥ or ဦ. Deva Nagri उ. Square Pali [illegible].

ဥ *ŏŏ*, has the sound of the "*oo*" in "*good;*" as ဘုန် *bhŏŏn*, "glory." When attached to an initial consonant, should there be no final consonant following, it frequently has the power of the inherent အ *ă;* as ပုဆိုး *pătshō*, not *pŏŏtshŏŏ*, "a garment." ဥ is a variety of the same character.

Burm. ဦ. Deva Nagri ऊ. Square Pali .

ဦ *ōō,* has the power of "*oo,*" in "*food;*" as ပူပေါင် *pōōpoung,* "to congregate." ဦ, is another variety of the same character.

Burm. ဧ. Deva Nagri ए. Square Pali .

ဧ *é,* has the power of the French *é,* or the "*a,*" in "*fame;*" as နေဝင် *né wĕng,* "sunset." ဧ, ဧ, are varieties.

Burm. ဢဲ. Deva Nagri ऐ. Square Pali, properly speaking, none.

ဢဲ *ey.* This vowel has the power of "*ei,*" in "*obeisance*" or the "*ey,*" in "*obey;*" as ဆဲဆို *tsheythsō,* "to abuse." It has no counterpart in the Pali language. ဢဲ, is another form of the character.

Burm. ဩ. Deva Nagri ओ. Square Pali .

ဩ *ăŭ,* has the power of "*oa,*" in "*moan;*" as ဂေါတမ *Găŭtămă;* and is expressed throughout the following pages by a short diphthong *ăŭ:* the Greek ω also expresses its power. When combined with a consonant, and immediately followed by က် *kă thăt-k,* or င် *gnă thăt-ng,* it has the power of "*ou*" in "*bound;*" as ကျောက် *kyouk,* "a stone;" ကောင်း *koung*း, "good:" frequently when initial it is written ဩော.

Burm. ဪ. Deva Nagri औ Square Pali, none.

ဪ *āū,* has the power of "*aw,*" in "*paw;*" as ပေါ်မှာ *pāūhma,* "above." There is no sound or character corresponding to this in Pali.

On the Consonants, ဗျည်း *byeen*း.

The first twenty-five Consonants are divided into five classes of five each; viz. five ကဏ္ဌဇ *kăṇhṭădză,* or Gutturals; five တာလုဇ *talōōdză,* or Palatals; five မုဒ္ဓဇ *mōōḍḍhădză,* or Linguals; five ဒန္တဇ *dăntădză,* or Dentals; and five ဩဋ္ဌဇ *ăŭṭhṭădză,* or Labials. Of the remainder ယ *yă,* is considered a palatal; ဟ *hă,* a guttural; ရ *ră,* and ဠ *llă,* as linguals; လ *lă,* and သ *thă,* as dentals; ဝ *wă,* is considered both dental and labial.

Table of Consonants, with their Class, Character, Name and Power.

Class.	Char.	Name.	Power.
Gutturals.	က	ကကြီး *kăgyeez,* "great kă."	*k.*
	ခ	ခခွေး *khăkhwé,* "curved khă."	*kh.*
	ဂ	ဂငယ် *găgnay,* "little gă."	*g.*
	ဃ	ဃကြီး *ghăgyeez,* "great ghă."	*gh.*
	င	င *gnă,* "gnă."	*gn.*
Palatals.	စ	စလုံး *tsălŏŏnz,* "round tsă."	*ts.*
	ဆ	ဆလိမ် *tshălien,* "twisted tshă."	*tsh.*
	ဇ	ဇကွဲ *dzăkhwey,* "broken dză."	*dz.*
	ဈ	ဈမျဉ်းဆွဲ *dzhămyĕngzdzwey,* "horse-bridle dzhă."	*dzh.*
	ည	ည *gnyă,* "gnyă."	*gny.*
Linguals.	ဋ	ဋသံလျင်းချိတ် *ṭăthănlyĕngz khyiet,* "ṭă like an iron hook."	*ṭ.*
	ဌ	ဌဝမ်းဘဲ *hṭăwŏnzbeyz,* "duck hṭă."	*hṭ.*
	ဍ	ဍရင်ကောက် *ḍărĕnggouk,* "ḍă with a convex breast."	*ḍ.*
	ဎ	ဎရေမှုတ် *ḍhăréhmŏŏk,* "water-dipper ḍhă."	*ḍh.*
	ဏ	ဏကြီး *ṇăgyeez,* "great ṇă."	*ṇ.*
Dentals.	တ	တဝမ်ပူ *tăwŏmbŏŏ,* "pot-bellied tă."	*t.*
	ထ	ထဆင်ထူး *htătshĕnghtōōz,* "htă like an elephant's foot-shackle."	*ht.*
	ဒ	ဒထွေး *dăhtwéz,* "dă rolled up."	*d.*
	ဓ	ဓအောက်ခြိုက် *dhăoukkhyŏik,* "dhă hollowed at the bottom."	*dh.*
	န	နငယ် *năgnay,* "little nă."	*n.*

Labials.	ပ	ပစောက် *pătsouk,* "pă upside down."	*p.*
	ဖ	ဖဦးထုပ် *hpă ōōshtŏŏk,* "hpă with a cap."	*hp.*
	ဗ	ဗထက်ခြိုက် *bă tăt khyŏik,* "bă scooped at top."	*b.*
	ဘ	ဘကုန်း *bhă gŏŏns,* "hump-back bhă."	*bh.*
	မ	မ *mă,* "mă."	*m.*
	ယ	ယပက်လက် *yă pătlăt,* "yă lying on its back."	*y.*
	ရ	ရကောက် *răgouk,* "crooked ră."	*r.*
	လ	လ *lă,* "lă."	*l.*
	ဝ	ဝ *wă,* "wă."	*w.*
	သ	သ *thă,* "thă."	*th.*
	ဟ	ဟ *hă,* "hă."	*h.*
	ဠ	ဠကြီး *llă gyees,* "great llā."	*ll.*
	အ	အ *ă,* "ă."	*mute.*
	အံ	သေးသေးတင် *thésthésteng,* "a minute mark placed."	*n final.*

The letters င *gnă,* ဉ *gnyă,* ဏ *ṇă,* န *nă,* and မ *mă,* are styled နှာလဒန် *hnalădănie,* "nasal."

On the mark ်

The mark ် called သတ် *thăt,* "to destroy," when placed over a consonant, has the power of annihilating the sound of the အ *ă,* otherwise inherent in it, and thereby rendering it mute; as ကန would be pronounced *kănă,* but ကန် would be pronounced *kăn.*

Every consonant has a vowel အ *ă,* inherent in it; as က *kă* not *k,* unless it have the mark ် superadded, or be the first member of a double consonant; as လတ္တန် *lăttạn,* not *lătătạn.*

Pronunciation of Consonants.

The first consonant of each class is the simple unmodified articulation itself. The second consonant of each class is the aspirate of the first. The third consonant of each class is the first hard and rough. The fourth is the aspirate of the third. And the fifth is the corresponding nasal. The permutations that take place in the sound of consonants are treated of in detail under that head.

Burm. က. Deva Nagri क. Square Pali က.

က *kă*, has the power of "*k*" in "*king*;" as ကာရ *kară*, "a letter." It sometimes has a power intermediate between a "*k*," and a "*g*;" as ကစား *gătsas*, "to play;" ကုဏ္ဍ: *gŏŏns*, "round;" ကတ် *kă thăt-k* when final in a syllable, and immediately preceded by an inherent အ *ă*, has its power permuted to *t*; as ရှက် "*shiet*," not "*shiek*."

Burm. ခ. Deva Nagri ख. Square Pali ခ.

ခ *khă*, has the power of an aspirated *k*; as ခဝါသည် *khăwathee*, "a washerman." ၶ is a variety.

Burm. ဂ. Deva Nagri ग. Square Pali ဂ.

ဂ *gă*, has the power of "*g*" in "*go*;" as ဂင်္ဂါ *gănga*, "the Ganges."

Burm. ဃ. Deva Nagri घ. Square Pali ဃ.

ဃ *ghă*, has the power of an aspirated "*g*," is initial in words of Pali origin; as ဃရ် *ghăr*, "a house." When final after the triphthong, it is mute, or at most very slightly articulated; မိုဃ် *mōgh*, "the sky." ဃ is a variety.

Burm. င. Deva Nagri ङ. Square Pali င.

င *gnă*, when initial has the power of "*gn*," in "*gnu*;" as ငါ *gna*, "I." When final it has the power of "*ng*," in "*king*;" as သင် *thĕng*, "thou." Sometimes its sound is softer intervening between the preceding and the French final "*n*;" as လင် *lăng*, "a husband." င် *ngă thăt-ng*, when in the middle of a word is often moved out of its place in the line, and placed over the succeeding letter; as သင်္ဘော for သင်ဘော *thĕngbhău*, "a ship," generally abbreviated into ် as သင်္ဘော. When combined with ြ the symbol of the letter ရ *ră;* as ငြ, it is frequently interchangeably written with ည *gnyă*.

Burm. စ. Deva Nagri च. Square Pali .

စ *tsă*, has the power of "*ts*," in "*hats*;" as စကား *tsăgas*, "a word." စ် *tsă thăt-ts*, when preceded by an inherent အ *ă*, has its power permuted to "*t*;" as စစ် *tseet*, not *tseets*, "war."

Burm. ဆ. Deva Nagri छ. Square Pali .

ဆ *tshă*, is the preceding sound aspirated; as ဆီ *tshee*, "oil, fat." [illegible] is a variety.

Burm. ဇ. Deva Nagri ज. Square Pali .

ဇ *dză*, has the power of "*j*" in "*jar*;" as ဇာတ် *dzat*, "race, kind." [illegible] is a variety.

Burm. ဈ. Deva Nagri झ. Square Pali .

ဈ *dzhă*, is the preceding sound aspirated; ဈေး *dzhés* "a Bazaar." ဆ is a variety.

Burm. ည. Deva Nagri ञ. Square Pali .

ည *gnyă*, has the power of "*gny*," or the Italian "*gn*" in "*signora*;" as ညမ *gnyămă*, "a younger sister:" ည် *gnyă thăt-gny* when preceded by an inherent အ *ă*, is quiescent; as ညည် *gnyee*, "to sigh." If the character ံ be superadded it has the power of a final "*n*;" as ညည့် *gnyeen*, "night." ဉ်, ဉ, are varieties.

Burm. ဋ. Deva Nagri ट. Square Pali [illegible].

ဋ *ṭă,* the lingual "*t,*" pronounced by placing the point of the tongue far back against the palate: is initial only in words of Pali origin. [illegible], [illegible], are varieties.

Burm. ဌ. Deva Nagri ठ. Square Pali [illegible].

ဌ *hṭă,* the aspirate of the preceding, with which it may have the same remarks applied. [illegible] a variety.

Burm. ဍ. Deva Nagri ड. Square Pali [illegible].

ဍ *ḍă,* is the lingual "*d,*" pronounced by the tip of the tongue thrown back on the palate: initial only in Pali words. [illegible] another form.

Burm. ဎ. Deva Nagri ढ. Square Pali [illegible].

ဎ *ḍhă,* is the aspirate of the preceding. [illegible], [illegible], other forms.

Burm. ဏ. Deva Nagri ण. Square Pali [illegible].

ဏ *ṇă,* is the lingual "*n,*" pronounced with the tongue on the palate: initial only in Pali words. [illegible], [illegible], other forms.

Burm. တ. Deva Nagri त. Square Pali [illegible].

တ *tă,* the common dental "*t,*" in "*ten;*" as တမန် *tămăn,* "a messenger;" တ် *tă thăt-t,* when preceded by the vowel ု *ŏŏ,* or a consonant combined with its symbol, has its power permuted to က်; as ကုတ် *kŏŏk,* "a lever," not *kŏŏt:* when preceded by the symbols of other vowels it is variously permuted, sometimes remaining unchanged; as in တစိတ်စီခလေး *tă tshiet tsie khălé,* "a very little," and sometimes under the same circumstances being changed to က် *k;* as ပိတ်ခန်း *pietskhăns,* "fine cotton."

Burm. ထ. Deva Nagri थ. Square Pali [illegible].

ထ *htă,* is the aspirate of the preceding; as ထောင် *htoung,* "a prison."

Burm. ဒ. Deva Nagri द. Square Pali ᨴ.

ဒ *dă,* is the common dental "*d,*" in "*den;*" as ဒူးလေး *dōōleĕ,* "a cross-bow." ၓ another variety.

Burm. ဓ. Deva Nagri ध. Square Pali ᨵ.

ဓ *dhă,* is the aspirate of the preceding; as ဓားပြ *dhaĕpyă,* "a robber." ဓ is the old form, whence its alphabetical name.

Burm. န. Deva Nagri न. Square Pali ᨶ.

န *nă,* the common dental "*n,*" in "*none;*" as နာမ *namă,* "a name;" န် *nă thăt-n,* when final in a syllable and preceded by the vowel အိ *ie,* or အု *ŏŏ,* or a consonant combined with their symbols, or when final in a word, has the power of the French "*n,*" in "*bon;*" as ပုန်ကန် *pŏŏngan,* "to rebel." It is also often interchangeably written with the character ံ, that is, when its power is as above stated; as ပုံကန် *pŏŏngan.*

Burm. ပ. Deva Nagri प. Square Pali ᨷ.

ပ *pă,* the common labial "*p*" in "*pan;*" as ပညာရှိ *păgnyashie,* "a wise man;" ပ် *pă that-p,* when preceded by an inherent အ *ă,* has its power permuted to "*t;*" as အပ် *ăt,* not *ăp,* "to deliver;" စပ် *tsăt,* not *tsăp,* "to join." When preceded by any other vowel its power is permuted to "*k.*" Sometimes when initial its sound approaches to "*b;*" as ပြေး *byeĕ,* "to run, flee."

Burm. ဖ. Deva Nagri फ. Square Pali ᨹ.

ဖ *hpă,* is the aspirate of the preceding, as the "*ph*" in "*uphanding;*" ဖိုးကြီး *hpōĕgyeeĕ,* "an old man."

Burm. ဗ. Deva Nagri ब. Square Pali ᨻ.

ဗ *bă,* has the power of "*b,*" in "*band;*" as ဗလ *bălă,* "strong."

Burm. ဘ. Deva Nagri भ. Square Pali [illegible].

ဘ *bhă*, is the aspirate of the preceding letter; as ဘယ်မှာ *bhayhma*, "where:" sometimes it has the sound of ဗ *bă*, or ပ *hpă*, and is interchangeably written with them.

Burm. မ. Deva Nagri म. Square Pali [illegible].

မ *mă*, has the power of "*m*," in "*man*;" as မင်းကြီး *mĕngtgyeet*, "a king:" မ် *mă thăt-m*, when final in a syllable, and preceded by the vowels ဣ *ie*, or ဥ *ŏŏ*, or consonants combined with their symbols, has the power of a final "*ng*;" as အိမ် *ieng*, "a house." In the word မြန်မာ the initial မ has its power permuted to "*b*," and is pronounced *byănma:* a similar permutation occurred in some of the dialects of Greece; as μυμορ for μυβορ—βυρμαξ for μυρμαξ. *Vide* Salmasius' Plin. Exercit.

Burm. ယ. Deva Nagri य. Square Pali [illegible].

ယ *yă*, has the power of "*y*," in "*yonder*;" as ယမ်း *yăn*, "gunpowder:" ယ် *yă thăt-y*, when occurring after the triphthong is quiescent, but the vocal sound is somewhat prolonged; as ကိုယ် *kōh*, "the body."

Burm. ရ. Deva Nagri र. Square Pali [illegible].

ရ *ră*, has the power of "*r*," in "*run*." The Burmese proper cannot pronounce an "*r*," but as a "*y*;" hence, ရ *ră* and ယ *yă*, are frequently interchangeably written. The Arracanese can pronounce the "*r*;" thus ရယ် "to laugh," would be pronounced "*ray*" by the Arracanese, and "*yay*" by the Burmese. ရ *ră*, when combined with ှ the symbol of the letter ဟ *hă*, is pronounced like the "*sh*," in *ship*;" as ရွှေ *shwé*, "gold." ရ် *ră thăt-r*, when final in a syllable and preceded by the triphthong, or its symbol, is always mute; as မြင်းမိုရ် *myĕngtmō*, "the sacred mount." ၍ is another form.

Burm. လ. Deva Nagri ल. Square Pali လ.

လ *lă*, has the sound of "*l*," in "*land;*" as လူ *lōō*, "man." When combined with ှျ, the symbols of the letters ဟ *hă*, and ယ *yă*, combined, it often has the sound of "*sh*," in "*ship;*" as လျှာ *sha*, not *hlya*, "the tongue." It sometimes has its power irregularly permuted when occurring in the middle of a word; as မင်းလုလင် *mĕngslŏŏlĕng*, or *mĕngsthŏŏlĕng*, "a constable;" လုံ့လ *lŏŏngă*, or *lŏŏnnă*, not *lŏŏllă*, "diligence."

Burm. ဝ. Deva Nagri व. Square Pali ဝ.

ဝ *wă*, has the power of "*w*," in "*war;*" as ဝါး *was*, "a bamboo." Its symbol when combined with a consonant has a sound somewhat approaching to "*oo;*" as ရွှေ *shooé*, or *shwé*, "gold;" when combined with a consonant which has the inherent vowel အ *ă*, and immediately preceding a တ် *tă thăt-t*, it always has the power of *ŏŏ;* as တဝတ် "a garment," pronounced *tăŏŏt*. ဝ် *wă thăt-w* is often placed expletively after the symbol of the triphthong ို at the end of a word; as ထိုဝ် *htō*, for ထို; သိုဝ် *thō*, for သို, no change is made in the sound.

Burm. သ. Deva Nagri स. Square Pali သ.

သ *thă*, is the only sibilant in the Burmese language approaching to an "*s*," combining the sound of a soft "*th*," as in "*thin*," with an "*s*," as in "*sin;*" as သူကြီး *thōōgyees*, or *sōōgyees*, "a chief;" သတိ *thădie*, "care, caution." When combined with ှျ the symbols of the consonants ဟ *hă*, and ယ *yă*, as သျှ, it has the power of "*sh*" in "*ship;*" as သျှာ *sha*, "the tongue," may be written either ရှာ, လျှာ, or သျှာ. *Vide* ရ, and လ.

Burm. ဟ. Deva Nagri ह. Square Pali ဟ.

ဟ *hă*, has the sound of "*h*," in "*hand;*" as ဟာ *ha*, "a thing."

Burm. ဠ. Deva Nagri ळ. Square Pali [illegible].

ဠ *llă*, is considered a lingual, but nearly similar in sound to a common "*l*." It is never initial in Burman words, but is found interchangeably written with လ *lă*, in the middle of words.

ံ *n*, final; this character called by the Burmese သေးသေးတင် *théthé těng*, (from သေးသေး *théthé*, "very small," and တင် *těng*, "to place or put upon,") or နိဂ္ဂဟိတ် *nieggăhiet*, has the power of a final French "*n*." It is final of itself, that is, has not a vowel inherent in it; as ပုံ *pŏŏn* not *pŏŏnă*, "a pattern." When placed over a consonant in which the vowel အ *ă*, is inherent, should such consonant be the initial of a dissyllable, it is generally mute, and may be said to be always so in words beginning with a တ *tă*; as တံငါး *tăngnăt*, "a fisherman," pronounced and often written တငါး *tăgnat*. This character is often found interchangeably written with a final န် *nă thăt*, and is used only in connection with the inherent vowel အ *ă*, the vowel အု *ŏŏ*, or consonants combined with their symbols.

အ *ă*, this has been introduced here as a mute consonant: if a consonant cannot be pronounced without the assistance of a vowel, the converse is as truly the case; that a consonant is required on which to append a pure vocal sound, which by itself is nothing but air; this mute consonant is formed by the constriction of the throat deeply down, and is therefore styled a guttural; it is the character to which the Burmese attach the symbols of the other vowels to express them.*

Compound Consonants.

Four consonants belonging to the miscellaneous or liquid class are,

* It is this mute consonant that has been styled by a writer on a cognate language "a sort of pivot on which the vowel points are arranged!"

when used in combination with other consonants, represented by symbols; these are ယ *yă*, ရ *ră*, ဝ *wă*, and ဟ *hă*.

Consonant.	Symbol	Name of Symbol.	Comb.	Power.
ယ *yă*.	ျ	ယပင် *yăpĕng*, "yă like a tree or plant."	မျ	*myă*.
ရ *ră*.	ြ	ရရစ် *ră reet*, "ră embracing."	မြ	*mră*.
ဝ *wă*.	ွ	ဝဆွဲ *wă tshwai*, "wă suspended."	မွ	*mwă*.
ဟ *hă*.	ှ	ဟထိုး *hă htōs*, "hă thrust out."	မှ	*hmă*.
ယ and ဝ	ျွ	ယပင်ဝဆွဲ *yă pĕng wă tshwai*, as above.	မျွ	*mywă*.
ယ and ဟ	ျှ	ယပင်ဟထိုး *yă peng hă htōs*, ditto.	မျှ	*hmyă*.
ရ and ဝ	ြွ	ရရစ်ဝဆွဲ *ră reet wă tshwai*, ditto.	မြွ	*mrwă*.
ရ and ဟ	ြှ	ရရစ်ဟထိုး *ră reet hă htōs*, ditto.	မြှ	*hmră*.
ဝ and ဟ	ွှ	ဝဆွဲဟထိုး *wă tshwai hă htōs*, ditto.	မွှ	*hmwă*.
ဟ,ရ and ဝ	ြွှ	ဟထိုးရရစ်ဝဆွဲ *hă htōs ră reet wă tshwai*, do.	မြွှ	*hmrwă*.

The symbol of the consonant ဟ *hă*, is combined only with the nasals, and the letters လ *lă*, ရ *ră*, သ *thă*, and ဝ *wă*.

Double Consonants.

Consonants frequently occur double; as က္က a double က *kă*, or two different consonants; as သ္မ *thmă*. It is to be borne in mind that the inherent vowel အ *ă*, never intervenes between the two consonants; as က္က is pronounced *kkă* not *kăkă*. When aspirated letters are thus doubled the first member is always commuted to its corresponding unaspirate; as a double ခ *khă*, would not be written ခ္ခ, but က္ခ *kkhă*; in the same way ဂ္ဃ *gghă*; စ္ဆ *tstshă*; ဇ္ဈ *dzdzhă*; ဋ္ဌ *hṭṭă*; ဍ္ဎ *ḍḍhă*; တ္ထ *httă*; ပ္ဖ *phpă*; ဒ္ဓ *ddhă*; ဗ္ဘ *bbhă*.

With the exception of င *gnă-thăt-gn*, the nasals are never compounded but with letters of their own class; as ဉ္စ *gnytsă*, ဏ္ဍ *ṇḍă*, န္တ *ntă*, &c.

It has been observed that in double consonants the inherent vowel does not intervene, for this reason a double consonant when occurring in a word may be written by separating them and placing the mark သတ် *thăt*, over the first; as *tsăkkŏŏ*, "paper," may be written either စက္ကူ or စက်ကူ.

Permutations of the Powers of Consonants.

The permutations of the powers of Consonants are of two kinds: 1st, when they occur in the middle of a word, and 2dly, when they are final.

Of the first kind:—In words of more than one syllable, should the first syllable begin with the first or second letter of any class, or in some cases with လ *lă*, or သ *thă*; or with အ *ă*. And at the same time should any of the following syllables begin with the first or second letter of any class, the initial letter of such following syllable takes the sound of the third letter of its class; as က *kă*, and ခ *khă*, take the sound of ဂ *gă*; စ *tsă*, and ဆ *tshă*, of ဇ *dză*; ဋ *ṭă*, and ဌ *htă*, that of ဍ *ḍă*; တ *tă*, and ထ *htă*, that of ဒ *dă*; and ပ *pă*, and ဖ *hpă*, that of ဗ *bă*; as in the following words:—

အတိုင်း *ădŏings*, "measure."

ကကောက် *kăgouk*, "the hollow of the knee."

ကင်းပုဇွန် *kĕngsbŏŏzwon*, "a scorpion."

ခတင် *khădĕng*, "a bed cot."

ခေါင်းပေါင်း *khoungsboungs*, "a turban."

ချိန်ခွင်ပေါင် *khiengwŏnboung*, "the beam of a balance."

စကားပြန် *tsăgasbyăn*, "an interpreter."

စက်ဆုတ် *tsĕtzŏŏk*, "disgusting."

တံစဉ် *tăzeen*, "a sickle."

တံပူ *tăbōō*, "a tooth-brush."

ထံတား *tădaȝ,* "a bridge."

ထံဆာ *tăza,* "an ornament."

တတိယ *tădieyă,* "third."

ပန်းချီ *păgyēē,* "a painter."

ပုကံပျား *pŏŏgănbyaȝ,* "a saucer."

ဖန်ကာတုန် *hpăgădŏŏn,* "a glass tumbler."

ထိဝ်စာ *liekza,* "the title of a book."

The same permutation occurs in the case of affixes; as လူတို့ *lōō dọ,* "men;" သွားပါ *thwaȝ ba,* "go:" or in compound roots; as ရွေးကောက် *rwéȝ-gouk,* "to choose;" သူကြီး *thōōgyeeȝ,* "a great man."

Of the second kind, viz. the Permutation of the Powers of Final Consonants and of inherent ဢ *ă.*

The permutation of the sounds of final consonants have been all remarked upon in their place under the head of pronunciation of consonants, and it will be necessary here to give tables of only the permutation of consonants when final in a word, and when preceded by the inherent vowel ဢ *ă,* which does itself in such situations generally have its own power permuted.

Permutation of the inherent vowel ဢ *ă,* with က် *kă thăt,* final into *ĕt.*

ကက် *kĕt.*	စက် *tsĕt.*	ဋက် *ṭĕt.*	တက် *tĕt.*	ပက် *pĕt.*	ယက် *yĕt.*
ခက် *khĕt.*	ဆက် *tshĕt.*	ဌက် *hṭĕt.*	ထက် *htĕt.*	ဖက် *hpĕt.*	ရက် *rĕt.*
ဂက် *gĕt.*	ဇက် *dzĕt.*	ဍက် *ḍĕt.*	ဒက် *dĕt.*	ဗက် *bĕt.*	လက် *lĕt.*
ဃက် *ghĕt.*	ဈက် *dzhĕt.*	ဎက် *ḍhĕt.*	ဓက် *dhĕt.*	ဘက် *bhĕt.*	ဝက် *wĕt.*
ငက် *gnĕt.*	ဉက် *gnyĕt.*	ဏက် *ṇĕt.*	နက် *nĕt.*	မက် *mẹt.*	သက် *thĕt.*

ဟက် *hĕt.* ဠက် *llĕt.*

The final "*t*," in all these is nearly quiescent; as ဖက် *hpĕt*, "aside," is pronounced more like *hpă*, and လက် *lĕt*, "the hand," like *lă*.

With င် *gnă thăt*, final into *ĕng*.

ကင် *kĕng*.	စင် *tsĕng*.	ဋင် *ţĕng*.	တင် *tĕng*.	ပင် *pĕng*.	ယင် *yĕng*.
ခင် *khĕng*.	ဆင် *tshĕng*.	ဌင် *hţĕng*.	ထင် *htĕng*.	ဖင် *hpĕng*.	ရင် *rĕng*.
ဂင် *gĕng*.	ဇင် *dzĕng*.	ဍင် *ḍĕng*.	ဒင် *dĕng*.	ဗင် *bĕng*.	လင် *lĕng*.
ဃင် *ghĕng*.	ဈင် *dzhĕng*.	ဎင် *ḍhĕng*.	ဓင် *dhĕng*.	ဘင် *bhĕng*.	ဝင် *wĕng*.
ငင် *gnĕng*.	ညင် *gnyĕng*.	ဏင် *ṇĕng*.	နင် *nĕng*.	မင် *mĕng*.	သင် *thĕng*.

ဟင် *hĕng*. ဠင် *llĕng*.

The final "*g*," in all these is quiescent, unless the heavy accent း ရှေးပေါက် *shéspouk*, is affixed; as နင် "thou" is pronounced *nĕn*; but မင်း "a governor," is pronounced *mĕngs*.

Permutation of the inherent အ *ă*, with စ် *tsă thăt*, final into *eet*.

ကစ် *keet*.	စစ် *tseet*.	ဋစ် *ţeet*.	တစ် *teet*.	ပစ် *peet*.	ယစ် *yeet*.
ခစ် *kheet*.	ဆစ် *tsheet*.	ဌစ် *hţeet*.	ထစ် *hteet*.	ဖစ် *hpeet*.	ရစ် *reet*.
ဂစ် *geet*.	ဇစ် *dzeet*.	ဍစ် *ḍeet*.	ဒစ် *deet*.	ဗစ် *beet*.	လစ် *leet*.
ဃစ် *gheet*.	ဈစ် *dzheet*.	ဎစ် *ḍheet*.	ဓစ် *dheet*.	ဘစ် *bheet*.	ဝစ် *weet*.
ငစ် *gneet*.	ညစ် *gnyeet*.	ဏစ် *ṇeet*.	နစ် *neet*.	မစ် *meet*.	သစ် *theet*.

ဟစ် *heet*. ဠစ် *lleet*.

Permutation of inherent အ *ă*, with ည် *gnyă thăt*, final into *ee*, or *een*.

ကည် *kee*.	စည် *tsee*.	ဋည် *ţee*.	တည် *tee*.	ပည် *pee*.	ယည် *yee*.
ခည် *khee*.	ဆည် *tshee*.	ဌည် *hţee*.	ထည် *htee*.	ဖည် *hpee*.	ရည် *ree*.
ဂည် *gee*.	ဇည် *dzee*.	ဍည် *ḍee*.	ဒည် *dee*.	ဗည် *bee*.	လည် *lee*.
ဃည် *ghee*.	ဈည် *dzhee*.	ဎည် *ḍhee*.	ဓည် *dhee*.	ဘည် *bhee*.	ဝည် *wee*.
ငည် *gnee*.	ညည် *gnyee*.	ဏည် *ṇee*.	နည် *nee*.	မည် *mee*.	သည် *thee*.

ဟည် *hee*. ဠည် *llee*.

In all these, ည် is quiescent unless the character • သေးသေးတင် *théthés-tĕng*, be superadded, as ညံ် when it has the power of a nasal *n.*

Permutation of the inherent အ *ă*, with ပ် *pă thăt*, final into *ăt*.

ကပ် *kăt.*	စပ် *tsăt.*	ဋပ် *ṭăt.*	တပ် *tăt.*	ပပ် *păt.*	ယပ် *yăt.*
ခပ် *khăt.*	ဆပ် *tshăt.*	ဌပ် *hṭăt.*	ထပ် *htăt.*	ဖပ် *hpăt.*	ရပ် *răt.*
ဂပ် *găt.*	ဇပ် *dzăt.*	ဍပ် *ḍăt.*	ဒပ် *dăt.*	ဗပ် *băt.*	လပ် *lăt.*
ဃပ် *ghăt.*	ဈပ် *dzhăt.*	ဎပ် *ḍhăt.*	ဓပ် *dhăt.*	ဘပ် *bhăt.*	ဝပ် *wăt.*
ငပ် *ngăt.*	ညပ် *gnyăt.*	ဏပ် *ṇăt.*	နပ် *năt.*	မပ် *măt.*	သပ် *thăt.*

ဟပ် *hăt.* ဠပ် *llăt.*

In all these the final "*t*," is short.

Permutations of ပ် *pă thăt*, final with all other vowels into က် *k.*

အာပ် *āk*, အိပ် *iek*, အီပ် *eek*, အုပ် *ŏŏk* အူပ် *ōōk*, အေပ် *ék*, အဲပ် *eyk*, အောပ် *ăŭk*, အော်ပ် *āūk*, အိုပ် *ŏik*, and so on, if the vowels be combined with consonants simple or compound.

Permutation of မ် *mă thăt*, final with inherent အ *ă*, into *ăn*.

ကမ် *kăn.*	စမ် *tsăn.*	ဋမ် *ṭăn.*	တမ် *tăn.*	ပမ် *păn.*	ယမ် *yăn.*
ခမ် *khăn.*	ဆမ် *tshăn.*	ဌမ် *hṭăn.*	ထမ် *htăn.*	ဖမ် *hpăn.*	ရမ် *răn.*
ဂမ် *găn.*	ဇမ် *dzăn.*	ဍမ် *ḍăn.*	ဒမ် *dăn.*	ဗမ် *băn.*	လမ် *lăn.*
ဃမ် *ghăn.*	ဈမ် *dzhăn.*	ဎမ် *ḍhăn.*	ဓမ် *dhăn.*	ဘမ် *bhăn.*	ဝမ် *wăn.*
ငမ် *gnăn.*	ညမ် *gnyăn.*	ဏမ် *ṇăn.*	နမ် *năn.*	မမ် *măn.*	သမ် *thăn.*

ဟမ် *hăn.* ဠမ် *llăn.*

In all these the final "*n*," is nasal.

Permutations of မ် *mă thăt*, final, with the vowels အိ *ie*, or အု *ŏŏ*, or their symbols into *ng;* as အိမ် *ieng*, အုမ် *ŏŏng*, ခြိမ်း *khiengs*, "thunder." Permutations of န် *nă thăt*, final with the vowels အိ *ie*, and အု *ŏŏ*, or their symbols into *ng;* as အိဉ် *ieng,* အုဉ် *ŏŏng,* ချိဉ် *khyieng,* "to weigh;" in all these cases the final *g,* is pronounced soft.

With reference to other final consonants, with the exception of the nasals, they undergo a similar permutation that the first letter of their class would under similar circumstances; as ခ် *khă thăt,* ဂ် *gă thăt,* ဃ် *ghă thăt,* undergo the same permutations that က် *kă thăt,* would; as မက် is pronounced *mĕt,* not *mĕg.* All in the စ *tsă,* class are permuted the same as စ် *tsă thăt,* final. All in the တ *tă,* class as တ် *tă thăt,* final, and all in the ပ *pă,* class as ပ် *pă thăt,* final. This rule holds good with other vowels besides the inherent အ *ă.*

Accents.

In the Burman language there are only two accents, the short or acute, and the heavy, or grave.

The short or acute accent ့ (called originally အံ့မြစ် *ặn myeet,* or the "*ặn* stop," being formerly a little အံ့ placed below a letter), but at present styled အောက်မြစ် *oukmyeet,* or "the stop below," is placed below a letter; thus ည့်, and is only used with the vowels ေ *é,* အဲ *ey,* ေအာ *ăŭ,* the triphthong အို *ŏi;* as also with the inherent vowel အ *ă,* or the vowel အိ *ie,* when they precede the character ံ *n,* final, or a nasal consonant;* as နှင့် *hnĕng,* "with."

The grave accent း called ရှေ့ပေါက် *shẹpouk,* "dot or stop in front," is placed after the letter; as ရှေး *shé,* "before;" and only used with the vowels အာ *a,* ဤ *ee,* ဦ *ŏŏ,* ေ *é,* with the triphthong အို *ŏi,* as also the inherent vowel အ *ă,* or the vowel အိ *ie,* when they precede the nasal consonants; and is considered inherent in the vowel အဲ *ey,* unless superceded by the light accent.

* It is most unphilosophical to say, that this accent is used with the nasal consonants, a consonant can no more be accentuated, than a vowel can be mute.

The remaining vowels never admit of an accent.

By the use of these accents, three distinct words may be formed out of the same combination of letters; as ဆို *tshō*, "to speak," ဆိုး *tshōs*, "to be vile, wicked," and ဆို့ *tshọ̄*, "to stop up, obstruct."

Punctuation.

The Burmese have only one stop in the way of punctuation, viz., ။, which is used either as a full stop at the end of a sentence; or as a colon, or semicolon, to part off the different clauses, or subdivisions of clauses, if in any way independent; and lastly it occurs as a comma, separating the various clauses, or substantives falling under the same government, as ရွှေ။ငွေ။ကြေး။ငါ့အားမရှိဘူ *shwẹ́* ။ *gnwé* ။ *kyé* ။ *gna aas mă shie bōō*, "gold, silver, copper, I have not." A peculiar use of this stop is, that it is sometimes used in the place of the connective or relative particle သော *thăū*, that is dividing off the word or words qualifying the rest of the sentence, or on which the sentence turns: as ကောင်းမြတ်။လူတယောက်မျှမရှိပါ *koungsmyăt* ။ *lōō tă youk hmyă mă shie ba*, "good, excellent; there is not so much as one man," for ကောင်းမြတ်သောလူ, &c.

Final Remarks on the Alphabet.

It may be necessary to remark that the vocal sound implied by "the inherent *ă*;" is the simplest sound that can be formed, as for instance: No consonant can be pronounced unless a vowel follow; this sound varies in the English alphabet; in the letter "p" it is an "e" as "pe;" but if an attempt were made to pronounce the "p" without the succeeding "e," the nearest approximation to it would be something like the first "pa" in "papa;" this is exactly the sound considered by the Burmese to be naturally inherent in every consonant. The mark ် *thăt,* as has been already stated, annihilates the inherent *ă,* and thereby necessarily causes the consonant to be mute; as က would be "*kă,*" but က် would be "*k,*" remaining in the throat, and requiring the after breath of the "*ă,*" to bring it out, and therefore becoming mute. It will then be enquired why the က် *kă thăt,* or mute, is said to be permuted into a "*t.*" Although the letter "*k,*" is not to be pronounced, it is to be *formed* in the mouth, and by trying any English word it will soon be perceived how the same vowel differs in sound by having a final consonant of two different classes immediately following it; this is caused by the closing sound of the vowel being affected by the different positions in which the organs of speech are placed in the formation of different letters. The learner must be careful to *form* these mute letters, but to stop the sound suddenly; therefore, when a mute "*k*" is said to be permuted into a mute "*t,*" the latter letter must be formed.

The aspirate "*h,*" being a guttural, has the quality when properly attached, of hardening the sound of a letter; as the "*t,*" in the word "often," even if pronounced distinctly, would be soft in comparison to what it would be in such a word as "ofthen" if care be taken to pronounce the "*h,*" the "*th,*" must not be pronounced; as the "*th,*" in "*then*" or "*thin,*" which is in reality a modification of an "*s.*" Indeed the sibilants form a class of sounds in the same way as the nasals.

ABBREVIATIONS.

In writing the undermentioned abbreviations are frequently used.

မ်ိ	for	မည် *mee.*
လ်ိ	for	လည် *lee.*
တ်ိ့	for	တည့် *t̤ee.*
စ်ိ	for	စည် *tsee.*
သ်ိ, or ၌	for	သည် *thee.*
ဥ်	for	ည် as in မဥ် for မည်, &c.
၍ or ...	for	ရွေ့ *ywé.*
၏	for	ဧည့် *éee,* or *ee.*
နှိ	for	နှိုက် *hnŏit.*
ေင်း	for	ကောင်း *koungs.*
ေင့်	for	ကြောင့် *gyoung.*
၎င် or ... or ...	for	လည်းကောင်း *leesgoungs,* when connective.
သ	for	သော *thău,* or သည် *thee.*
ၐ or ေၐ	for	သော *thău.*
˙ superadded	for	က် final, as ကော့ for ကောက် *kouk.*
... or ...	for	မ inferior, as ... or ... for ...း.
လုင်	for	လုလင် *lŏŏlĕng,* "a constable."
ျ interchangeably written	for	ယ especially after က် as လကျာ် for လက်ယာ *lĕtya,* "the right hand."
ၤ	for	င် superior especially when a guttural follows; as မဂ်လာ for မင်္ဂလာ *mĕngăla.*

ဋ္ဌ	for	ဋ *ṭă*, with ဌ *hṭă*, under it.
ၮ	for	ဍ *ḍă*, inferior; as ဘဏ္ၮာ for ဘဏ္ဍာ *bhăṇḍa*.
ဿ or သ္သ	for	a double သ *thă*.
ေသွ့ံ	for	ေသွေသာက် *thwéthouk*.
ေသ္ည	for	ေသသည် *théthee*.
၎	for	သင်ႇ့ *thărwé*.
ေသဝ်	for	ေသာဝ် *thăŭ*.

ဍ *ḍă*, with ဎ *ḍhă*, under it is found written ဍ္ဎ.

It may be here the proper place to remark, that the letters of the alphabet are sometimes found supplied by the use of numerals, either entirely or in part. In the one instance the symbols only of the vowels, and of the letters ဟ *hă*, ရ *ră*, ယ *yă*, and ဝ *wă*, are thus represented. All the consonants are divided into seven classes, corresponding to the seven days of the week, and presided over by what the Burmese consider the seven planets; thus က *kă*, ခ *khă*, ဂ *gă*, ဃ *ghă*, င *gnă*, are considered as belonging to the second day of the week တနင်္လာ *tănengla*, Monday, and are presided over by the Moon: စ *tsă*, ဆ *tshă*, ဇ *dză*, ဈ *dzhă*, ည *gnyă*, belong to the third day of the week အင်္ဂါ *ănga*, Tuesday, and are presided over by Mars: ဋ *ṭă*, ဌ *hṭă*, ဍ *ḍă*, ဎ *ḍhă*, ဏ *ṇă*, တ *tă*, ထ *htă*, ဒ *dă*, ဓ *dhă*, န *nă*, belong to the seventh day of the week စနေ *tsăné*, or Saturday, and are presided over by Saturn: ပ *pă*, ဖ *hpă*, ဗ *bă*, ဘ *bhă*, and မ *mă*, belong to the fifth day of the week ကြာသပတေး *kyathăbădé*, or

Thursday, and are presided over by Jupiter: ယ *yă,* ရ *ră,* ဝ *wă,* လ *lă,* and ဠ *llă,* belong to the fourth day of the week ဗုဒ္ဓဟူး *bŏŏddhăhōō,* Wednesday, and are presided over by Mercury: သ *thă,* and ဟ *hă,* belong to the sixth day of the week သောက်ကြာ *thoukkra,* Friday, and are presided over by Venus: And finally the mute consonant အ *ă,* which belongs to the first day of the week တနင်္ဂနွေ *tănĕngănwé,* Sunday, and is presided over by the Sun.

The two most common numerical modes of expressing the letters of the Alphabet (ဂဏန်း *gănănt,*) are first the ကျောက်စာဂဏန်း *kyouk tsa gănăn,* so styled, from being much used in inscriptions on stone (ကျောက် *kyouk*); and secondly the ဒူးဂဏန်း *dōōtgănănt,* perhaps a corruption of ထူး *htōōt,* "various, differing."

The ကျောက်စာဂဏန်း *kyouk tsa gănănt,*

Is merely a numerical representation of the symbols of the eight vowels belonging to the Pali system, of the mark ် သတ် *thăt,* and of the symbols of the consonants ယ *yă,* ရ *ră,* and ဝ *wă,* of which the latter letter is represented by its corresponding mark in the ဒူးဂဏန်း *dōōtgănănt,* system: the consonants suffer no alteration.

ာ the symbol of the vowel အာ *a,* is represented by the numeral ၁ placed above; ၁ 1 က၁ for ကာ *ka.*

ိ the symbol of the vowel ဣ *ie,* is represented by the numeral ၂ 2 placed above; .... ၂ 2 က၂ for ကိ *kie.*

ီ the symbol of the vowel ဤ *ee,* is represented by the numeral ၃ 3 placed above; .... ၃ 3 က၃ for ကီ *kee.*

ု	the symbol of the vowel ဥ *ŏŏ*, is represented by the numeral ၄ 4 placed below;	၄ 4	က၄ for ကု	*kŏŏ.*
ူ	the symbol of the vowel ဦ *ōō*, is represented by the numeral ၅ 5 placed below;	၅ 5	က၅ for ကူ	*kōō.*
ေ	the symbol of the vowel ေ *é*, is represented by the numeral ၆ 6 placed before;	၆ 6	၆က for ကေ	*ké.*
ေ-ာ	the symbol of the vowel ဪ *ăŭ*, is represented by the corresponding numerals ၆ 6 and ၁ 1 placed in their relative positions;	၆-၁ 6-1	၆က၁ for ကော	*kăŭ.*
်	the mark for သတ် *thăt*, is represented by the numeral ၇ 7 placed below;	၇ 7	က၇ for ကတ်	*k.*
ို	the symbol of the triphthong အို *ō*, is represented by the corresponding numerals ၂ 2, and ၄ 4 placed in their relative positions;	၂ 2 / ၄ 4	က၂၄ for ကို	*kō.*
ျ	the symbol of the letter ယ *yă*, is represented by the mark ါ placed after;	ကါ	for ကျ	*kyă.*
ြ	the symbol of the letter ရ *ră*, is represented by the vowel ေ *é*, placed below the letter;		ကေ for ကြ	*kră.*
ွ	the symbol of the letter ဝ *wă*, is represented by its corresponding mark in the			

ဒွေးဂဏန်း *dōōsgăṇăns,* system by two ၇ or sevens ;.............................. ဝ၇ for ကွ *kwă.*

It is common to find the above method of writing on the titles of Books, Inscriptions, &c.;

သု၄ဓမ္မစိရ်မင်၁းသမီးဖ၆တ၇်ထုံ၄ဓမ္မသတ၇်ရ၄ခိုင၇်လေး၆၄မဟာဒံ၇မင်၁းနံ၇စာ

Thŏŏdhămmă tsarie mĕngs thămees hpyăt htŏŏn dhămmă thăt Răkhŏing lésmyọ̄ măha dan mĕngs nam tsa.

"The legal decisions of the Princess *Thŏŏdhămmă Tsarie,* being the Book of Mengnam, the Mahadan of the four Provinces of Răkhŏing."

The ဒွေးဂဏန်း *dōōsgăṇăns.*

This is an occult mode of writing, which can be varied according to the pleasure of the writer, and can only be read when possessed of the key. One of the more common modes is where the consonants, with the exception of the third and fourth of each class, are represented by the first 9 numerals ("nine" being considered a mystical and holy number, whence its name ကိုး *kōs,* "to reverence,") either singly or repeated. In this system the vowels are sometimes represented by their usual symbols, or by the numerals given to them in the ကျောက်စာဂဏန်း *kyouk tsa găṇăns,* system, with the exception of ေ-သဝေထိုး *thăwéhtōs,* the symbol of the vowel ေ *é,* which is generally represented by four round dots, ꞉ ꞉.

က *kă,*	is represented by the numeral	၁	1	က	၁
ခ *khă,*	....	၂	2	ခ	၂
င *gnă,*	....	၃	3	င	၃
စ *tsă,*	....	၄	4	စ	၄
ဆ *tshă,*	....	၅	5	ဆ	၅

ည *gnyă,*	....	၆	6	ည	၆
တ *tă,*	....	၇	7	တ	၇
ထ *htă,*	....	၀	8	ထ	၀
န *nă,*	....	၉	9	န	၉
ပ *pă,* by two numerals,	....	၁/၁	1/1	ပ	၁/၁
ဖ *hpă,* ditto	....	၂/၂	2/2	ဖ	၂/၂
မ *mă,* ditto	....	၃/၃	3/3	မ	၃/၃
ယ *yă,* ditto	....	၄/၄	4/4	ယ	၄/၄
ရ *ră,* ditto	....	၅/၅	5/5	ရ	၅/၅
လ *lă,* ditto	....	၆/၆	6/6	လ	၆/၆
ဝ *wă,* ditto	....	၇/၇	7/7	ဝ	၇/၇
သ *thă,* ditto	....	၈/၈	8/8	သ	၈/၈
ဟ *hă,* ditto	....	၉/၉	9/9	ဟ	၉/၉
အ *ă,* by the mark called ကြက်ခြေ *krĕt khyé,* "fowl's foot,"				အ	+
၎ သဝေထိုး *thă wé htōႏ,* by	....	းး		၎	းး

ကောင်း *koungး,* "good," written thus, would be ၆ကၥ၃်း in the *kyouk tsä gă-ṇăn,* system; and းး ၁ါ၃်း in the *dōōႏgăṇăn,* system;—in this latter ါ the second symbol of the vowel အ *ă* is used with the numeral ၁ 1, to avoid confounding it with the letter ဘ *bhă;* and the final င် *ng* is represented by the numeral ၃ 3, with the mark *thăt,* over it. Or it might be ၆ဒ၃်း being a combination of the two systems.

PART II.

It may be here repeated, that in the Burmese language almost all words are derived from original roots, which by being used with affixes or prefixes, of which last there are only two, are converted into the different parts of speech; as ကောင်း *koungး,* "good;" အကောင်း *ăkoungး,* "goodness;" ကောင်းစွာ *koungးtswa,* "goodlily;" and so on. These roots are monosyllabic, consisting of one or more letters, but the final letter is always a simple one, and mute. It must be borne in mind, that these roots, in their original form, are not to be considered as conveying any idea but that of an abstract principle or property, as for instance, ကောင်း *koungး* does not convey the idea of any thing or person that is good, or any relative idea of goodness, but goodness considered as an abstract mental quality, then by the use of prefixes or affixes, we can resolve this abstract quality into its various relations, as "good*ness*," good*ly*, good*lily*, good*ish*, &c. &c.

As the whole genius of the language, therefore, depends upon the use of these affixes, it will be proper to give a clear and succinct definition of the different classes of affixes, and an explanation of the terms by which they are expressed.

1. A *causal* affix is so styled because when affixed to a noun it expresses those of its relations, which are generally styled its cases; as လူ *lōō,* "man," လူအား *lōō aaး,* "to man."

2. A *modal* affix is affixed to a verbal root to express the *mode*, or *manner* in which the action, or state expressed by the verb exists, and expresses those of its relations which are commonly called its *moods;* as သွား *thwaः*, "to go," သွားနိုင် *thwaःhnoing*, "can go."

3. A *temporal* affix is a word affixed to a verbal root to express the *time* in which the action, or state of the verb exists; they express those of its relations commonly styled its *tenses*. It is thus evident that they must come after the *Modal* affixes; for the state or action of the verb must be first given, whether modified or not, and then its time, hence it is an invariable rule, that *temporal* affixes never intervene between a *modal* affix and its root; thus သွားနိုင် *thwaःhnoing*, "can go" သွားနိုင်ပြီး *thwaःhnoing byeeः*, "can have gone."

4. A *numeral* affix is one that expresses the *plural number* of the word to which it is attached, (there is no affix of the singular number) thus, လူ *lōō*, "man," လူတို့ *lōō dō*, "men," သွား *thwaः*, "go," (singular,) သွားကြ *thwaःkyă*, "go," (plural)—hence it is always attached to the root itself, and invariably precedes all other affixes. We have thus an easy mode of determining whether, when two roots are together, they form a compound verb, or whether the latter member expresses some modal or other relation of the verb; thus in the clause သွားနိုင်သည် *thwaः hnoing thee*, we are unable (except by the context) to determine, whether it implies, "(he) is able to go," or the potential mood "(he) can go;" but the plural number သွားကြနိုင်သည် *thwaःkyă hnoing thee*, at once conveys the idea of the potential mood, "(they) can go;" here နိုင် *hnoing* expresses a modal relation "can" of သွားကြ *thwaःkyă*, "a plural state of going;" but သွားနိုင်ကြ

သွားနိုင်ကြသည် *thwas hnoing kyă thee,* conveys the idea at once of "a plural state of ability to go;" နိုင် *hnoing,* expressing in this instance, not a *modal* relation of the verb သွား *thwas,* "to go," but forming with it a *compound verbal root.*

5. A *generic* affix is one that expresses the *genus, class,* or *kind* of the noun in connection with which it is used; as they are generally attached to the cardinal or ordinal numbers, they are sometimes styled *Numeral Generic Affixes;* as လူ *lōō,* "man;" လူတယောက် *lōō tă youk,* "one man," ယောက် *youk,* being the generic affix for human beings.

6. A *connective* affix is, as its terms expresses, an affix that *connects* two words; as they generally join a verbal qualifying root, with the noun qualified, they perform the functions of relative pronouns in other languages, and have therefore been sometimes styled *Relative Increments;* as ကောင်း *koungs,* "good," and လူ *lōō,* "man;" ကောင်းသောလူ *koungsthăŭlōō,* "a good man;" for a further analysis of the nature of this class of affixes. Vide *Introduction.*

OF THE NOUN နာမ် *NAM.*

The substantive is the only real Noun.

Noun Substantives

May be divided into two classes, Original Nouns, and Derivative Nouns.

Of Original Nouns.

The subdivisions may be two, 1st. Nouns Proper, or proper names of individuals, whether of men, or other objects; as မောင်လောက် *Moung-louk,* "the name of a man," and ရခိုင် *Răkhoing,* "Arracan." 2ndly.

Common Nouns, or terms implying things, species, or objects of sense; as မြင်း *myengः*, "a horse;" တောင် *toung*, "a hill;" အိမ် *ieng*, "a house," &c.

Sometimes with reference to common nouns, when the name of any animal or thing is expressed, the term implying its species is frequently superadded, as ငှက် *gnhet*, "a bird," to the names of birds; ကောင် *goung*, "a brute beast," to the names of beasts; ပင် *peng*, "a plant," to the names of objects that grow from roots; and sometimes ပိုး *pō*, "an insect," to the names of insects: as စာငှက် *tsagnhet*, "a sparrow;" နွား ကောင် *nwaःgoung*, "an ox;" မြက်ပင် *myetpeng*, "grass;" ဆံပင် *tshăn peng*, "hair."

Derivative Nouns

Are those formed from verbal roots *by prefixing*,

အ *ă*, as စား *tsăः*, "to eat," အစာ *ătsa*, "food;" (in this instance the accent is dropped in the latter compound); ကျောင်း *kyoungः*, "to take care of, to herd as cattle," အကျောင်း *ăgyoungः*, "a herdsman;" ကျန် *kyăn*, "to remain, be left behind," အကျန် *ăgyăn*, "a residue," &c; ဝတ် *ŏŏt*, "to wear," (as clothes), &c. အဝတ် *ăŏŏt*, "a garment." This class of substantives, when derivatives of a root implying any quality, have sometimes an affix of gender attached, and then convey the idea of a person of that gender, either as the agent, or subject of the quality implied in the root; as အရူးမ *ărōōmă*, "a mad woman;" from ရူး *rōō*, "mad." အကြီးဖိုလ် *ăgyeeःbō*, "a great male animal;" from ကြီး *gyeeः*, "great," and ဖိုလ် *hpō*, "the masculine affix for animals."

In compounds consisting of simple derivative nouns, the initial အ *ă*, is frequently omitted; as ညစာ *gnyătsa*, "supper," from အညာ *ăgnyă*, "evening," and အစာ *ătsa*, "food."

This formative prefix အ *ă*, must not be confounded with the အ *ă*, "the—a privative" of the Pali language; which is often found in use in the Burmese language with words of Pali origin; as မင်္ဂလာ *mengăla*, "blessed," အမင်္ဂလာ *ămengăla*, "unblessed" or "accursed."

Or by affixing, 1st:

ခြင်း *khrengး*, or ချင်း *khyengး*, the compounds so formed conveying the idea of the abstract property, principle or action implied in the root; as စားခြင်း *tsaးkhyengး*, "the act, fact, property or principle of eating;" ကျန်ခြင်း *kyănkhyengး*, "the act, fact, principle or property of remaining or being left behind." This is the affix most commonly used for forming substantives from verbal roots; it may be applied to any root whether simple, or compound, and the compounds so formed may have affixes attached to them like any other substantives; as ကယ် *kay*, "to save," ကယ်ခြင်း *kaykhyengး*, "salvation;" မုံးထား *möönးhtaး*, "to hate," မုံးထားခြင်း *möönးhtaးkhyengး*, "hatred." Thus the meaning may be made to vary, as the termination is attached to an active, or neuter root; as ကြောက် *krouk*, "to be afraid," ကြောက်ခြင်း *kroukkhyengး*, "fear," i. e. "neuter fear;" ခြောက် *khrouk*, "to frighten," ခြောက်ခြင်း *khroukkhyengး*, "fright," i. e. "active fear;" ပွင့် *pwęng*, "to open," neuter, ပွင့်ခြင်း *pwęng khyengး*, "an opening," neuter, as "a door when opened;" ဖွင့် *hpwęng*, "to open," active, ဖွင့်ခြင်း *hpwęngkhyengs*, "an opening," active, as "a door in the act of opening."

These compounds admit of two plural numbers, according as the termination ခြင်း *khyengs*, is attached to a verbal root in the singular, or plural number; as သွားခြင်း *thwaskhyengs*, expresses "the *singular* going of a *singular* person," သွားခြင်းတို့ *thwaskhyengsdō*, "the *plural* goings of a *singular* person;" the root သွား *thwas*, "to go," being in the singular number in both instances, but the compound as a *substantive* being placed in the *plural* number, in the latter instance, by the addition of the numeral affix တို့ *dō*. Again သွားကြခြင်း *thwaskyăkhyengs*, implies "the *singular* going of *plural* persons;" the root သွား *thwas*, "to go," being placed in the plural number by the numeral affix of verbs ကြ *kră*, expresses that "the going is plural," but the compound as a *substantive* being in the *singular* number (not having the plural affix တို့ *dō*, attached) expresses that "the *instance* of going is *singular*;" သွားကြခြင်းတို့ *thwaskyăkhyengsdō*, again implies "the *plural* goings of *plural* persons,"—both the verb and the substantive being placed in the *plural* number, the one by the affix တို့ *dō*, the other by the affix ကြ *kyă*.

Verbals of this class take nouns in the possessive case, (like substantives,) and sometimes in the objective case, (like verbs.)

Or, 2dly:

စရာ *tsăra*, ရန် *răn*, or ရဲ *răn*, and the compounds so formed indicate the object or subject of the principle, property or action implied in the root as စားစရာ *tsastsăra*, or စားရန် *tsasrăn*, "an object to be eaten or subject to be eaten or for the purpose of being eaten," as "cooked meat;" ကျန်စရာ *kyăntsăra,* or ကျန်ရန် *kyănrăn,* "what is intended or subject to be left behind, refuse;" ပေး *pés,* "to give," ပေးစရာ *péstsăra,* or ပေးရန် *pésrăn,* "what is meant, &c. to be given, alms." These compounds sometimes have an active signification; as ကြား *kyas,* "to hear," ကြားစရာ *kyastsăra,* or ကြားရန် *kyasrăn,* "what is meant to hear, the ear."

Or, 3rdly:

ရာ *ra,* from အရာ *ăra,* "matter, concern." The compound so formed has a variety of meanings. Thus it may denote an object done or made for the property principle or act implied in the root; as စားရာ *tsasra,* "a thing made to be eaten;" ကျန်ရာ *kyănra,* "a thing made or done for the purpose of being left behind;" ထိုင် *htoing,* "to sit," ထိုင်ရာ *htoingra,* "a chair or seat;" ပယ်ပြစ် *paypyect,* "to throw away," ပယ်ပြစ်ရာ *paypyeetra,* "a place for throwing away,—a bolting hutch;" ဝင် *weng,* "to enter," ဝင်ရာ *wengra,* "an entrance gate;" အိမ် *ieng,* "a house," အိမ်ရာ *iengra,* "a household object,—a wife;" စည်းဝေး *tseeswés,* "to assemble," စည်းဝေးရာ *tseeswésra,* "a place of assemblage;" အိပ် *iek,* "to sleep," အိပ်ရာ *iekra,* "a bed;" or with compound roots, as ဆိတ် *tshiet,* "to be silent," and ကွယ် *kway,* "to hide" form ဆိတ်ကွယ်ရာ *tshietkway ra,* "a thing hidden by silence, a secret;" ရေနက်ရာ *rénătra,* or ရေနက်ရာအရပ် *rénătraărăt,* "a place where the water is deep," from ရေ *ré,* "water," နက် *năt,* "deep," and အရပ် *ărăt,* "a place;" သွားရာလမ်း *thwasra lăns,* "a road for going in," from သွား *thwas,* "to go," and

လမ်း *läns,* "a road;" နိုင်ရာမဲ့သူ *hnoingra mại thōō,* "a man without an equal," from နိုင် *hnoing,* "to overcome," မဲ့ *mại,* "to be without," and သူ *thōō,* "a person;" ထိုလူနေရာအရပ် *htō lōō néra ărăt,* "the place where that man is stopping." It is also found sometimes to imply the principle of the root substantively considered or "the act implied by the root;" as ပြော *pyăŭ,* "to speak," ပြောရာ *pyăŭra,* "a speech;" ပေး *pés,* "to give," ပေးရာ *pésra,* "a gift." A curious, and common application of it is with the causal affix သို့ *thọ̆,* "towards;" and one that shews the true meaning of that word to be "the active principle of progression;" as သို့ရာ *thọ̄ra,* "thus;" သို့ရာတွင် *thọ̄ra dweng,* "thus, in this way, such being the case."

Sometimes the expletive လေ *lé,* precedes this affix; as ကပ် *kăt,* "to take refuge," ကပ်လေရာ *kătléra,* "a place of refuge."

Or, 4thly:

ဖို့ *hpọ̄,* from အဖို့ *ăhpọ̄,* "a part or portion," is sometimes used in the place of ရာ *ra,* or they are often found interchangeably compounded; as ဖို့ရာ *hpọ̄ra;* ရာဖို့ *ra hpọ̄;* ရာအဖို့ *ra ăhpọ̄.*

Or, 5thly:

ချက် *khyet,* from အချက် *ăkhyet,* "a subject, matter;" and the compound so formed implies the present subject of the principle, property or action implied in the root; this affix is chiefly confined to roots implying mental, or bodily action; as ပြော *pyăŭ,* "to speak," ပြောချက် *pyăŭkhyet,* "the present subject of conversation;" ပြု *pyŏŏ,* "to do," ပြုချက် *pyŏŏkhyĕt,* "the present subject of action;" ရယ် *ray,* "to laugh," ရယ်ချက် *raykhyet,* "the present subject of laughter."

Another class of verbals implying quality, and therefore similar to our adjectives and participles are formed by affixing:

ဖွယ် *hpway*, ဘွယ် *bhway*, or စဘွယ် *tsăbway*, and the word so formed implies being fit, worthy, or desirable to be, or become the principle, property or action implied by the root; as စားဖွယ် *tsaahpway*, not only "what is fit to be eaten," but "what is desirably so,—delicious;" ချစ် *khyeet*, "to love," ချစ်ဖွယ် *khyeetbhway*, not only "what is deserving of love," but "what cannot but be loved,—loveable."

ဘွယ် *bhway*, ဖွယ် *hpway*, စဖွယ် *tsăhpway*, စဘွယ် *tsăbhway*, စလိ *tsălie*, စလိလိ *tsălielie*, လိဘွယ် *liebhway*, ခမန် *khămăn*, or ဂမန် *gămăn*, or any of these combined, when affixed to a word convey the idea of being possessed of the property implied in the root; as အံ့ဘွယ် *ăn bhway*, အံ့လိဘွယ် *ănliebhway*, အံ့ဂမန် *ăngămăn*, all imply "wonderful," from အံ့ *ăn*, "to wonder."

All these affixes, especially those terminating in ချင်း *khyengs*, are not confined to simple roots, like စား *tsaa*, "to eat," &c. &c., but may be applied to a verbal substantive combined with its adjective, and implies the principle, &c. of the verbal so qualified; as အစာ *ătsa*, "food," and ခေါင်းပါး *khoungsbaa*, "scarce," whence အစာ ခေါင်းပါးချင်း *ătsa khoungsbaa khyengs*,* "scarcity of food,—a famine."

Compound Substantives.

Some nouns are compounded of two different roots, the latter mem-

* It is to be stated that the remark made at p. 34, in reference to verbals ending in ချင်း *khyengs*, admitting of two plural numbers, may be equally applied to all the other verbals.

ber of the word, being either a substantive, or a verb; this class is so numerous that all could not be particularised.

ခလေ *khălé*, or ဂလေ *gălé*, from အခလေ *ăkhălé*, "the young of any animal," is attached to the names of living things to form a corresponding diminutive or to express the young of such animals; as လူ *lōō*, "a man," လူဂလေ *lōōgălé*, "a boy;" မြင်း *myengs*, "a horse," မြင်းဂလေ *myengsgălé*, "a poney."

ဖုတ် *hpŏŏk*, an adjective; improperly written ဘို *bhō*, is affixed to the names of inanimate objects to express their diminutives; as တောင် *toung*, "a hill," တောင်ဖုတ် *tounghpŏŏk*, "a little hill."

စ *tsă*, from အစ *ătsă*, "a bit," is affixed to solids to imply a "bit of;" as သံ *thăn*, "iron," သံစ *thăntsă*, "a bit of iron;" ကျောက် *kyouk*, "a stone," ကျောက်စ *kyouktsă*, "a bit of stone."

သား *thas*, from အသား *ăthas*, "offspring," is affixed to proper names of towns or countries, or to nouns implying places to denote their inhabitants or natives; as မြန်မာသား *Byămma thas*, "a son of Burma, a Burman;" ရွာသား *rwathas*, "a villager," from ရွာ *rwa*, "a village;" လယ်သား *laythas*, "a countryman," from လယ် *lay*, "a field;" in contradistinction to မြို့သား *myōthas*, "a townsman," from မြို့ *myō*, "a city:" သား *thas*, is also applied to the names of the days of the week to imply born on that day; as အင်္ဂါသား *ăhgathas*, "a son of Tuesday, —born on a Tuesday." When particularising females in any of the above compounds သမီး *thămees*, "a daughter," is used; as ရွာသမီး *rwathămees*, "a village woman;" &c.

သည် *thee*, from အသည် *ăthee*, "an owner," and သယ် *thay*, from အသယ်

ăthay, "business, performance," are affixed to denote a person of the employment or profession of the word to which it is attached; as ဆီသည် *tsheethee,* or ဆီသယ် *thsheethay,* "an oilman," from ဆီ *tshee,* "oil;" လယ် *lay,* "a field," လယ်သည် *laythee,* "a husbandman;" ခရီး *khăreeး,* "a way," ခရီးသည် *khăreeးthee,* "a wayfaring, man." When applied to a verbal root it expresses the agent of the act, fact, property or principle implied in the root; as ပြော *pyău,* "to speak," ပြောသည် *pyăuthee,* "a speaker." v. Introduction.

သမား *thămaး,* "an artificer," is affixed to words implying tools, substances, or work to imply persons employed with such things; as ဆေး *tshéး,* "medicine," ဆေးသမား *tshéးthămaး,* "a doctor;" လက် *lĕt,* "the hand," လက်သမား *letthămaး,* "a handicraft's man;" ချုပ် *khyŏŏk,* "to sew," ချုပ်သမား *khyŏŏkthămaး,* a tailor;" လွှ *hlwă,* "a saw," လွှသမား *hlwăthămaး,* "a sawyer."

ချင်း *khyengး,* from အချင်း *ăkhyengး,* "a companion," is affixed to names of men's trade or occupation to express "a fellow;" as ကျွန် *kwyŏn,* "a slave," ကျွန်ချင်း *kwyŏnkhyengး,* "a fellow-slave."

ခိုက် *khoik,* from အခိုက် *ăkhoik,* "a state of being," is used in the following manner; ငယ် *gnay,* "little," ငယ်ခိုက် *gnaykhoik,* "the time of littleness or childhood;" ပျို *pyō,* "prime," ပျိုခိုက် *pyōkhoik,* "the time of prime, manhood;" &c.

တတ် *tăt,* "to know;" as ခရာ *khăra,* "a wind instrument," ခရာတတ် *khăra tăt,* "a bugler."

စား *tsaး,* "to eat;" as အခ *ăkhă,* "wages," အခစား *ăkhătsaး,* "a hired servant;" ကိုယ် *kōh,* "the body," ကိုယ်စား *kōhtsaး,* "an agent or substitute;" မြီ *myee*, "a debt," မြီစား *myeetsat*, "a creditor;" နေ့ *nẹ́*, "a day," နေ့စား *nẹ́tsat*, "a day-laborer."

ပြ *pyă*, "to shew;" as ဓား *dhas*, "a sword or knife," ဓားပြ *dhaspyă*, "a robber;" လမ်း *lăns*, "a road," လမ်းပြ *lănspyă*, "a guide."

မ *mă*, "chief, principal;" as တက် *tĕt*, "a paddle," တက်မ *tĕtmă*, "a rudder."

သီး *thees*, from အသီး *ăthees*, "fruit or any thing of that shape;" လက် *lĕt*, "the hand," လက်သီး *lĕtthees*, "the fist;" နို့ *nō̤*, "the mammæ," နို့သီး *nō̤thees*, "the nipple;" နှာ *hna*, "the nose," နှာသီး *hnathees*, "the tip of the nose."

ရှိ *shie*, "to be;" as အသရေ *ăthăré*, "character," အသရေရှိ *ăthăréshie*, a person of character;" အရာ *ăra*, "business, affair," အရာရှိ *ărashie*, "an employé," applied to Government officials.

ဝန် *wŏn*, "a burden;" as မြို့ *myō̤*, "a chief city or district," မြို့ဝန် *myō̤wŏn*, "a Governor of ditto;" အခွန် *ăkhwon*, "territorial revenue," အခွန်ဝန် *ăkhwŏnwŏn*, "a head revenue officer.

မှူး *hmōōs*, from အမှူး *ăhmōōs*, "superintendence;" as ထောင် *htoung*, "a jail," ထောင်မှူး *htounghmōōs*, "a jailer."

ရှင် *sheng*, from အရှင် *ăsheng*, "an owner;" as မြီ *myee*, "a debt," မြီရှင် *myeesheng*, "a creditor;" အိမ် *ieng*, "a house;" အိမ်ရှင် *iengsheng*, "a householder;" စည်းစိမ် *tseestsien*, "wealth," စည်းစိမ်ရှင် *tseestsien sheng*, "a wealthy person."

ရံ *răn*, or ယံ *yăn*, from အရံ *ărăn*, "a season," is often expletively attached to words of "time;" as ညဉ့်ယံ *gnyeenyăn*, "night time."

ချိန် *khyien*, from အချိန် *ăkhyien*, "time," is used in the same way as the preceding.

အိမ် *ieng,* "a house;" as ဓား *dhas,* "a sword," ဓားအိမ် *dhas ieng,* "a scabbard;" မီး *mees,* "fire, light;" မီးအိမ် *mees ieng,* "a lanthorn."

ရည် *ree,* from အရည် *ăree,* "a liquid;" as အုန်း *ŏŏns,* "a cocoanut," အုန်းရည် *ŏŏns ree,* "cocoanut milk;" ရာသီ *rathee,* "a moon," ရာသီရည် *rathee ree,* "the menses;" ပျား *pyas,* "a bee," ပျားရည် *pyas ree,* "honey."

သူ *thōō,* "a person," is sometimes prefixed; as ခိုး *khōs,* "to steal," သူခိုး *thōōkhōs,* "a thief;" ကြီး *gyees,* "great," သူကြီး *thōō gyees,* "a great person."

These compound nouns are inflected, and passed as simple nouns, although they may be partly compounded of a verb; as တောင်းစား *toungstsas,* "a beggar," တောင်းစားတို့ *toungstsasdō,* "beggars;" or the first member may have an adjective, or the honoric affix တော် *dāū,* attached; as အခွန်တော်ဝန် *akhwon dāū wŏn,* "head collector of the royal revenue;" မြေကြီးပုံ *myé gyees pŏŏn,* "a map of the great earth, i. e. of the world;" မြေပုံကြီး *myé pŏŏn gyees,* "a great map of land."

NUMBER OF NOUNS.

The number of nouns are two; "Singular," and "Plural." The singular number is expressed by the simple root; as လူ *lōō* "man;" စားခြင်း *tsas khyengs,* "an eating."

The Plural is formed by affixing တို့ *dō;* as လူတို့ *lōō dō,* "men;" စားချင်းတို့ *tsas khyengs dō,* "eatings." This affix is *always* attached to the root, all other affixes following it; as လူတို့အား *lōō dō aas,* "to men."

This increment may also be attached to a succession of proper names.

When an indefinite plural is to be expressed, the adjective များ *myas,* "many" is either substituted for တို့ *dō*, or used in connection with it; as လူများ *lōō myas*, "a number of men," လူများတို့ *lōō myasdō*, "many men;" ဤလောကဝေဒနာများ *ee läügă wédăna myas*, "the afflictions of this world." များ *myas* is also used when several substantives follow in immediate connection with each other; as ခေါင်း။လက်။ခြေ။မျက်စိများ *khoungs‖ lĕt‖ khyé‖ myettsie myas*, "the head, hands, feet, eyes."

To express various or indefinite numbers of a verbal substantive, the noun is often reduplicated, the initial အ *ă*, omitted in the last compound, and the numeral affix is then appended; as အရပ် *ărăt*, "a place," from ရပ် *răt*, "to stay," အရပ်ရပ်တို့ *ărăt răt dō*, "various places, an indefinite number of places;" အမျိုးမျိုးတို့အား *ămyōs myōs dō aas*, "to various generations."

Genders of Nouns.

The masculine gender of nouns implying intellectual beings is expressed by affixing ယောက်ျား *youkyas*, "a male," and the feminine by မိမ္မ *meimmă*, "a woman;" as သား *thas*, "offspring," သားယောက်ျား *thas youkyas*, "a son," သားမိမ္မ *thasmeimmă*, "a daughter;" but this circumlocution is very rarely used, the gender of such words being formed irregularly; as သမီး *thămees*, "a daughter," သား *thas*, "a son;" အဖ *ăhpă*, ဖ *hpă*, or ဖခင် *hpăkheng*, "a father," အမိ *ămie*, မိ *mie*, or မိခင် *miekheng*, "a mother;" ရှင်ဘုရင် *shengbhŏŏreng*, "a monarch," မိဘုရား *miebhŏŏras*, "a queen;" အရှင် *ăsheng*, "Sir, Master," မယ်ရှင် *maysheng*, "Mistress, Madam."

ထီး *htees*, from အထီး *ăhtees*, "a male," is affixed to the names of brute beasts, and in some cases of human beings, to express the male; and

မ *mă*, from အမ *ămă*, "a mother, or female," to express the female; as ခွေးထီး *khwé:htee:*, "a dog," ခွေးမ *khwé:mă*, "a bitch." Those animals which custom subjects to castration, when entire are expressed either by the use of the affix ထီး *htee:*, or လား *la:*, the final syllable of the word အလား *ăla:*, "uncastrated;" as နွားလား *nwa:la:*, or နွားထီး *nwa:htee:*, "a bull,' နွားမ *nwa:mă*, "a cow." The castrated animal is particularised by ပြီး *byee:*, "finished, done;" as နွားပြီး *nwa:byee:*, "an ox;" any root implying castration may likewise be affixed.

ဖ *hpă*, from အဖ *ăhpă*, "a father," is used to particularise the male gender of birds; as ဒေါင်းဖ *doung:hpă*, "a pea cock," ဒေါင်းမ *doung:mă*, "a pea hen;" ကြက်ဖ *krĕthpă*, "a cock," ကြက်မ *krĕtmă*, "a hen."

သိုး *thō:*, from အသို *ăthō*, "a penis," is likewise sometimes affixed to express the male of animals; as နွားသိုး *nwa:thō:*, "a bull."

ဖိုလ် pronounced, and often written ဖို *hpō*, and incorrectly ဘို *bhō*, from အဖိုလ် *ăhpō*, a term applied to barren females; and which perhaps, from the Pali ဗလ *bălă*, "strength, power," is indiscriminately applied to the male of certain animals, birds, or beasts, and in one instance to human beings; as, ငန်းဖိုလ် *gnăn:bō*, "a gander," ငန်းမ *gnăn:mă*, "a goose;" မျောက်ဖိုလ် *myoukbō*, "a male monkey," မျောက်မ *myoukmă*, "a female monkey;" မုတ်ဆိုးဖိုလ် *mŏŏktshō:bō*, "a widower," မုတ်ဆိုးမ *mŏŏktshō:mă*, "a widow."

Cases of Nouns.

In the Burmese language the different relations of Noun Substantives, in reference to their cases, are expressed by the appendage of certain affixes, which may be styled *causal affixes* or *affixes of case*

These affixes may, for the sake of arrangement, be divided into two classes. 1st, Those that express a simple or unmodified relation of a noun; and 2dly, Those that express a compound or modified relation.

Of the first class the meaning of the roots of some may be traced; as ဖို့ *hpō*, "for," from အဖို့ *ăhpō*, "a part or portion," but of others the meaning, if there was any, is lost; as မှာ *hma*, "in."

သည် *thee*, is the most common affix of the nominative case; as သူသည်ပြုသည် *thōōthee pyōōthee*, "he does it." When the agent of a passive verb is to be expressed, this affix is sometimes used in place of the instrumental affix ဖြင့် *hpyeng*; as ငါသည်ဖန်လုပ်သောသေတ္တာကောင်းရှိပါသည် *gna thee hpăn lōōk thăü theetda koungး shie ba thee*, "the trunk I made is good," for "the trunk made," ငါဖြင့် *gna hpyeng*, "by me." In colloquial discourse this affix is by an ellipse generally omitted. သည် *thee*, is found used after မှ *hmă*, and က *gă*, "from"—in the following manner, and having a connective power keeps the clause open; thus အငုံမှသည်အပွင့်ဖြစ်၏။အပွင့်မှသည်အသီးဖြစ်၏ *ăgnōōn hmă thee ăpweng hpyeet ee*။ *ăpweng hmă thee ătheeး hpyeet ee*။, "after the bud *then* comes the blossom; after the blossom *then* comes the fruit."

ကား *gaး*, is also an affix of the nominative case; it is used either emphatically; as ဤပညတ္တိကားဖြစ်သည် *Ee pägnyättie gaး hpyeet thee*, "this is the divine commandment," or in particularising and recapitulating; as ငါသည်ဝယ်သောဥစ္စာတို့တွင်။တခုကားဓါး။တခုကားလှံ။တခုကားလွှရှိသည် *gna thee way thăü ōōtstsa dō dweng tăkhōō gaး dhaး*။ *tăkhōō gaး hlăn*။ *tăkhōō gaး hlwă shie thee*, "of the goods I have bought the one is a dao, the one a spear, and the one a saw." It may in this manner be used emphatically after other affixes without changing the cases of their nouns; as စာကိုကားဖတ်တတ်သည်လော *tsa gō gaꞋhpăt tăt thee lăü,* "the letter to read, do you know how;" ထိုနေ့၌ကား *htō nę hnoit gaꞋ,* "for in that day, verily in that day." In the same way it is sometimes used to mark a contrast; as သားခလေးကိုကားနမ်းရှုသည်သမီးကိုကားဆုံးမှကြွပ်ညှပ်သည် *thaꞋkhălé gō gaꞋ nănꞋ shōō thee thămeeꞋ gō gaꞋ tshōōmmă kwĕt gnyhĕt thee,* "the little son indeed he kissed, but the daughter he rebuked." ကား *gaꞋ,* is also used emphatically at the close of a simple sentence; as ငါဆိုသည်ကား *gna tshō thee gaꞋ,* "for I say, now I tell you." Also to shew the point on which an allusion turns; as သူပြောသည်ကားအဘယ်သို့နည်း *thōō pyăü thee gaꞋ ăbhay thō neeꞋ,* "how then is it he speaks." ကား *gaꞋ,* မူကား *mōōgaꞋ,* ရကား *răgaꞋ,* မူ *mōō,* are likewise used when the idiom of "having," is to be rendered by that of "being to;" as ငှက်တို့မူကားအသိုက်တို့ရှိကြသည် *gnhĕt dō mōōgaꞋ ăthoik dō shie kyă thee,* "Birds have nests." မူကား *mōōgaꞋ,* is used in connection with အကြောင်း *ăgyoungꞋ,* "a reason," or any of its compounds; as အဘယ်ကြောင်း *ăbhay gyoungꞋ,* and has the meaning "for what reason," "for this reason," "for that reason;" according to the pronoun with which compounded; as သည်ကြောင်းမူကား *thee gyoungꞋ mōōgaꞋ,* "for this reason;" to obviate the tautology of သည်ကြောင်းကြောင့် *thee gyoungꞋ gyoung.*

These affixes ကား *gaꞋ,* မူကား *mōōgaꞋ,* ရကား *răgaꞋ,* and မူ *mōō,* may be styled particularising causal affixes, and imply "in respect of, in reference to, as to, concerning, in regard to;" &c.

က *ga,* the ablative affix is likewise found used as a nominative affix, and is emphatic; as ငါကဆိုသည် *gnă gă tshō thee,* "*I* say it." It is chiefly used as a nominative affix, when a clause intervenes between the nominative and its verb ; မိန္မတယောက်ကငါသည်အဝတ်တော်ကိုသာတို့လျှင်ချမ်းသာရမည်ဟုစိတ်ထင်လာ၍ "a certain woman, having in her mind, if his garment only I could but touch I should be healed ; came, &c ;" here the nominative, "a certain woman," is separated by a long clause from its verb "came," and takes the affix က *gă.*

ကို *gō,* is the affix of the objective or accusative case, and is the affix of the noun immediately governed by all transitive verbs. This affix is rendered by a variety of different prepositions in English ; as ငါးကိုထောင် *gnaː gō htoung,* "catch fish ;" အကျင့်ကိုထောက် *ăgyęng gō htouk,* "deliberate on the deed ;" ငါကိုကူထောက် *gna gō kōō htouk,* "assist me ;" ကျမ်းစာကိုဖတ်၍ရှာတော့ *kyănː tsa gō hpĕt rwę̄ sha dăŭ,* "search, and read the scriptures." It is often used as the affix of the dative case "To," in such instances the object itself has no affix at all ; as ငါခင်ပွားကိုဒင်္ဂါးတပြားပေးမည် *gna khengbyaː gō dingaː tă byaː péː mee,* "I will give thee, friend, a rupee :" ကို *gō,* also implies "at," in reference to time ; as သုံးနာရီအချိန်ကို *thŏŏnː naree ăkhien gō,* "at three o'clock." Likewise "of ;" as in သံကိုလုပ်သည် *thăn gō lŏŏk thee,* "made of iron." It is likewise also sometimes used particularisingly after other affixes ; as ဤမြို့ကကိုထိုမြို့ရောက် *ee myō̤ gă gō htō myō̤ rouk,* "from this city to that city ;" when used in this way after the nominative affix သည် *thee,* the latter is often not expressed ; as ငါ၏လေးယောက်သောသားတို့ကိုအလွန်စွာမကောင်းယုတ်ဖြစ်ကြသည် *gna ee lę̄ːyouk thăŭ thaːdō̤ gō ăhlwon tswa mă koungːyŏŏk hpyeet kyă thee,* "my four sons are extremely depraved and wicked : ကို *ko,* is also sometimes possessive ; as ငှက်တို့ကိုအသိုက်တို့ရှိကြသည် *gnhĕt* *dọ̄ gō ăthŏik dọ̄ shie kyă thee,* "Birds have nests." In the same way it is used as the genitive with verbals, v. p. 34; as ရန်ပြုခြင်းကိုအလိုရှိချင်း *rănpyŏŏ khyeng: gō ălō shie khyeng:,* "a desire for quarrelling and fighting." Sometimes it implies" "in the direction of;" as ရှေ့ကိုကြည့် *shẹ́ gō kyẹe,* "look to the front." Other instances of the use of ကို *kō,* are as follows; သခင်ကိုမေ့ာက် *thăkheng gō shouk,* "ask of the master;" သူသည်ပညတ်ကိုလွန်ကျူးသည် *thōō thee păgnyăttie gō hlwăn kyŏŏ: thee,* "he transgresses the divine precept;" တယောက်ကိုတယောက်စကားပြောကြသည် *tă-youk gō tăyouk tsăga: pyăŭ kyă thee,* "one person speaking to another," i. e. "speaking to each other;" တယောက်ကိုတယောက်တွေ့ကြပြီး *tăyouk gō tăyouk twẹ́ kyă byee:,* "two persons meeting each other."* ကို *kō* is also sometimes used as the affix of the object of verbs of "motion;" as သည်ကိုလာခဲ့ *thee gō la gại,* "come here;" ငါ့အိမ်ကိုသွားတော့ *gna ieng gō thwa: dặŭ,* "go to my house."

သို့ *thọ̄,* implies the principle of motion towards or progression, whether "mental;" as designing, intending, or "bodily;" as going, proceeding &c, and answers to the preposition "to, towards," and is the affix of the object of verbs of motion; as မိမိတို့ပြည်သို့သူတို့သွားကြသည် *miemie dọ̄ pyee thọ̄ thōō: dọ̄ thwa: kyă thee,* "they go to their own country," i. e. "towards their own country." This critical distinction however, is seldom attended to; as မိမိနေရာသို့သူရောက်လာပြီး *miemie nẹ́ra thọ̄ thōō rouk la byee:,* "he arrived at his dwelling;" အိမ်သို့ဝင်သည် *ieng thọ̄ weng thee,* "he enters the house." သို့ *thọ̄,* has the meaning of "to, unto;" as in

* It will be here remarked that the idea of "mutuality," is expressed in Burmese by the verb in the *plural* number agreeing with a nominative in the *singular* number; thus as it were drawing in the *object,* to assist with the *agent* in making the concord true, and vice versâ.

လွှတ်ရုံးတော်သို့အပ်နှံ *hlŏŏt yŏŏn꞉dāū thọ̄ ăt hnăn,* "deliver over to the supreme tribunal." Since သို့ *thọ̄,* implies " mental progression towards, " as well as " bodily progression towards," it in some cases is to be rendered into English by the words " according to, in proportion to ;" as ရောက်လိုရာသို့လျှင်မြန်စွာသွားသည် *rouk lō ra thọ̄ hlyeng myăn tswa thwa꞉ thee,* " he goes with a speed in proportion to desire of arrival." When used as the causal affix of the object of words implying " seeing, beholding, hearing &c," its inherent meaning of motion affects the sentence, and such words imply " going to see, " going to hear,to visit, &c ;" အိမ်သို့ကြည့်မြင်ရသည် *ieng thọ̄ kyẹe myeng ră thee,* " to visit a house," lit. " to see to or towards a house." When combined with a demonstrative pronoun its peculiar power affects the compound and it implies " manner, mode &c ;" as ဤ *ee,* " this," ဤသို့ *ee thọ̄,* " thus, after this fashion," i. e. " progressing to this ;" ထို *htō,* " that," ထိုသို့ *htō thọ̄,* " In that wise, so, &c." Its power when used as a demonstrative pronoun by itself will now be easily perceived ; သို့ဟုတ်လျှင် *thọ̄ hō hlyeng,* " should such be the case, if so."

၏ *ee,* is the affix of the possessive case, and is generally omitted by an ellipse, when not used emphatically ; as ငါ၏ပညာအစွမ်းဖြင့် *gna eepăynya ătswon hpyẹng,* " By the power of my wisdom," or ငါ၏ပညာ၏အစွမ်းဖြင့် *gna eepăgnya ee atswonhpyẹng.* In one instance, that of the first personal pronoun ငါ *gna,* " I," not only is it omitted by an ellipse, but likewise the pronoun is abbreviated into င *gnă ;* as ငအဖ *gnă ăhpă,* " my father ;" ငသမီး *gnă thămee꞉,* " my daughter."

အား *aa꞉,* is the affix of the dative case, implying " to ;" as ကောင်းသောလူခ

လေးအားငါပေးမည် *koungs thăŭ lōōgălé aas gna pés mee,* "I will give (it) to a good boy;" ငါ့အားပြောသည် *gna aas pyăŭ thee,"* (he) speaks to me;" ငါ့အားတံခါးဖွင့်တော့ *gna aas tăkhăs hpwęng dăŭ,* "open the door to me. It may also be rendered "of, from;" as in ဟိုသိကြားအားတောင်းပန်ပြီး *hōthiegyas aas toungs păn byees,* "thus (he) respectfully solicited of the angel." It is used as the affix of nouns governed by words denoting "fitness, &c.;" as ငါ့၏သားအားထိုက်တန်သောမယား *gna ee thas aas htoik tăn thăŭ măyas,* "a wife fitting, or becoming my son;" ငါ့အားတော်လျော်သောနေရာ *gna aas tāū lyāū thăŭ né ra,* "a dwelling becoming me;" အမိန့်တော်အားလျော်စွာ *ămień dāū aas lyāū tswa,* "agreeably to the divine commandment." The following are a variety of its applications; ဘေးပြုသူတို့အားဘေးကြီးရောက်လိမ့်မည် *bhés pyŏŏ thōō dō aas bhés gyees rouk liem mee,* "on evil doers evil will come;" ငှက်တို့အားအသိုက်တို့ရှိကြသည် *gnhĕt dō aas ăthoik dō shie kyă thee,* "birds have nests;" ဘေးထင်သူအားဘေးကြီးဖြစ်စေ *bhés hteng thōō aas bhés gyees hpyeet tsé,* "evil to him who evil thinks;" ငါ့အားပြုချင်သမျှကိုငါပြုသည် *gna aas pyŏŏ khyeng thă hmyă gō gna pyŏŏ thee,* "I do as I list:" အား *aas,* is also rendered by "by," as in ရေအားရောက်ပြီးမှကြည်းအားပြန်သွားမည်လော *ré aas rouk byees hmă kyees aas pyăn thwas mee lăŭ,* "after having come by water will you return by land."

ငှါ *gnha,* "for, in order to;" before this affix such a word, as အလို *ălō,* "desire, wish," may be considered as understood; its use is chiefly confined to verbal roots; and, when used in connection with a future affix, it is the means of expressing the infinitive mood; as ငတ်ခြင်းကိုဝပြောစေငှါ *gnĕt khyengs gō wă pyăŭ tsé gnha,* or ငတ်ခြင်းကိုဝပြောစေအလိုငှါ *gnĕt khyengs gōwă pyăŭ tsé ălō gnha,* or ငတ်ခြင်းကိုဝပြေအံ့သောငှါ *gnĕt khyengs gō wă pyăŭ ăn thăŭ gnha,* "in order to appease hunger," "with the desire of appeasing hunger," "so as to appease hunger."

ကြောင့် *gyoung,* "because," "on account of," is likewise chiefly used with verbal roots, or verbal nouns; as အမိန့်တော်ကြောင့် *ămieṇ dāū gyoung,* "on account of the sacred mandate;" ငါအပြစ်သောကြောင့် *gna ăpyeet thăŭ gyoung,* "on account of my transgression."

နှင့် *hneṇg,* is the instrumental affix "with, by means of, together with," and is very various in its signification; မျက်စိနှင့်မြင်သည်။နားရွက်နှင့်နားကြားသည် *myettsie hneṇg myeng thee* ॥ *nas rwĕt hneṇg nas kyas thee,* "(he) sees with the eye, and hears with the ear;" နီသောအထည်နှင့်မဖာရဘူ *nee thăŭ ădee hneṇg mă hpa yă bhōō,* "(you) must not mend it with red-cloth;" စာနှင့်မှာကြားသည် *tsa hneṇg hma kyasthee,* "(he) sends information by letter;" ရေနှင့်ပြည့် *ré hneṇg byeẹ,* "filled with water;" ရေအပြည့်နှင့် *ré ăbyeẹ hneṇg,* "with a fulness of water." ကြောက်ခြင်းနှင့်ပြေးသွားသည် *kyouk khyengs hneṇg byés thwas thee,* "(he) runs through fear; မင်းကြီးလည်းထိုအနာနှင့်လွန်တော်မူလေ၏ *myengs gyees lee htō ăna hneṇg lwon dăŭ mōō lé ee,* "then the king died of that disease:" နှင့် *hneṇg,* also implies "in," in reference to "time;" as in ဤမြို့မှသည်ထိုမြို့သို့အရောက်ရက်ပေါင်းသုံးဆယ်ရက်နှင့်ရောက်သည် *ee myọ hmă thee htō myọ thọ ărouk ret poungs thŏŏns tshay ret hneṇg rouk thee,* "from this city to that city; the total days of arrival were arrived in thirty days;" i. e. "(we) arrived from this city to that city in thirty days." နှင့် *hneṇg,* is also a connective affix, and as such has various applications: when in the sense of "together with," "similar to," the words အတူ

ăkwă, အတူ *ătōō,* implying "similarity, likeness," are often superadded. Sometimes the initial အ *ă,* of these words is dropped or its place supplied with the formative prefix တ *tă;* as တကွ *tăkwă,* တတူ *tătōō,* or they may be used variously combined or reduplicated; as ငါနှင့် *gna hnẹng,* or ငါနှင့်အတူ *gna hnẹng ătōō,* or ငါနှင့်အတူတူ *gna hnẹng ătōō dōō,* or ငါနှင့်တတူတူ *gna hnẹng tătōō dōō,* or ငါနှင့်အကွ *gna hnẹng ăkwă,* ငါနှင့်အကွကွ *gna hnẹng ăkwă kwă,* or ငါနှင့်တကွကွ *gna hnẹng tă kwă kwă,* &c. &c. &c. all imply either "together with me," or "similar to me," according to the contest; as ငါနှင့်အတူရှိသည် *gna hnẹng ătōō shie thee,* may imply either "similar to me," or "together with me;" ငါနှင့်အတူဖြူသည် *gna hnẹng ătōō hpyōō thee,* "as fair as I am;" ငါနှင့်အတူလာခဲ့ပြီး *gna hnẹng atōō la gại byeeः,* "(he) came with me;" ငါနှင့်စပ်ဆိုင်သောသူ *gna hnẹng tsăt tshoing thăŭ thōō,* "a person connected with me, a neighbour;" လူမိုက်နှင့်ပုံပြု *lōō moik hnẹng pŏŏn pyŏŏ,* "to liken to a fool, compare to a fool;" ကိုယ်နှင့်အမျှချစ်တော့ *koh hnẹng ăhmyă khyeet dặŭ,* "love (him) as thyself:" နှင့် *hnẹng* is also found having a negative connective meaning; as မယားနှင့်ကွာလိုချင်သည် *măyaः hnẹng kwa lō khyeng thee,* "(he) wishes to be separated from his wife," lit. "with his wife;" ထိုသူတို့နှင့်မနီး *htō thōō dộ hnẹng mă neeः,* "not near those persons;" သည်အိမ်နှင့်ဝေးပါသည် *thee ieng hnẹng wéः ba thẹe,* "(it) is far from this house," lit. "in connection with this house it is far;" သည်မြို့နှင့်တနေ့ခရီး *thee myộ hnẹng tă nẹ́ khăreeः,* "a day's journey from this city:" နှင့် *hneng,* is also used to express the present participle, which use of it will be treated of in its proper place. It is also the only conjunctive, answering to the copulative conjunction "and;" as

မောင်လောက်နှင့်ရွှေမောင် *Mounglouk hnęng Shwémoung* ; "Mounglouk and Shwémoung," literally "Mounglouk with Shwémoung;" မင်းသား မင်းသမီးနှင့်မြင်ကြ၏ *mengः thaः mengः thămeeः hnęng myeng kyă ee,* "the Prince and Princess saw each other," here the "Prince" and "the Princess," are both the object and the agent; the seer and the seen; but the clause might infer that they both saw a third object.

ဖြင့် *hpyęng,* or အားဖြင့် *aaःhpyęng,* or in its neuter form ပြင့် *pyęng,* implies "by, by means of;" and as an instrumental affix is interchangeably used with နှင့် *hnęng*; မျက်စိဖြင့်မြင်သည်။နားရွက်ဖြင့်နားကြားသည် *myettsie hpyęng myeng thee*॥ *naः rwĕt hpyęng naः kyaः thee,* "(he) sees with the eye, and hears with the ear;" အားဖြင့် *aaः hpyęng,* is somewhat more emphatic; as ငါလက်ျာလက်ရုံးတံခိုးအားဖြင့် *gna lĕtya lĕt yŏŏnः tănkhōः aaः hpyęng,* "by the power of my right hand." It is sometimes used in a somewhat peculiar instrumental signification; as in အမျိုးမျိုးဘာသာစကားအားဖြင့်ပြောတတ်သည် *ămyōः myōः bhatha tsăgaः aaः hpyęng pyău tăt thee,* "(he) can speak various languages," lit. "by means of various languages:" another peculiar instance in which it is found used is after a numeral; as လူနှစ်ယောက်ဖြင့် *lōō hneet youk hpyęng,* "men two in number." It has also sometimes the power of ကြောင့် *gyoung,* especially after the word အကြောင်း *ăgyoungः,* "reason, matter, concern;" ဤအကြောင်းဖြင့် *ee ăgyoungः hpyęng,* "on account of this affair, by reason of this circumstance."

နှိုက် *hnoit,* when used in writing abbreviated to ၌, is a locative affix implying "in," or "on;" but is variously rendered in English; as အိမ်၌ ရှိသည် *ieng hnoit shie thee,* "(he) is in the house;" ရွာ၌ရှိသမျှ *rwa hnoit shie thă hmyă,* "as many as there are in the village;" စားပွဲ၌ထိုင်ပါ *tsa: bwai hnoit htoing ba,* "sit at the table;" ဗေဒင်အရာ၌တတ်သောဆရာ *bédeng ăra hnoit tăt thăŭ tshăra,* "a teacher skilled in astrology." Also applied to dates; as အင်္ဂါနေ့၌ *ănga nẹ́ hnoit,* "on Tuesday." A few of its various applications are as follows; ငါတို့၌မရှိ *gna dọ̄ hnoit mă shie,* "not among us;" မင်းကြီးလည်းသူတို့ကိုအာဏာသား၌အပ်တော်မူ၏ *meng: gyee: lee thōō dọ̄ gō aaṇatha: hnoit ăt dāū mōō ee,* "then the king delivered them over to the executioner;" ကိုယ်၌သူတပါးပြုစေလိုသည်အတိုင်း *kōh hnoit thōō tăba: pyŏŏ tsé lō thee ădoing:,* "according as you wish others to do unto you;" အလိုအတိုင်းသင်၌ဖြစ်စေ *ălō ădoing: theng hnoit hpyeet tsé,* "according to your wish be it unto you;" ငါ၌ပြောပြီး *gnă hnoit pyăŭ byee:,* "he spoke unto me;" ငါ၌များစွာသောစည်းစိမ် *gna hnoit mya: tswa thăŭ tseetsien,* "my plentiful wealth;" ငါ၌သား *gna hnoit tha:,* "my son;" ထိုလူ၌ငါများစွာခံရပြီး *htō lōō hnoit gna mya: tswa khăn yă byee:,* "from that man I have suffered much." In the following instance it is an affix of the nominative case; ငါ၌။မယူသောကြောင့် *gna hnoit* ॥ *mă yōō thăŭ gyọung,* "because I have not brought," or perhaps more literally; "as to me, because I have not brought, &c."

တွင် *dweng,* is a locative affix implying "among, in;" as ငါဝယ်သောဥစ္စာတွင် *gna way thăŭ ŏŏtstsa dweng,* "among the goods I bought;" ထိုလူစုတွင် *hto lōō tsŏŏ dweng,* "among that company of men." It also implies "at," or "in," in reference to time; as သုံးနာရီအချိန်တွင် *thŏŏn: naree ăkhien dweng,* "at three o'clock;" တတိယရက်တွင် *tădieyă rĕt dweng,* "on the third day." With verbal roots it implies "during," and is therefore used as a present participial affix; as ထိုင်နေသည်တွင် *htoing né thee dweng*, "during the sitting, as he sat, whilst sitting." ဟောပြောတော်မူသောအခါတွင် *höö dāū mōō thāū dweng*, "whilst he was preaching."

ဝယ် *way*, is likewise a locative affix implying "in, among," and found generally used with neuter nouns; ရခိုင်ရွှေပြည်ဝယ် *Răkhoing shwé pyee way*, "in the kingdom of Arracan;" ထိုအခါဝယ်မဟာသဂရမင်းသည်ဖြစ်၏ *htō ăkha way măhathăgără meng thee hpyeet ee*, "in, or at that time Măhathăgără became king;" ဤမင်းသမီးဝယ်ဖြစ်လတ္တံ့သောသား *Ee meng thămee way hpyeet lăttăn thāū tha*, "The son that shall hereafter be begotten in this princess."

မှာ *hma*, is a locative affix implying "in, in presence of, among;" as အိမ်မှာရှိသည် *ieng hma shie thee*, "(he) is in the house;" ဤလူတို့မှာတယောက်ကားကောင်းတယောက်ကားမကောင်းဖြစ်ပါသည် *ee lōō dō hma tă youk ga koung tayouk ga măkoung hpyeet ba thee*, "among these men one is good, one bad." It is also a particularising and nominative affix implying "as to, in reference to;" as ဤအရာမှာ *ee ără hma*, "as to this affair, in reference to this subject; ခေါင်းမှာနဂါးခေါင်းကဲ့သို့ *khoung hma năga khoung gaitho*, "the head like a naga's head, i. e. as to the head, like a naga's head;" ကိုယ်မှာသံကိုလုပ်သည် *koh hma thàn gō löök thee*, "the body made of iron." With participles and verbals it implies "whilst," &c., and is a present participial affix.

မှ *hmă*, is an affix implying "from, out of;" as တောမှလာသည် *tāū hmă la thee*, "he comes from the wood;" အရှေ့ဖက်မှပေါ်လာသည် *ăshe phĕt hmă pāū la thee*, "makes its appearance from the east." မှ *hmă*, is likewise disconnective and opposed to နှင့် *hneng*; as ဤနှင့်တတူ *ee hneng tă tōō*, "similar to this;" ဤမှတပါး *ee hmă tăba*, "different from this;" ငါမှတပါးအဘယ်သူမျှမဝင်ရပြီး *gna hmă tăbas ăbhay thōō hmyă mă weng yă byees,* "other than myself no one has entered"; ထိုမှတပါး *htō hmă tăbas,* "besides that, moreover;" the word တပါး *tăbas,* may be omitted, especially after the demonstrative pronouns; as ဤမှ *ee hmă* "besides this;" ထိုမှ *htō hmă,* "besides that;" ငါမှ *gna hmă,* "besides me." မှ *hmă,* is often found used with စ *tsă,* a root implying "to begin, commence," and connected to a succeeding clause having the affix သို့ *thō,* either expressed or understood; its application and meaning will be best understood by various examples; either the affix သည် *thee,* or ၍ *rwę* is used to connect the clauses; as တောမှစသည်မြို့သို့ *tăŭ hmă tsă thee myō thō,* or တောမှစ၍မြို့သို့ *tăŭ hmă tsă rwę myō thō,* "from the woods to the city;" the particle စ *tsă,* is often omitted before သည် *thee,* especially when the affix သို့ *thō,* is expressed; as တောမှသည်မြို့သို့ *tăŭ hmă thee myō thō,* "from the woods to the city;" တအိမ်မှသည် တအိမ်သို့သွားလာသောသူ *tă ieng hmă thee tă ieng thō thwăs la thăŭ thōō,* "a man coming and going from one house to another." When the whole sentence is required to be inflected, the latter clause has the affix သို့ *tho,* omitted, and the affix of the objective, or other inflective attached; as သူသည်ငါ၏နေရာမှစ၍။နွားရ။ဥယျာဉ်။ဥစ္စာ။အလုံးရှိသမျှတို့ကိုလုယူပြီးဘုရား *thōō thee gna ee né ra hmă tsă rwę nwastsōō ။ ŏŏyeen ။ ŏŏtstsa ။ ălŏŏns shie thă hmyă dō gō lŏŏ yōō byees hpŏrăs,* "he has seized my dwelling, my cattle, my garden, my goods, my all, my Lord;" (lit.) "he has seized, beginning from my dwelling inclusive, my, &c. &c." အိမ်မှ စ၍အိမ်နှင့်ရှိသမျှသောဥစ္စာတို့သည် *ieng hmă tsă rwę ieng hnoit shie thă hmyă thăŭ ŏŏtstsa dō thee,* "the house, and all the goods in the house."

When the second clause is found wanting and the sentence terminates abruptly with မှစ၍ *hmă tsă rwę́*, the meaning is implied of "&c. so forth;" as ထိုနေ့မှစ၍ *htō nę́ hmă tsă rwę́*, "from that day forth;" ထိုခဏချင်းမှစ၍ *htō khăṇă khyengः hmă tsă rwę́*, "from that moment forth;" or the sentence may be closed according to circumstances; as ခြောက်နှစ်အရွယ်မှစ၍အောက် *khyouk hneet ărway hmă tsă rwę́ ouk*, "from the age of six years and under;" ခြောက်နှစ်အရွယ်မှစ၍အထက် *khyouk hneet ărway hmă tsă rwę́ ăhlĕt*, "from the age of six years and upwards;" ထိုအခါမှစ၍သူအိမ်နှင့်နေလျက်ရှိ *htō ăkha hmă tsă rwę́ thōō ieng hnoit nę́ lyet ee*, "from that time forth he used to remain in the house." When used with words of time, the affix တိုင်အောင် *toingoung*, "until" is used in place of သို့ *thō̤* "unto;" as ယခုမှစ၍ငါပြန်လာအခါတိုင်အောင် *yăkhŏŏ hmă tsă rwę́ nga pyăn la ăkha toingoung*, "from this day forth until I return." Sometimes သော *thău*, is found immediately succeeding the first clause; as မင်းကြီးမှစသောမိဘုရားတော်များနှင့်တကွရာဇဝင်စာ *mengः gyeeः hmă tsă rwę́ thău miephoraःdāū myaः hnę́ng takwă radză wengtsa*, "a chronicle of the king with his royal queens;" here the သော *thău*, is the connective of the qualified substantive ရာဇဝင်စာ *radză wengtsa*.

က *gă*, is an affix exactly synonymous to the preceding one; as တောကလာသည် *tău gă la thee*, "comes from the wood;" ထိုနေ့ကစ၍ *htō nę́ gă tsă rwę́*, "from that day forth." It is sometimes vocative and often nominative, and is used when a long sentence, such as a speech, &c. intervenes between the nominative and its verb; as မင်းကြီးကလည်း &c. &c. *mengः gyeeः gă lee*, "then the king, &c."

ကဲ့သို့ *gaị thō̤*, "like, like as, as, similar to," might perhaps be more correctly styled a compound affix being composed of the root ကဲ့ *gại*, implying "degree, amount," and သို့ *thọ̄*, a causal affix implying "motion towards." Its application is; as in အဖိုးကြီးကဲ့သို့ *ahpōs gyee gại thọ̄*, "like an old man;" သင်မကဲ့သို့လှသည်လော *thĕngsmă gại thọ̄ hlă thee la*, "is she as beautiful as you?" When used with verbal roots it is connected to them by သ *thă*, a contraction of the connective affix သော *thău*; as သွားသကဲ့သို့ *thwas thă gại thọ̄*, "like going." As an adjective it is often used after a noun and in connection with တူ *tōō*; as စေတီကဲ့သို့တူသောတိုက် *tsédee gại thọ̄ tōō thău tŏik*, "a building like a pagoda."

ဖို့ *hpọ̄*, subst. form အဖို့ *ăhpọ̄*, "a part, portion," implies "for, for the use of;" as မြင်းဖို့မြက် *myĕngs hpọ̆ myĕt*, "grass for the horse."

လျှာ or လျာ *hlya*, or *lya*, subst. form အလျှာ *ăhlya*, "a part, portion," is used precisely in the same way.

The above are the simple affixes of case. The vocative case is expressed either by use of the interjection အို *ō*, or the affix လေ *lé*; as အိုအဖ *ō ăhpă*, "oh father;" အဖလေ *ăhpă lé*, "ditto."

Compound Causal Affixes.

Many of the relations of nouns cannot be expressed in the Burmese language, but by the use of affixes compounded of a simple causal affix, and a root conveying some relative idea; these relations are of a compound nature, such as in the preposition "into," which combines the ideas of position "in" and motion "to;" as in the sentence အင်းထဲသို့ကျပြီး *ăngs dai thọ̄ khyă byees*, "he fell into the pond," lit. "to the *in* of the pond." "Into" being rendered by ထဲ *htai*, the root of the word အထဲ *ăhtai,* "an inner part," and သို့ *thọ̄,* the causal affix implying "motion to." The noun to which these affixes are attached is always in the possessive case, having the possessive affix ၏ *ee,* expressed or understood; as အင်း၏ထဲသို့ *ăngး ee dai thọ̄,* or more fully အင်း၏အထဲသို့ *ăngး ee ădai thọ̄.*

ROOTS THUS COMBINED.

ပေါ် *pāū,* subst. form အပေါ် *ăpāū,* "an upper part;" as အိမ်ပေါ်မှာရှိသည် *ieng pāū hma shie thee,* "(it) is on the top of the house," or ပေါ်၌ *pāū hnŏit,* or ပေါ်တွင် *pāū dwĕng;* တောင်ပေါ်သို့တက်၏ *toung pāū thọ̄ tĕt ee,* "he ascends the hill;" တောင်ပေါ်မှ or ပေါ်ကဆင်းကြွပြီး *toung pāū hmă,* or *pāū gă tshĕngး kywă byeeး,* "he descended from the hill."

အောက် *ouk,* "an under part;" as အိမ်အောက်မှာ *ieng oukh hma,* or အောက်၌ *ouk hnŏit,* or အောက်တွင် *ouk dwĕng,* "under the house;" အိမ်မိုးအောက်သို့လာ *ieng mōး ouk thọ̄ la,* "come under the roof of the house."

ထက် *htĕt,* subst. form အထက် *ăhtĕt,* "an upper part," both in reference to time or place; as ပြသာဒ်ထက်မှာ *pyăththĕd htĕt hma,* or ထက်၌ *htĕt hnŏit,* or ထက်တွင် *htĕt dwĕng,* "in the top of the tower;" ထက်သို့ *htĕt thọ̄,* "to the top of;" ထက်မှ *htĕt hmă,* or ထက်က *htĕt gă,* "from the top of." ထက် *htĕt,* when used by itself implies "beyond;" as အတိုင်းထက် *ădŏingး htĕt,* "beyond measure."

ရှေ့ *shḙ,* subst. form အရှေ့ *ăshḙ,* "an anterior part;" as အိမ်ရှေ့မှာ *ieng shḙ hma,* or ရှေ့၌ *shḙ hnŏit,* ရှေ့တွင် *shḙ dwĕng,* "in front of" or "before the house;" ရှေ့သို့ *shḙ thọ̄,* "to the front;" ရှေ့မှ *shḙ hmă,* and ရှေ့က *shḙ gă,* "from the front of."

နောက် *nouk,* subst. form အနောက် *ănouk,* "a posterior part;" as အိမ်နောက်မှာ *ieng nouk hma,* or နောက်၌ *nouk hnŏit,* or နောက်တွင် *nouk dwĕng,* "behind, abaft, in rear of the house;" ငါနောက်သို့လိုက်ပါ *gna nouk thọ̆ lŏik ba,* "follow after me, follow me;" ငါနောက်မှ *gna nouk hmă,* or နောက်ကထွက်သွား *gna nouk gă htwĕt thwas,* "depart from after," or "begone from me." When referring to time, the simple causal affix is omitted and အခါ *ăkha,* "time," is understood or expressed; as မင်းကြီးလာတော်မူသောနောက်အိမ်ရှေ့မင်းတက်၍ *mĕngs gyees la dāū mōō thăū nouk ieng shẹ́ mĕngs tĕt rwẹ́,* "after the arrival of the king, the heir-apparent rose and," &c.

ပါး *pas,* subst. form အပါး *ăpas,* "contiguity;" as နားပါးမှာ *nas pas hma,* or ပါး၌ *pas hnŏit,* or နားပါးတွင်သာသာပြောသည် *nas pas dwĕng thatha pyăū thee,* "(he) whispers in the ear," lit. "speaks gently in the contiguity of the ear."

ပြင် *pyĕng,* subst. form အပြင် *ăpyĕng,* "an outer part;" as အိမ်ပြင်မှာ *ieng pyĕng hma,* or ပြင်၌ *pyĕng hnŏit,* or ပြင်တွင် *pyeng dwĕng,* "without the house;" ပင်လယ်ပြင်သို့သွားပြီး *pĕnglay pyĕng thọ̆ thwas byees,* "(he) went out to sea;" ပြင်မှ *pyĕng hmă,* or ပြင်က *pyĕng gă,* "from out."

ပ *pă,* subst. form အပ *ăpă,* "an outer part;" the same in application as the preceding one.

ဦး *ōōs,* subst. form အဦး *ăōōs,* "a head, or beginning;" as ကမ္ဘာဦးမှ *kănbhă ōōs hmă,* "from the beginning of creation;" ကမ္ဘာဦးမှာ *kănbhă ōōs hma,* or ဦး၌ *ōōs hnŏit,* or ဦးတွင် *ōōs dwĕng,* "in the beginning of the creation."

လယ် *lay,* subst. form အလယ် *ălay,* "a middle part, the midst;" as

အိမ်လယ်မှာ *ieng lay hma,* or လယ်၌ *lay hnŏit,* or လယ်တွင် *lay dwĕng,* "in the midst of the house;" အိမ်လယ်သို့ *ieng lay thō,* "to the midst of the house."

ထဲ *htai,* subst. form အထဲ *ăhtai,* "an interior part;" as အိမ်ထဲမှာ *ieng htai hma,* or ထဲ၌ *htai hnŏit,* or ထဲတွင် *htai dwĕng,* "within the house;" အိမ်ထဲက *ieng htai gă,* or ထဲမှထွက်သွား *htai hmă twĕt thwas,* "depart from out of the house;" ထဲသို့ *htai thō,* "in unto."

နား *nas,* subst. form အနား *ănas,* "a side part;" as အိမ်နားမှာ *ieng nas hma,* or နား၌ *nas hnŏit,* or နားတွင် *nas dwĕng,* "alongside the house, by the house;" သင်္ဘောနားသို့ *thĕng bhău nas thō,* "up to and alongside of the ship;" နားမှ *nas hmă,* or နားက *nas gă,* "from alongside."

နီး *nees,* subst. form အနီး *ănees,* "a near part;" as အိမ်နီးမှာ *ieng nees hma,* or နီး၌ *nees hnŏit,* နီးတွင် *nees dwĕng,* "near the house;" နီးသို့ *nees thō,* "up to near;" နီးမှ *nees hmă,* or နီးက *nees gă,* "from near."

ရင်း *rĕngs,* "to be near, close;" used in the same way as နီး *nees.*

ဝေး *wés,* subst. form အဝေး *ăwés,* "distance;" as အိမ်ဝေးမှာ *ieng wés hma,* or ဝေး၌ *wés hnŏit,* ဝေးတွင် *wés dwĕng,* "afar from the house;" အိမ်ဝေးသို့ *ieng wés thō,* "to a distance from the house;" အိမ်ဝေးမှ *ieng wés hmă,* or ဝေးက *wés gă,* "from a distance from the house."

ထံ *htăn,* subst. form အထံ *ăhtăn,* "nearness, presence;" used only with the names of animate objects; as မင်းကြီးထံသို့ပြေးပြီး *mĕngs gyees htăn thō byés byees,* "(he) fled to the presence of the king;" ထံ၌ *htăn hnŏit,* ထံမှာ *htăn hma,* or ထံတွင် *htăn dwĕng,* "in the presence of;" ထံမှ *htăn hmă,* or ထံက *htăn gă,* "from the presence."

ဆီ *tshee,* subst. form အဆီ *ătshee,* "presence, nearness;" the same in-meaning and application, as the preceding; as မင်းကြီးဆီသို့ *mĕngး gyeeး tsheethō̤*, "to the presence of the king."

ဆုံး *tshŏŏnး*, subst. form အဆုံး *ătshŏŏnး*, "an end, final," is chiefly used in the comparison of adjectives but when with nouns, it implies "throughout, to the end of;" as အသက်ဆုံးသို့ *ăthĕt tshŏŏnး thō̤*, "through life;" sometimes the root ထက် *htĕt*, implying "upper, uppermost," precedes, and then the final causal affix is omitted; as အသက်ထက်ဆုံး *ăthĕt htĕt tshŏŏnး* "to the end of life, throughout life."

ညာ *gnya*, subst. form အညာ *ăgnya*, "an upper or superior part," applied only to position; as ပြည်ညာသို့ *pyee gnya thō̤*, "up the country;" မြစ်ညာသို့ *myeet gnya thō̤*, "up the river."

ကျေ *kyé*, subst. form အကျေ *ăkyé*, "a lower or inferior part," only used in reference to position; as မြစ်ကျေသို့ *myeet kyé thō̤*, "down the river;" လမ်းကျေသို့ *lănး kyé thō̤*, "down the road." This, and the preceding one are seldom used combined with any other causal affix than သို့ *thō̤*, they are also used adjectively without an affix; as အထက်မြစ်ညာမြို့များက *ăhtĕt myeet gnya myō̤ myaး gă*, "from the various towns up the river,"

တွင်း *twĕngး*, subst. form အတွင်း *ătwĕngး*, "an inner part;" as အိမ်တွင်းမှာ *ieng twĕngး hma* or တွင်းနှိ *twĕngး hnŏit*, or တွင်းတွင် *twĕngး dwĕng*, "in the house;" အိမ်တွင်းသို့ရောက်ပြီးမှ *ieng twĕngး thō̤ rouk byeeး hmă*, "having arrived into the interior of the house."

ရှိရာ *shie ra*, from ရှိ *shie*, "to be," and ရာ *ra*, a participial termination, vide p. 35; as in အသေကောင်ရှိရာနှိ *ăthé goung shie ra hnŏit*, rendered "where the carcase is," lit. "in the sphere of existence of the carcase."

The above are in most common use, they can scarcely be styled causal affixes, except in that they are used to express certain relations of nouns. Sometimes the final simple causal affix is omitted; as in အိမ်နားရှောက်သောလမ်း *iengnas shouk thăüs lăns,* "the road passing near the house," here နား *nas,* "near," has no causal affix after it; စစ်သူကြီးဆီရောက်လျှင် *tseet thōō gyees tshee rouk hlyĕng,* "having arrived in presence of the General." Also frequently after a participle; as ပြောသည်နောက် *pyăü thee nouk,* "after the speaking." For the use of the honorific affix တော် *dāü,* in connection with this class of affixes; vide page, 66.

The following roots also express some of the relations of nouns and may therefore be considered causal affixes:

အတိုင်း *ădŏings,* from တိုင်း *tŏings,* "to measure, estimate," implies "according to;" as မှတ်စာရင်းအတိုင်း *hmăt tsarengs ădŏings,* "according to the catalogue." Sometimes abbreviated to တိုင်း *tŏings.*

အညီ *ăgnyee,* from ညီ *gnyee,* "to be even, like," has the same signification as the preceding, but chiefly used in connection with the affix နှင့် *hnęng;* as နှင့်အညီ *hnęng ăgnyee,* "like as," &c.

တိုင်အောင် *tŏingoung,* subst. form အတိုင် *ătŏing,* "arrival at, attainment," and အောင် *oung,* "completion, fulness;" implies, "as far as;" as အိမ်တိုင်အောင် *ieng tŏing oung,* "as far as the house." After words of time, or participles of active verbs, it implies "until;" as ဤနေ့တိုင်အောင် *ee nę́ tŏingoung,* "until this day;" သွားသည်တိုင်အောင် *thwas thee tŏingoung,* "until the going or until he goes." Sometimes in the first example the causal affix တွင် *dwĕng,* "in," or a synonymous one is superadded; as ညီနေ့တိုင်အောင်တွင် *ee nę tŏing oung dwĕng,* "On, and up to the present day;" တိုင်အောင် *tŏing oung,* has the objective affixes expressed, or understood with the noun it governs.

တိုင်တိုင် *tŏing tŏing,* subst. form အတိုင် *ătŏing,* as above reduplicated; implies " through, throughout;" as ပြည်တိုင်တိုင် *pyee tŏing tŏing,* " through or throughout the country." With words of time, or the participles of active verbs, it implies "during;" as မွန်းလွဲတိုင်တိုင် *mwŏn: lwai tŏing tŏing,* " during the afternoon;" သွားသည်တိုင်တိုင် " *thwa:thee tŏing tŏing,* " during the going."

ဝန်းကြင် *wŏn:kyĕng,* " a circle;" ဝန်းပတ် *wŏn:păt,* ditto, from အဝန်း *ăwŏn:,* " a circle," and အပတ် *ăpăt,* " a circle," and ပတ်လည် *pătlee,* from အပတ် *ăpăt,* " a circle;" and လည် *lee,* " to turn," all imply " around;" as အိမ်ဝန်းကြင် *ieng wŏn:kyĕng,* or အိမ်ဝန်းပတ် *ieng wŏn:păt,* or အိမ်ပတ်လည် *ieng pătlee,* " around or round about the house."

ပတ်လုံး *păt lŏŏn:,* from အပတ် *ăpăt,* " a circle;" and ပန်လုံး *păn lŏŏn:,* from အပန် *ăpăn,* " a circle," and အလုံး *ălŏŏn:,* " rotundity," are applied to nouns of time, and imply " during;" as တလပတ်လုံး *tă lă păt lŏŏn:,* " during a month, in the whole period of a month;" တလပန်လုံး *tă lă păn lŏŏn:,* ditto.

လျှာ *lya,* " all, the whole," implies, when used with words of time, " during;" as တသက်လျှာ *tă thĕt lya,* " during life."

ရွေ့ *rwę,* a conjunction, implying " as much as," is often connected with a noun by သ *thă,* a contraction of the connective affix သော *thău,* and implies, when affixed to words of time, " during;" as အသက်သရွေ့ *ăthĕt thărwę,* " during life."

အလျောက် *ălyouk,* "to be fit, suitable, consistent with," is used as an affix to imply "according to;" as အပြစ်မှားအလျောက် *ăpyeet hmas ălyouk,* "according to one's sins;" အလိုတော်အလျောက် *ălō dāū ălyouk* "according to the royal wish."

ရောက် *rouk,* "to arrive at, obtain," implies "up to, unto;" as ဤမှစ၍မြို့ရောက် *ee hmă tsă rwę́ myǭ rouk,* "from here unto the city;" တရှောက်လုံးမြို့ရောက် *tă shouk lŏŏns myǭ rouk,* "all the way to the city."

အရင် *ărĕng,* "before," in reference to time; as ငါအရင်လာရောက်ပြီး *gna ărĕng la rouk byees,* "he arrived before me." It is also an adjective; as အရင်မယား *ărĕng măyas,* "a former wife."

ရှောက် *shouk,* "to cross over," is used as an affix implying "across, over;" as တံတါးရှောက် *tădas shouk,* "across the bridge."

ကြောင်း *gyoungs,* "business, affair," is used in the sense of "by," as in the sentence; ဤမြို့ကထိုမြို့ရောက်ရေကြောင်း *ee myǭ gă htō myǭs rouk ré gyoungs,* "from this city to that city by water."

The application of these causal affixes is by no means confined to nouns substantives, but any word however compounded or even a a whole sentence, if it be the agent, or subject of a verb, and in the participial form of သည် *thee,* may be inflected with the corresponding affixes; as လူတယောက်သည်ကုလားထိုင်၌ထိုင်နေသည်ကိုမြင်လျှင် *lŏŏ tă youk thee kŏŏlas htŏing hnŏit htŏing né thee gō myĕng hlyĕng,* "should you see a person sitting in a chair;" here the whole sentence, except the two last words, is the object ("a person sitting in a chair,") of the verb "see," and therefore takes the objective affix ကို *gō;* and so with any other causal affix the construction may require.

Causal affixes are sometimes found connected to their nouns by the connective affix သော *thău*, or သည် *thee*; as ဘုရားသခင်မျက်နှာတော်သောအားဖြင့် *phŏŏraŧthăkhĕng myĕthna dāū thău aaŧhpyĕng*, "by means of the countenance of the Deity."

But only those causal affixes, that express some substantive quality are thus connected; as အားဖြင့် *aaŧhpyĕng*, which is composed of အား *aaŧ*, "force," and ဖြင့် *hpyĕng*, "ditto;" such an affix as ကို *kō*, could not be so connected except to convey an *indefinite* idea; such as of time in the phrase တနေ့သနှိုက်ား *tă nĕ thă hnŏit gaŧ*, "for once upon a time, on a certain day;" here the indefinite idea is conveyed by the use of the connective affix သ *thă*, with a causal affix နှိုက် *hnŏit*, which does not express any substantive idea.

The above will be sufficient to shew the manner in which compounds are formed to express the various relations of nouns rendered in other languages by the use of prepositions.

On the use and application of THE HONORIFIC AFFIX OR INCREMEMT တော် *dāū*, in connection with nouns.

တော် *dāū*, the honorific affix, is an adjective implying "excellent, superlative," (i e. not an inherent quality of excellence, as an "*excellent* man;" but rather, "appertaining or belonging to what is excellent") and is affixed to the names, or to the nouns implying the actions, words, property or any thing in any way connected with divine, regal, or sacred persons or things, and is always attached immediately to the noun, before all other affixes whether of gender, number, or case;

ကျွန် *kywŏn*, " a slave;" ကျွန်တော် *kywŏn dāū*, " the slave of an excellent person," i. e. " your excellency's slave;" "I," (inferior;) ကျွန်တော်တို့ *kywŏn dāū dō̤*, the same in the plural " We," inferior; ကျွန်မ *kywŏn mă*, " a female slave;" ကျွန်တော်မ *kywŏn dāū mă*, " I," (feminine inferior;) ကျွန်တော်မတို့ *kwŏn dāū mă dō̤*, " We," (fem. plur. inf.) When used with nouns to which a compound causal affix is attached, တော် *dāū*, is not applied to the original noun, but to the root of the affix; as သခင်ဘုရား။ကိုယ်နောက်တော်သို့ငါလိုက်ပါမည် *thăkïng hpŏŏra*း။ *kōh nouk dāū thō̤ gna lŏik ba mee*, " my Lord and Master, thee will I follow." For the application and use of this affix with verbs, Vide under Verb, *honorific mood.*

Pronouns.

In the Burmese language there are no pronouns adjective, or pronouns relative, both being expressed by the modified use of the pronoun substantive.

Pronoun Substantives.

ငါ *gna*, " I," mas. or fem. used when addressing an inferior, or when speaking to, or of one's self.

ငါတို့ *gna dō̤*, " We," plur. of the above, mas. or fem. Also when great personages are speaking of themselves, sometimes in such cases the final တို့ *dō̤* is only used; as ငါတို့၏အမှာတော်အတိုင်း *gna dō̤ ee ăhma dāū ădŏing*း, " according to our order," or တို့၏အမှာ *dō̤ ee ăhma*, &c.

ကျွန်နုပ် *kywŏnnŏŏk*, or အကျွန်နုပ် *ăkywŏnnŏŏk*, " I," mas. or fem. used when addressing an equal, or speaking in a familiar manner of one's self; is pronounced, and commonly written; ကျနုပ် *kyănŏŏk*, and sometimes

ကျုပ် *kyŏŏk.* ကျွန်နုပ်တို့ *kywŏnnŏŏkdō̤,* plur. of the above; also ကျနုပ်တို့ *kyănŏŏkdō̤,* or ကျုပ်တို့ *kyŏŏkdō̤.*

ကျွန်တော် *kywŏndāū,* "I," mas. sing. used to a superior, "your slave, servant."

ကျွန်တော်တို့ *kywŏn dāū dō̤* plur. of the above.

ကျွန်တော်မ *kywŏn dāū mă,* fem. of ကျွန်တော် *kywŏndāū.*

ကျွန်တော်မတို့ *kywŏn dāū mă dō̤,* plur. of the preceding.

အကျွန် *ăkywŏn,* "I," mas. used when addressing a superior, "your slave," &c.

အကျွန်တို့ *ăkywŏndō̤,* plur. of the preceding

ကျွန်မ *kywŏn mă,* or by abbrev. ကျမ *kyă mă,* is the feminine of အကျွန် *ăkywŏn.* All these last are compounds of the root အကျွန် *ăkywŏn,* "a slave, subject."

တပည့်တော် *tăbyee̤dāū,* "I," mas. used only when addressing a priest, or religious teacher, from တပည့် *tăbyee̤,* "a disciple," and တော် *dāū,* honorific.

ကိုယ် *kōh,* "one's self, myself, thyself, himself," according to the context, and either mas. or fem. When by itself, it implies "thou thyself: sometimes the personal pronouns are superadded; as ငါကိုယ် *gna kōh,* "I myself;" သင်ကိုယ် *thĕngkōh,* "thou thyself;" သူကိုယ် *thōō kōh,* "he himself."

ကိုယ်တို့ *kōhdō̤,* by corruption ကိုယ်ရို့ *kōh rō,* plur. of the preceding; when by itself, it implies "ye yourselves;" ငါတို့ကိုယ် *gna dō̤ kōh,* "we ourselves;" သူတို့ကိုယ် *thōō dō̤ kōh,* "they themselves." It is often variously reduplicated with မိမိ *miemie,* and other cognate words; as

မိမိကိုယ် *miemie kōh,* ကိုယ်ရှင် *kōhshĕng,* ကိုယ်ကြပ် *kōh gyăt,* ကိုယ်တိုင် *kōh dŏing.*

မိမိ *miemie,* same as ကိုယ် *kōh,* မိမိတို့ *miemie dō̤,* plur. မိမိ *miemie,* is used chiefly, when speaking of the 2nd, and 3rd persons.

ကိုယ်တော် *kōhdāū,* " Thou," mas. or fem. used when addressing superiors.

တကာ *tăga,* " Thou," used by a priest when addressing a layman respectfully, implies " a supporter of religious characters and institutions."

တကာမ *tăgamă,* fem. of the preceding.

ကွယ် *kway,* mas. and fem. " Thou," used when addressing equals, and kindly to inferiors; ကွယ်တို့ *kwaydō̤,* the corresponding plur. sometimes corrupted into ကွယ်ရို့ *kwayrō,* and ကရို့ *kărō,*

မင်း *mĕng:,* mas. and sometimes fem. " Thou," used to inferiors, or familiarly to equals; မင်းမ *mĕng:mă,* fem. of the preceding.

မောင်မင်း *moungmĕng:,* mas. " Thou," used to inferiors.

မောင်ရှင် *moungshĕng,* a term of compellation, addressed to men younger than one's self, and commonly by women.

ကိုရှင် *kōshĕng,* a term of compellation used to men; from အစ်ကို *ăkkō,* " an elder brother," and အရှင် *ăshĕng,* " Sir."

သင် *thĕng,* mas. and fem. " Thou," when used colloquially somewhat inferior, chiefly used in writing, and has no reference to relative condition; သင်တို့ *thĕngdō̤,* the plural, when used in reference to a single person, is honorific; as ဘုရားသင်တို့အမှာတော်အတိုင်း *hpŏŏra:thĕngdō̤ ăhma dāū ădŏing:,* " My Lord, in conformity to your Lordly mandate." သင်မ *thĕngmă* is also used in the feminine.

နင် *nĕng,* mas. and fem. " Thou," used to inferiors, and to animals.

ချင်း *khyĕngı,* " You," mas. or fem. used only in the phraseology of the Courts of Law, from အချင်း *ăkhyĕngı,* " a companion."

သူ *thōō,* " he, she, or it," is chiefly used substantively, implying " a person ;" as ကောင်းသောသူ *koungıthăŭ thōō,* " he that is good, a good person ;" ထိုသူ *htōthōō,* " that person." သူ *thōō* is used by implication as a substantive, exactly similar to the words " he" and " she," in the sentence " I am he, I am she."

PRONOUN ADJECTIVES

Are expressed in the Burmese language by the use of the possessive case of their respective personal pronouns ; the affix ၏ *ee,* of the possessive case is however seldom expressed ; as ငါအိမ် *gna ieng,* " my house," for ငါ၏အိမ် *gna ee ieng,* " the house of me ;" ကျွန်နုပ်မယား *kywŏnnŏŏk măyaı,* " my wife." When those pronouns are used which are compounds of the honorific affix တော် *dāū,* it (the honorific affix) is always applied to the substantive ; as ကိုယ်တော် *kōh dāū,* " your excellency," ကိုယ်အဖတော် *kōh ăhpă dāū,* " your excellency's father."

Pronominal adjectives may be connected to nouns by the relative increment သော *thăŭ,* in the same way as common adjectives ; as သူသောဥစ္စာ *thŏŏ thăŭ ŏŏtstsa,* " another's goods ;" or သူ၏ဥစ္စာ *thŏŏ ee ŏŏtstsă,* " the goods of another." This is because သော *thăŭ,* is an affix of the present time, as is also the time inherent in the possessive case of a noun ; so that either may be attached to a pronoun, when used with an appellative to express a present pronominal attribute of such appellative.

သူ *thŏŏ,* is used to express " of or belonging to another ;" as သူ့ဥစ္စာ *thŏŏ ŏŏtstsa*, "another's goods;" သူ့အသရေ *thŏŏ ăthăré*, "another's reputation."

ရင်း *rĕngː*, "one's own," seems indefinitely applied and may be either prefixed, or affixed. In the latter case the personal pronoun in the possessive case is prefixed, and it then refers to that person; as ရင်းဥစ္စာ *rĕngː ŏŏtstsa*, implies "one's own property, i. e. "personal property" indefinitely considered; ငါ၏ဥစ္စာရင်း *gna ee ŏŏtstsa rĕngː*, "my own property."

THE DEMONSTRATIVE AND INTERROGATIVE PRONOUNS

Are properly adjectives, and connected to the noun substantive by the usual connective သော *thău*, which however is seldom expressed; as ထိုသူ *htō thōō*, "that person," properly ထိုသောသူ *htō thău thōō*, "the person who is that."

ဤ *ee*, or သည် *thee*, "this;" as ဤသူ *ee thŏŏ*, "this person;" သည်လူ *thee lōō*, "this man;" used according to the euphony.

ထို *htō*, "that;" as ထိုလူ *htō lōō*, "that man." Sometimes reduplicated to form a plural; as ထိုထို *htō htō*, "those others;" ထိုထိုမင်းတို့ *htō htō mĕngː dọ*, "kings of other countries, foreign monarchs."

ယင် *yĕng*, "that, that same;" ယင်အခါ၌ *yĕng ăkha hnŏit*, "at that same time," alluding to something past.

ဟောက် *houk*, ဟို *hō*, ဟုက် *hŏŏ*, "that," generally used in conversation, where the thing is pointed at. Vide Adverbial Compounds of these pronouns.

အနည် *ănee*, အို *ō*, "that," used when a thing is pointed at; the first is somewhat exclamatory.

သင်း *thĕngs,* mas. fem. or neut. "this or that;" chiefly used substantively; as ဘယ်သင်း *bhaythĕngs,* "who or what;" ထိုသင်း *htōthĕngs,* "that;" ကောင်းသင်း *koungsthĕngs,* "that, or this good person, or thing."

ကဲ့သို့ *gaithō,* the causal affix "like, such as," is used adjectively in connection with any of the demonstrative pronouns; as ဤကဲ့သို့သောလူ *ee gaithōthău lōō,* "a man such as this;" ထိုကဲ့သို့သောလူ *htō gaithō thău lōō,* "a man such as that."

အဘိ *ădie,* "what?" interrogative pronoun.

အဘယ် *ăbhay,* "what," most common; frequently when combined with words it is contracted to အဘဲ *ăbhai,* or ဘယ် *bhay;* and when compounded with either the pronoun သူ *thōō,* or the causal affix သို့ *thō,* it is often contracted to အ *ă;* as အသူ *ăthōō,* "who? what person?" for အဘယ်သူ *ăbhaythōō;* အသို့ *ăthō,* "how? in what manner, or sort?" for အဘယ်သို့ *ăbhaythō.* ဘယ် *bhay,* when combined with ဟာ *ha,* "matter, concern," especially when used interjectionally, is often contracted to ဘာ *bha;* as ဘာလည်း *bhalees,* "what? what is it?"—in full ဘယ်ဟာရှိသည်လည်း *bhayhashie theelees,* "what thing, or matter is it?" Sometimes, provincially, the initial ဘ *bhă,* is permuted to ဇ *dză;* as ဇာလည်း *dzalees,* for ဘာလည်း *bhalees.* In ancient parlance ဘယ် *bhay,* was abbreviated into ပ *pă;* as ပသို့ *păthō,* for ဘယ်သို့ *bhaythō.*

When used with words of time, နံ *năn,* from အနံ *ănăn,* (the specific idea of time; as "a date, birth-day, anniversary, &c.") is affixed; as အဘယ်နံအရက် *ăbhay năn ărĕt,* "what date or day."

When used in asking questions of number; as "how many?" the numeral နှစ် *hneet,* "two," is used as a numeral adjunct, and intervenes between it and the generic affix ; as လူဘယ်နှစ်ယောက်ရှိသည်လာ *lōō bhay hneet youk shie thee la,* " how many men are there?" ပုလင်းဘယ်နှစ်လုံးရှိသည်လာ *pălĕngs bhay hneet lōōns shie thee la,* " how many bottles are there?* When asking an indefinite question, မျှ *hmyă,* " as much as" is used in connection with the interrogative pronouns ; as ဘယ်မျှရှိသနည်း *bhay hmyă shie thă nees,* " how much is there? how many may there be?"

အချား *ăkhyas,* " other ;" တချား *tăkhyas,* " another."

မည် *mee,* မည်သည် *mee thee,* မည်ရွာ *mee rwa,* မည်ဝါ *mee wa,* with their various reduplications, all express " what, whatever ;" as မည်သူ *mee thōō,* " who ever." Sometimes the interrogative အဘယ် *ăbhay,* is superadded ; as အဘယ်မည်သောသူ *ăbhay mee thăŭ thōō,* " whosoever," antecedent, and relative combined.

ဤမည် *ee mee,* " such," indefinite.

အကြင် *ăkyĕng,* " whatever ;" as အကြင်သူ *ăkyĕng thōō,* " whoever." When used with words of time နံ *năn,* is superadded.

သို့ *thō,* the affix of the objective case is often found having a signification in the Burmese language, which can only be rendered by the English pronoun " thus, like that ;" it must be borne in mind that this root conveys the abstract idea of motion towards, and then its use may be more easily understood, it is seldom used except in compounds ; as သို့က *thōgă,* " hence ;" သို့မဟုတ် *thōmăhō,* " if such be not the case, or else."

When သို့ *thō,* is affixed to a demonstrative or interrogative pronoun it has a similar power ; as ဤသို့သောသူ *ee thō thăŭ thōō,* " a man such as

* This idiomatic peculiarity perhaps arose from the probable mode of counting being by couples.

this, a man who has attained to this;" ဤသို့သောအရာ *eethọ̄ thăŭ ăra,* "an affair such as this;" ထိုသို့ *htō thọ̄,* "such as that;" ဘယ်သို့ *bhay thọ̄,* "such as what?" Or to express its meaning exactly, သို့ *thọ̄,* in signification bears exactly the same relation to ထို *htō,* "*that*;" that "*there for,*" does to "*there.*"

နို့ *nọ̄,* "thus," a corruption of the preceding.

The demonstrative and interrogative pronouns are compounded with the causal and other affixes, to form cognate adverbs, conjunctions, &c.

ဤ *ee,* and its compounds.

ဤက *eegă,* and ဤမှ *eehmă,* "hence," from ဤ *ee,* "this," and က *gă,* and မှ *hmă,* "from."

ဤကြောင့် *eegyoụng,* "on this account," from ကြောင့် *gyoụng,* causal affix.

ဤမှာ *eehma,* "thus," from မှာ *hma,* "in," causal affix.

ဤမူကား *eemōō gas,* "thus, in reference to this," from မူကား *mōō gas,* causal affix, q. v.

ဤသို့ *eethọ̄,* "such as this, of such a kind or tendency as this," from သို့ *thọ̄,* causal affix, q. v.

ဤသို့မှ *eethọ̄hmă,* or ဤသို့က *eethọ̄gă,* "hence, from such sort," from ဤသို့ *eethọ̄,* and မှ *hmă,* and က *gă.*

ဤသို့ကြောင့် *eethọ̄ gyoụng,* or ဤသို့သောကြောင့် *eethọ̄thăŭgyoụng,* "on account of such being the case, therefore," from ဤသို့ *eethọ̄,* and ကြောင့် *gyoụng,* causal affix, q. v.

ဤမဟုတ် *ee mă hō,* "or,—or else,—otherwise,—if not thus," from ဤ *ee,* "this," မ *mă,* "not," and ဟုတ် *hō,* "true, right, the case."

ဤနည်းတူ *eeneestōō,* "such as this," from ဤ *ee,* "this," နည်း *nees,* "manner," and တူ *tōō,* "similar."

သည် *thee,* may be used instead of ဤ *ee,* with any of the above compounds where euphony requires.

ထို *htō,* and its compounds.

ထို *htō,* has exactly the same compounds as the preceding, "that" being inserted in the place of "this."

ယင် *yĕng,* and its compounds.

ယင်သို့ *yĕngthō̤,* "it being thus, if so;" ယင်သို့မဟုတ် *yĕng thō̤ mă hō,* "it not being so, if not so."

အဘယ် *ăbhay,* or ဘယ် *bhay,* and its compounds.

အဘယ်သို့ *ăbhaythō̤,* or ဘယ်သို့ *bhaythō̤,* abbrev. အသို့ *ăthō̤,* and corrupted to အနို့ *ănō̤,* "how? where to?" from သို့ *thō̤,* causal affix, q. v. နည်း *nees,* "manner, kind," is sometimes added; as အဘယ်သို့နည်း *ăbhay thō̤ nees,* "in what like manner?"

ဘာပြုလို့ *bhapyŏŏ̤lō,* "why? wherefore?" from ဘယ် *bhay,* "what?" ဟာ *ha,* "thing," ပြု *pyŏŏ̤s,* "to do," and လို *lō,* "to want," lit. "wanting to do what thing?" often colloquially pronounced ဘာဘူ *bhabhōō,* and provincialized to ဇာပြုလို့ *dza pyŏŏ lō.*

ဘယ်က *bhaygă,* or ဘယ်မှ *bhay hmă,* "whence?" from မှ *hmă,* "from," causal affix, q. v.

ဘယ်ကို *bhay gō,* "what? whence?" from ကို *gō,* causal affix, q. v.

ဘယ်မှာ *bhay hma,* "where? wherein?" from မှာ *hma,* "in," causal affix.

ဘယ်ကြောင့် *bhay gyoung,* "why? wherefore? for what reason?" from ကြောင့် *gyoung,* causal affix, q. v.

ဘယ်သို့က *bhaythọ gă,* or ဘယ်သို့မှ *bhay thọ hmă,* " how? why? wherefrom? whence?" from ဘယ်သို့ *bhay thọ,* " such as what?" and မှ *hmă,* and က *gă,* causal affixes.

ဘယ်သို့မှာ *bhay thọ hma,* " whence? wherein? in which case?" from ဘယ်သို့ *bhay thọ,* and မှာ *hma,* causal affix.

ဘယ်ကြောင့်နည်းဟူမူကား *bhay gyoung neeः hŏŏ mōōgaः,* or ဘယ်သောကြောင့်နည်း &c. *bhay thău gyoung neeः, &c.*; or ဘယ်သို့ကြောင့်နည်း &c. *bhaythọ gyoung neeः, &c.*; or ဘယ်သို့သောကြောင့်နည်းဟူမူကား *bhay thọ thău gyoung neeः hŏŏ mōō gaः,* " on account of which matter, to wit, wherefore, (not interrogative) because," from ဘယ် *bhay,* or ဘယ်သို့ *bhay thọ,* ကြောင့် *gyoung,* causal affix, နည်း *neeः,* " manner, way, method," ဟူ *hŏŏ,* connective affix, and မူကား *mōōgaः,* causal affix.

သို့ *thọ,* and its compounds.

သို့ရာ *thọ ra,* " thus," v. p. 36.

သို့ကြောင့် *thọ gyoungः,* " wherefore, (not interrogative) on that, or this account," from သို့ *thọ,* and ကြောင့် *gyoung,* causal affix.

သို့ဝင် *thọ tsĕng,* " as much as, the same as," from သို့ *thọ,* " unto," and ဝင် *tsĕng,* " to attain."

သို့တပြီး *thọ tă byeeः,* or သို့တပြီးကား *thọ tă byeeः gaः,* " therefore, although being so," from သို့ *thọ,* " unto," တ *tă,* formative prefix, ပြီး *byeeः,* " fulfilment, attainment to," and ကား *gaः,* causal affix, lit. " having attained to this point; because of attainment to this point."

သို့ပြီး *thọ byeeः,* " if so, being so, as having been so," from သို့း *thō,* & ပြီး *byeeः.*

သို့ပြီးမှ *thọ byeeः hmă,* " after being so, when it has been so," from သို့ပြီး *thọ byeeः,* and မှ *hmă,* causal affix.

သို့ဖြစ် *thọ̄ hpyeet,* "wherefore, therefore," from သို့ *thọ̄,* and ဖြစ် *hpyeet,* "to be;" it is generally connected to the rest of the sentence by ၍ *rwẹ́;* သို့ဖြစ်လျှင် *thọ̄ hpyeet hlyĕng,* "such having been the case," or "should such be the case."

သို့မို့ *thọ̄ mọ̄,* "therefore, if so," from သို့ *thọ̄,* and မို့ *mọ̄,* "because;" နို့မို့ *nọ̄ mọ̄,* corrupt.

သို့မှ *thọ̄ hmă,* or သို့က *thọ̄ gă,* "hence, from this, whence," applied to place or manner, from မှ *hmă,* and က *gă,* causal affix.

သို့မှာ *thọ̄ hma,* "therein, wherein;" applied to manner, or place.

သို့မဟုတ် *thọ̄ măhō,* "or else, if not so, such not the case," from သို့ *thọ̄,* "thus," မ *mă,* "not," and ဟုတ် *họ̄,* "right, true, the case."

သို့တရုန် *thọ̄ tă mọ̆n,* "as much as, the same as, about the same;" from သို့ *thọ̄,* တ *tă,* formative prefix, and အရုန် *ămọ̆n,* "again."

သို့တမူကား *thọ̄ tă mōō gas,* "therefore, for the above reason," also the exceptive conjunction "but," from သို့ *thọ̄,* တ *tă,* formative prefix, မူကား *mōōgas,* causal affix, "regarding, in reference to."

သို့မချည်း *thọ̄ mă khyees,* "if not so, therefore," in the sense of "because not so, if not so," from သို့ *thọ̄,* မ *mă,* "not," and ချည်း *khyees,* "nothing but."

သို့သောလည် *thọ̄ thăŭ lee,* "notwithstanding it is so, nevertheless," from သို့ *thọ̄,* သော *thăŭ,* connect. affix, and လည် *lee,* "moreover."

သို့မျှ *thọ̄ hmyă,* "so much," from သို့ *thọ̄,* and မျှ *hmyă,* "as much as."

မည် *mee,* and its compounds.

မည်သို့ *mee thọ̄,* "of what sort?" မည်သို့လူ *mee thọ̄ lōō,* "what sort of man?" မည်သို့သောအရာ *mee thọ̄ thăŭ ăra,* "what sort of an affair?"

မည်မျှ *mee hmyă,* "so much," indefinite; as အဖိုးမည်မျှထိုက်၏ *ăhpōt mee hmyă htŏik ee,* "the price is so and so."

အချားသို့ *ăkhyatthō̧,* "aside, apart, elsewhere," from အချား *ăkhyat,* "another, separate," and သို့ *thō̧,* "to, towards."

ဟို *hō* is combined with the locative affixes မှာ *hma,* "in," and မှ *hmă,* "from," to form adverbs of place when the object is pointed at or otherwise designated; the sound of the pronoun is prolonged or shortened according to the relative distance; as ဟုတ်မှာ *ho hma,* "there," when comparatively near; ဟိုမှာ *hō hma,* when further; and ဟောက်မှာ *hou hma,* when at a still greater distance.

On rendering of the Pronoun Adjective—*None.*

The only way of expressing the idea of "*none,*" in the Burmese language, is by the use of the interrogative pronoun ဘယ် *bhay,* "what?" မျှ *hmyă,* "as much as," and မ *mă,* "not;" as ဘယ်သူမျှမရှိပါ *bhay thōō hmyă mă shie ba,* "there is no one," lit. "there is not so much as what person;" it is to be borne in mind that all causal affixes always precede the adverb မျှ *hmyă;* as ဘယ်သူအားမျှမဆိုနှင့် *bhay thōō aat hmyă mă tshō hnę̄ng,* "tell it to no one," lit. "tell it not so much as to what person:" or မျှ *hmyă,* may be omitted; as အဘယ်သူအားမပြောနှင့် *ăbhay thōō aat mă pyăŭ hnę̄ng,* "speak not to what person," i. e. "to no one." ဘာမယူ *bha mă yōō,* "take not any thing;" ဘာကိုမျှငါမတွေ့နိုင်ပြီး *bha gō hmyă gna mă twę̄ hnŏing byeet,* "I have been able to find nothing," lit. "I have not been able to find so much as what thing;" sometimes မည်သည် *meethee,* "whatever," is substituted for ဘယ် *bhay;* as မည်သည်သူမရှိ *meethee thōō mă shie,* "there is none."

The same idea is also conveyed by the use of the numeral တ *tă*, "one;" a generic affix; the word မျှ *hmyă;* and the negative particle မ *mă*, and then no individual of the class expressed by the generic affix is implied; as လူဘယ်နှစ်ယောက်ရှိသည်လော *lōō bhay hneet youk shie thee la*, "how many men are there?" တယောက်မျှမဟိ *tă youk hmyă mă hie*, "no one, i. e. "not so much as one person;" sometimes the word မျှ *hmyă* is omitted, and the persistive affix လေ *lé*, introduced; as တပြားလေမဟိ *tă byas lé mă hie*, "there is not a single flat thing," i. e. "piece of money." Sometimes an interrogative verbal affix is used in connection with the negative; as ဘာလည်း *bha lees*, "what?" ဘာလည်းမဟိ *bha lees mă hie*, "nothing," lit. "there is not what."

"NEVER" is thus expressed; တရံတခါမျှမ *tă răn tă kha hmyă mă*, "not so much as once;" from အခါ *ăkha*, and အယံ *ăyăn*, "time."

THE RELATIVE INCREMENT သော *thău*.

There is no relative pronoun properly so called in the Burmese language, but its place is supplied by the use of the connective affix သည် *thee*, or သော *thău*, connecting the adjective with its noun; as ကောင်းသောလူ *koungs thău lōō*, "the man who is good." In the same way any sentence however complicated may be connected with its noun; as ငါကိုနေ့တိုင်းနေ့တိုင်းရိုက်လျက်သောသူ *gna gō nẹ̆ dŏings nẹ̆ dŏings rŏit lyĕt thău thōō*, "the man who keeps beating me day after day;" when a verb in the present tense expresses the relative, the affix သည် *thee*, becomes the connecting affix; as ပြုသည်သူ *pyọ̆ọ̆ thee thōō*, "the man who does, the doer;" ပြေးသည်သူ *byés thee thōō*, "the man who runs, the runner;" လာမည်သောသူ *a mee thău thōō*, "the man who shall come."

ADJECTIVES.

The adjective, as has been already stated, (*Introduction*) expresses the *present* attribute of an apellative, for this reason, any compound sentence, or any part of speech, if connected to the substantive by an affix of the present time, or by the substantive verb in the present tense, or by the affix ၏ *ee*, of the possessive case, which last, as has been remarked, (vide *Introduction*,) is itself but an affix of the present tense; becomes an adjective; as လှသော နှင်းဆီပွင့် *hlă thău hnĕngs, tshee pwĕng*, or လှရှိသော နှင်းဆီပွင့် *hlă shie thău hnĕngs tshee pwĕng*, "a beautiful rose;" သစ်ပင်၏အသီး *theet pĕng ee ăthees*, or သစ်ပင်၏ရှိသောအသီး *theet pĕng ee shie thău ăthees*, "the fruit of the tree;" မြို့သို့လမ်း *myō thō lăns*, or မြို့သို့သောလမ်း *myō thō thău lăns*, or မြို့သို့ရှိသောလမ်း *myō thō shie thău lăns*, "the road to the city;" ယခုလူတို့ *yă khŏŏ lōō dō*, or ယခုရှိကြသောလူတို့ *yă khŏŏ shie kyă thău lōō dō*, "the men that are now." But it will be necessary to dwell, here, only upon the following three methods which are the most commonly in use.

1st. By *prefixing* the simple root, connected to the noun by the connective affixes သည် *thee*, or သော *thău*; as ကောင်းသည်လူ *koungs thee lōō*, or ကောင်းသောလူ *koungs thău lōō*, "the good," or "a good man;" ငယ်သည်လူခလေး *gnay thee lōō gălé*, or ငယ်သောလူခလေး *gnay thău lōō gălé*, "a little boy;" လှသောမိန်းမ *hlă thău miens mă*, "a beautiful woman."

2ndly. By *affixing* the simple root itself without any connecting affixes; as လူကောင်း *lōō koungs*, "a good man;" လူခလေးငယ် *lōō gălé gnay*, "a little boy;" မိန်းမလှ *miens mă hlă*, "a beautiful woman."

3rd. By *prefixing* the root in the form of the 1st class of derivative nouns without any connective affix; as အကောင်းလူ *ăgoung: lōō,* "a good man;" အငယ်လူခလေ *ăgnay lōō gălé,* "a little boy;" အလှမိန်းမ *ăhlă mien: mă,* "a beautiful woman." In this case the qualifying root is properly a substantive in the possessive case, the affix ၏ *ee,* being understood; as အကောင်း၏လူ *ăgoung: ee lōō,* "a man of goodness;" and so on with the other examples. In this case, also the connective affix သော *thău,* may be used; as အကောင်းသောလူ *ăgoung: thău lōō,* "a good man;" အလိမ္မာသောလူ *ăliemma thău lōō,* "a wise man."

Should it be necessary to express the relations of any of these qualified nouns; in the first and third cases, the noun itself is inflected with the causal affixes, or affix of number; as ကောင်းသောလူ၏ *koung: thău lōō ee,* or အကောင်းလူ၏ *ăgoung: lōō ee,* "of a good man;" ငယ်သောလူခလေဖို့ *gnay thău lōō gălé hpọ̄,* or အငယ်လူခလေဖို့ *ăgnay lōō gălé hpọ̄,* "for a little boy;" ကောင်းသောလူတို့ *koung: thău lōō dọ̄,* or အကောင်းလူတို့ *ăgoung: lōō dọ̄,* "good men;" လှသောမိန်းမတို့ *hlă thău mien: mă dọ̄,* "beautiful women."

But in the 2nd case, where the simple root is affixed to the noun, the qualifying root or adjective, and not the noun becomes inflected with all affixes, whether of number, of case, or gender; as နွားကြီးမ *nwa: gyee: mă,* "a big cow;" နွားကြီးမတို့ *nwa: gyee: mă dọ̄,* "big cows;" လူကောင်း၏ *lōō koung: ee,* "of or belonging to a good man;" လူခလေငယ်တို့အား *lōō gălé gnay dọ̄ aa:,* "to little boys;" မိန်းမလှတို့သည် *mien: mă hlă dọ̄ thee,* "the beautiful women;" ခွေးရူးမတို့ကြောင့် *khwé: rōō mă dọ̄ gyoung,* "on account of the mad bitches."

In the first instance, where the simple root is connected to the noun by the connective affixes သည် *thee,* or သော *thăü,* the root, if a verbal one, will admit of being inflected with its own numeral affix; as စားသောနေရာ *tsa: thăü né ra,* "an eating place;" စားသောနေရာတို့ *tsa: thăü né ra dō̤,* "eating places;" စားကြသောနေရာ *tsa: kyă thăü né ra,* "a place where a plural number of persons eat;" စားကြသောနေရာတို့ *tsa: kyă thăü né ra dō̤,* "places where a plural number of persons eat."—v. p. 34.

When a substantive verb is to be qualified, the adjective is generally used in the form of the third case; as အကောင်းဖြစ် *ăgoung: hpyeet,* "to be," or "become good;" ဤလူတို့အမိုက်ဖြစ်ကြသည် *ee lōō dō̤ ămŏik hpyeet kyă thee,* "these men are become foolish."

When a substantive has two qualifying roots or adjectives, it is often repeated with each; as လူကောင်းလူငယ် *lōō koung: lōō gnay,* "a good man a little man," i.e. "a good little man;" or sometimes one adjective precedes in the substantive form, and the other is affixed as in the third and second methods; as အဖြူမြင်းကြီး *ăhpyōō myĕng: gyee:,* "a great white horse."

Sometimes the root in an adverbial form is used; as များစွာသောသူ *mya: tswa thăü thōō,* "numerous persons;" or a compound sentence may be the qualifier; as ရှိသမျှသောသူ *shie thă hmyă thăü thōō,* "as many persons as there are." The forms of these qualifying roots are very various; as အဆင့်ဆင့် *ătshĕ̤ng tshĕ̤ng;* is an adverbial form of the root ဆင့် *tshĕ̤ng,* "to accumulate, put one on another," and implies "one after another," as "day after day;" အသွယ်သွယ် *ăthway thway,* is the same form of the root သွယ် *thway,* "to be in a continuous row, to flow as a river," and they, (in the adverbial form) imply an indefinite degree of the qualities expressed by the root; hence အဆင့်ဆင့်အသွယ်သွယ်အခန်းတို့ *ătshĕngtshĕng ăthway thway ăkhăns dō*, implies "rooms," affected with those qualities, that is "different stories, and continued suits of apartments."

ON THE COMPARISON OF ADJECTIVES.

The first or most imperfect degree of comparison may be formed in some cases by the reduplicating of the simple root, and adding the short accent; as ငန် *gnăn*, "salt," ငန့်ငန့် *gnăngnăn*, "saltish;" ချို *khyō*, "sweet," ချို့ချို့ *khyō khyō*, "sweetish;" or, where a heavy accent is expressed in the original, the root may be shortened by omitting the vowel; as ခါး *khas*, "bitter," ခခ *khăkhă*, "bitterish."

The most usual way of expressing, what in English is styled the comparative degree, is by the use of the affix ထက် *htĕt*, (from အထက် *ăhtĕt*, "an upper" or "a superior part,") attached to the noun *against which the comparison is made*, (synonymous to the English "*than*" in the same position,) and by the word သာ *tha*, a root signifying "to increase, surpass," being used in connection with the *adjective, agreeing with or the root qualifying the substantive, whose comparison is wished to be expressed.* The root သာ *tha*, in such situations generally has the connective affix ၍ *rwé*, attached; as သာ၍ *tharwé;* though သာ *tha* is the root in most common use, any synonymous one may be employed; as လွန်၍ *lwŏnrwé*, from လွန် *lwŏn*, "to excel, surpass;" တိုး၍ *tōsrwé*, from တိုး *tōs*, "to advance, increase;" ပွါး၍ *pwasrwé*, from ပွါး *pwas*, "to increase;" စီး၍ *tseesrwé*, from စီး *tsees*, "to increase." Examples: ထိုလူထက်ဤလူသာ၍ကောင်းရှိပါသည် *htō lōō htĕt ee lōō tha rwé koungs shiepathee,* "this man is better than that man," lit. "than that man," or "above that man, this man surpasses, and is good;" ထိုကုလားသွီးထက်ကျွန်မလှွန်၍လှပါ၏မဟုတ်လော *htō kŏŏlaːthămeeːhlĕt kywŏnmă hlwŏn rwę hlăpa ee măhōla,* "am I not more beautiful than that foreign woman?" lit. "than that daughter of a foreigner, I excel and am beautiful, is it not so?" It will be perceived that the noun to which ထက် *htĕt,* is affixed, is in the objective case. Instead of the connective affix ၍ *rwę,* the root, to which it is generally attached, is sometimes placed in the past participial form by the instrumental affix သဖြင့် *thăhpyęng,* "by, by means of," in its character of a past participial affix; as ဤလူထက်ထိုလူလွန်သဖြင့်ကောင်းသည် *ee lōō htĕt htō lōō hlwŏn thăhpyęng koungːthee,* or လွန်သဖြင့်သာ၍ကောင်းသည် *hlwŏn thăhpyęng tha rwę koungːthee,* "that man is better than this man," lit. "than this man, that man by means of excelling is good."

Sometimes, and more correctly, the relative positions of the agent and nominative or the noun whose comparison is asserted, and that of the object or the noun against which the comparison is made, together with its affixes, are changed; the one being last and the other first; as ဤလူသည်ထိုလူထက်သာ၍ကောင်းဖြစ်ပါသည် *ee lōō thee htō lōō htĕt tha rwę koungː hpyeet pa thee,* "this man, than that man is better."

When an inferior, or lesser comparative degree of comparison is to be expressed, the word အောက် *ouk,* "below," may be substituted for ထက် *htĕt;* as ဤလူထိုလူအောက်သာ၍ကြီးသည် *ee lōō htō lōō ouk tha rwę gyeeː thee,* "this man is less than that man," lit. "this man less than that man excels, and is great;" ထိုလူခလေအောက်သာ၍ဆိုးသည် *htō lōō gălé ouk tha rwę tshōး thee,* " less wicked than that boy," and so on.

When the idea of the comparison *not* existing, or being the case, is to be expressed, the adjective or qualifying root attached to the noun, is negatived by the prefix of negation မ *mă,* as is also the root connected to the said qualifying root ; as ဤလူထိုလူထက်မသာ၍မကောင်းသည် *ee lōō htō lōō htĕt mă tharwę mă koungး thee,* " this man is not greater than that man," lit. " this man more than that man, does not excel, and is not good ;" ကျွန်သည်ကိုယ်သခင်ထက်မသာ၍မကြီးရှိပါသည် *kywŏn thee kōh thăkhĕng htĕt mă tharwę mă gyee shie thee,* " the slave is not greater than his Lord ;" or မသာ *mă tha,* may be omitted ; as ဤလူထိုလူထက်မကောင်းရှိပါသည် *ee lōō htō lōō htĕt mă koungး shie ba thee,* " this man is not greater than that man."

In all these cases the adjuncts သာ၍ *tharwę,* လွန်၍ *lwŏn rwę,* &c., may be omitted, and ထက် *htĕt* alone be used; as တရိစ္ဆာန်ထက်မြတ်သည်လူတို့ *tărietstshan htĕt myăt thee lōō dō,* " man that is more excellent than the beast ;" ဤလူကလေးထိုလူကလေးထက်ငယ်သည် *ee lōō gălé htō lōō gălé htĕt gnay thee,* " this boy is less than that boy."

As the idea of similarity implies a previous idea of comparison, it may not be out of place to mention that if in the above case the substantive against which the comparison is made, instead of being in the objective case, and having the affix ထက် *htĕt ;* have the connective affix နှင့် *hnęng,* attached ; either by itself or compounded with တူ *tōō,* or ညီ *gnyee,* both implying " equal ;" the idea of similarity will be expressed ; as ဤလူသည်ထိုလူနှင့်တူသာ၍ကောင်းသည် *ee lōō thee htō lōō hnęng tōō tha rwę koungး thee,* " this man is as good as that man;" ကျွန်မသည်ထိုကုလားသမီးနှင့်လွန်၍လှပါသည် *kywŏnmăthee htōkŏŏlas thă mees hnęng lwŏn rwę hlă pa thee,* "your handmaid is as beautiful as that daughter of a stranger."

When နှင့်တူ *hnęng tōō,* alone are used to express similarity, they are sometimes found separated; the first, viz., (နှင့် *hnęng,*) is attached to the noun, with which the comparison is made; the other (တူ *tōō,*) is used as an adjective with the noun, whose similarity is asserted; တူ *tōō* may even be made into the superlative degree; as မျောက်တို့နှင့်ဤမြို့သားတို့တူလှ၏ *myouk dǫ hnęng ee myǫ thas dǫ tōō hlă ee,* "the inhabitants of this city are very like monkeys."

A kind of comparative degree may in the same way be formed in connection with a verb; as မြစ်ညာသို့ထက်ကျေးသို့သာ၍သွားလိမ့်မည် *myeet gnya thǫ htĕt kyés thǫ tha rwę thwas liem mee,* "(you) will go easier down than up a river," lit. "you will go more down, &c.;" လူထက်ဘုရားသခင်တော်ကိုသာ၍ကြောက်ကြလော့ *lōō htĕt phŏŏras thăkhĕng dāū gō tha rwę kyouk läūs,* "fear (ye) God, rather than man." Or the adjunct သာ၍ *tha rwę,* may be omitted, and ထက် *htĕt,* alone expressed; သမီးထက်သားကိုငါနှစ်ချစ်၏ *thămees htĕt thas gō gna hneet khyeet ee,* "I love the son, more than the daughter." Or when an absolute comparison is not meant to be expressed, ထက် *htĕt* is omitted, and သာ *tha,* alone used; as ဤသို့ပြောသဖြင့်သာ၍ရလိမ့်မည် *ee thǫ pyăū thăhpyęng tha rwę yă liem mee,* "by speaking thus (you) will obtain more." This formation obeys the same rule as the comparison of adjectives; as should the negative, &c. be wished to be expressed, it would be in the same manner; as ဘုရားသခင်တော်ထက်လူတို့ကိုမသာ၍မကြောက်ကြနှင့် *phŏŏras thăkhĕng dāū htĕt lōō dǫ gō mă tha rwę mă kyouk kyă hnęng*, " fear (ye) not men, rather than God.''

ထက် *htĕt*, when used alone, may be rendered "beyond;" as အတိုင်းထက် *ădŏings htĕt*, " beyond measure."

THE SUPERLATIVE DEGREE.

ဆုံး *tshŏŏns*, from အဆုံး *ătshŏŏns*, " an end, termination," may be considered as the affix of the superlative degree, and may be appended to any word; as နောက်ဆုံး *nouk tshŏŏns*, " the last, or hindermost," from နောက် *nouk*, " behind;" နောက်မှ *nouk hnŏit*, " afterwards," နောက်ဆုံးမှ *nouk tshŏŏns hnŏit*, " at last;" ကောင်းဆုံး *koungs tshŏŏns*, " the best," from ကောင်း *koungs*, " good." The superlative degree may likewise be expressed by reduplicating the root, and connecting it to its substantive by the connective affix သော *thău*; as ကောင်းကောင်းသောသူ *koungs koungs thău thōō*, " a very good person."

Or by prefixing.

တယ် *tay*, " to be very," either connected to the root by the affix ရွေ့ *rwę*, or not; as တယ်ကောင်းသောသူ *tay koungs thău thōō*, or တယ်ရွေ့ကောင်းသောသူ *tay rwę koungs thău thōō*, " a very good man;" တယ်လှ *tay hlă*, or တယ်ရွေ့လှသောမိန်းမ *tay rwę hlă thău mienz mă*, " a very beautiful woman."

Or

အလွန် *ăhlwŏn*, " exceedingly," from လွန် *hlwŏn*, " to exceed, surpass;" as အလွန်ကောင်းသောသူ *ăhlwŏn koungs thău thōō*, " a very," or " exceedingly good person." When the superlative comparison is to be asserted the noun against which the comparison is made is necessarily in the plural number, and has the affix တွင် *dwĕng*, " in, among," or some similar one attached; and the adjunct သာ *tha*, or သာရွေ့ *tharwę*, or တယ်

tay, or တယ်၍ *tay rwę́*, is used; as ဤလူတို့တွင်ထိုလူသာ၍အလွန်ကောင်းသည် *ee lōō dǫ dwĕng htō lōō tha rwę́ ăhlwŏn koungs thee*, or ဤလူတို့တွင်ထိုလူတယ်၍အလွန်ကောင်းသည် *ee lōō dǫ dwĕng htō lōō tay rwę́ ăhlwŏn koungs thee*, or ဤလူတို့တွင်ထိုလူသာ၍အကောင်းဆုံးရှိပါသည် *ee lōō dǫ dwĕng htō lōō tha rwę́ ăgoungs tshŏŏns shie ba thee*, or ဤလူတို့တွင်ထိုလူတယ်၍အကောင်းဆုံးရှိသည် *ee lōō dǫ dwĕng htō lōō tay rwę́ ăkoungs tshŏŏns shie thee*, all mean "among these men that one is the best."

Sometimes the adverbial form of the root terminating in စွာ *tswa*, has a superlative signification; as များစွာသောလူတို့ *myas tswa thău lōō dǫ*, "very many persons;" နီးစွာသောအိမ်တို့ *nees tswa thău ieng dǫ*, "the nearest houses;" ကြီးစွာနိမိတ် *gyees tswa niemiet*, "a mighty sign." When in this form; အလွန် *ăhlwŏn*, or တယ် *tay*, may be prefixed, and it then forms a very strong superlative; as အလွန်လှစွာမိန်းမ *ăhlwŏn hlă tswa miens mă*, or တယ်လှစွာမိန်းမ *tay hlă tswa miens mă*, "an exceedingly beautiful woman:" sometimes လှ *hlă*, in its adverbial form is found *affixed;* as အရာနှိတ်တတ်လှစွာသောဆရာ *ăra hnŏit tăt hlă tswa thău tshăra*, "a teacher exceedingly skilled in affairs."

စွန်း *tswŏns*, "to be extreme, final," also forms a superlative; as အထက်စွန်း *ăhtęt tswŏns*, "the topmost;" အောက်စွန်း *ouk tswŏns*, "the lowermost;" or it may imply the "top and bottom," without any idea of comparison. မြေကြီးစွန်း *myé gyees tswŏns*, "the uttermost part of the earth."

များ *myas*. A superlative is likewise formed by the use of the word များ *myas*, "to be many," especially with such compounds; as ကျောက်ပေါ *kyouk pau*, "rocky," from ကျောက် *kyouk*, "a stone," and ပေါ *pau*, "numerous;" ကျောက်ပေါများ *kyouk pau myas*, "very rocky."

မြတ် *myăt.* With some roots' မြတ် *myăt,* "to exceed," is compounded to form a superlative; as မြင့်မြတ် *myĕng myăt,* "exceeding lofty."

With adjectives implying number, amount, or quantity; the substantive form used after the noun, implies a superlative or increased degree; as လူအများရှိပါသည် *lōō ămyaः shie pa thee,* "there are a good many men;" မိန်းမအနည်းရှိပါသည် *mienःmă ăneeः shie pa thee,* "there are a small number, very few women."

PART III.

The Numeral system of the Burmese is decimal, and similar in structure and application to that of the Pali and Sanscrit.

Most of the names of the numerals have some signification in the language, but it will be necessary to notice only two of them, which bear evident marks of allusion to the tenets of the Boodhist faith; they are သုံး *thŏŏns,* "three," and ကိုး *kōs,* "nine," and are both sacred numbers; the first typifies the Boodhist triad ဗုဒ္ဓ *bŏŏddhă,* ဓမ္မ *dhămmă,* သင်္ဃာ *thĕnggha,* "God, His Law, and the Congregation of his Saints;" according to Boodhism, from God proceeded the Law; and from the Law came those who fulfilled it; for that human intelligence has in itself the power of transcendental perfectibility, is the diagnostic dogma, the foundation stone of Boodhism as a religion: for this reason သုံး *thŏŏns,* "three," implies likewise, so to perform one's moral exigencies, as, by becoming enrolled in the latter member of the tri-une Three, (the သင်္ဃာ *thĕnggha,*) to become also a component part of the Supreme Triad the သရဏဂုဏ် *thărăṇăgŏŏṇ,* "the Supreme, and final attributes beyond which there is no passing." The number "*nine,*" in the same manner is a *triple* combination of "*three;*" a trebly expressive symbol, therefore, of the expressive *three;* and, being the product of that number into itself, it emblematises the active energy of the Supreme Triad teeming in itself; hence ကိုး *kŏs*, "nine," implies likewise, "to reverence, worship, trust in, &c."

It is usual in epistolary writing, &c. to make a mark or pause, as a sort of starting point; the figure ၅, 5, is often used in this way, because it refers to the ပဉ္စင်း *pĕgnytsĕngs*, "the five parts," or သီလ *theelă*, "precepts," or "commandments;" viz. refraining from, 1st, ပါဏာတိပါတာ *panatiepata*, "destroying life;" 2d, အဒိန္နာဒါနာ *ădiennadana*, "theft;" 3d, ကာမေသုမိစ္ဆာစာရာ *kaméthŏŏmietstshatsara*, "adultery;" 4th, မုသာဝါဒါ *mŏŏthawada*, "falsehood;" 5th, သုရာမေရယမဇ္ဇပမာဒဋ္ဌာနာ *thŏŏ ramérăyămădzdzhăpămadăṭhṭana*, "intoxicating drinks:" and its use in this instance implies that the writer has kept in mind these commandments whilst writing his letter; as also that the reader should do the same, and not put an evil interpretation on any part of it.

TABLE OF NUMERALS.

Eng. Figure.	Burmese Figure.	*Burmese Cardinals.*	*Corresponding Pali Ordinals.*
1	၁	တစ် *teet*, generally contracted to တ *tă*.	ပဌမ *păhṭămă*.
2	၂	နှစ် *hneet*, sometimes contracted to နှ *hnă*.	ဒုတိယံ *dŏŏtieyă*.
3	၃	သုံး *thŏŏns*.	တတိယာ *tătieyă*.
4	၄	လေး *lés*.	စတုတ္ထ *tsădŏŏttă*.
5	၅	ငါး *gnas*.	ပဉ္စမ *pĕgnytsămă*.
6	၆	ခြောက် *khyouk*.	ဆဌမ *tshăhṭămă*.

Eng. Fig.	Burm. Fig.	*Burmese Cardinals.*	*Corresponding Pali Ordinals.*
7	၇	ခွံနှစ် *khwŏnhneet,* sometimes ခုနှစ် *khŏọ̆hneet.*	သတ္တမ *thăttămă.*
8	၈	ရှစ် *sheet,* pronounced *shé.*	အဋ္ဌမ *ăhṭămă.*
9	၉	ကိုး *kōı.*	နဝမ *năwămă.*
10	၁၀	ဆယ် *tshay,* or တဆယ် *tătshay.*	ဒသမ *dăthămă.*
11	၁၁	တဆယ်တစ် *tătshay teet.*	ဧကာဒသမ *ékadăthămă.*
12	၁၂	တဆယ်နှစ် *tătshay hneet.*	ဒွါဒသမ *dwadăthămă,* or ဗါရသ *bară thă.*
13	၁၃	တဆယ်သုံး *tătshhay thŏŏnı.*	တေရသ *térăthă,* or တေလသ *télătha.*
14	၁၄	တဆယ်လေး *tătshay léı.*	စုဒ္ဒသ *tsŏŏddăthă,* or စတုဒ္ဒသ *tsătŏŏd dăthă.*
15	၁၅	တဆယ်ငါး *tătshay gnaı.*	ပဉ္စသ *pĕgnytsăthă* or ပန္နရသ *pănnă răthă.*
16	၁၆	တဆယ်ခြောက် *tătshay khyouk.*	သောဠသ *thăŭllăthă,* or သောရသ *thăŭ răthă.*
17	၁၇	တဆယ်ခွံနှစ် *tătshay khwŏnhneet.*	သတ္တရသ *thăttărăthă,* or သတ္တဒသ *thăttădăthă.*
18	၁၈	တဆယ်ရှစ် *tătshay sheet.*	အဋ္ဌာရသ *ăhṭarăthă,* or အဋ္ဌာဒသ *ăhṭ adăthă.*
19	၁၉	တဆယ်ကိုး *tătshay kōı.*	နဝါဒသ *năwadăthă,* or ဧကုနဝတိ *ekŏŏ năwălie.*

Eng. Fig.	Burm. Fig.	*Burmese Cardinals.*	*Corresponding Pali Ordinals.*
20	၂၀	နှစ်ဆယ် *hneet tshay.*	ဝီသတိ *weethătie.*
21	၂၁	နှဆယ်တစ် *hneet tshay teet.*	ဧကဝီသတိ *ékăweethătie.*
22	၂၂	နှစ်ဆယ်နှစ် *hneet tshay hneet.*	ဒွါဝီသတိ *dwaweethătie.*
23	၂၃	နှစ်ဆယ်သုံး *hneet tshay thŏŏns.*	တေဝီသတိ *téweethătie.*
24	၂၄	နှဆယ်လေး *hneet tshay lés.*	စတုဝီသတိ *tsătŏŏweethătie.*
25	၂၅	နှဆယ်ငါး *hneet tshay gnas.*	ပဉ္စဝီသတိ *pĕgnytsăweethătie.*
26	၂၆	နှစ်ဆယ်ချောက် *hneet tshay khyouk.*	ဆဝီသတိ *tshăweethătie.*
27	၂၇	နှစ်ဆယ်ခွံနှစ် *hneet tshay khwŏnhneet.*	သတ္တဝီသတိ *thăttăweethătie.*
28	၂၈	နှစ်ဆယ်ရှစ် *hneet tshay sheet.*	အဋ္ဌဝီသတိ *ăhṭăweethătie.*
29	၂၉	နှစ်ဆယ်ကိုး *hneet tshay kōs.*	နဝဝီသတိ *năŭweethătie.*
30	၃၀	သုံးဆယ် *thŏŏns tshăy.*	တိံသ *tiengthă.*
31	၃၁	သုံးဆယ်တစ် *thŏŏns tshay teet.*	ဧကတိံသ *ékătiengthă.*
32	၃၂	သုံးဆယ်နှစ် *thŏŏns tshay hneets.*	ဒွါတိံသ *dwatiengthă.*
33	၃၃	သုံးဆယ်သုံး *thŏŏns tshay thŏŏns.*	တေတိံသ *tétiengthă.*
34	၃၄	သုံးဆယ်လေး *thŏŏns tshay lés.*	စတုတိံသ *tsădŏŏtiengthă.*
35	၃၅	သုံးဆယ်ငါး *thŏŏns tshay gnas.*	ပဉ္စတိံသ *pégnytsătiengthă.*
36	၃၆	သုံးဆယ်ချောက် *thŏŏns tshay khyouk.*	ဆတိံသ *tshătiengthă.*
37	၃၇	သုံးဆယ်ခွံနှစ် *thŏŏns tshay khwŏnhneet.*	သတ္တတိံသ *thăttătiengthă.*
38	၃၈	သုံးဆယ်ရှစ် *thŏŏns tshay sheet.*	အဋ္ဌတိံသ *ăhṭătiengthă.*
39	၃၉	သုံးဆယ်ကိုး *thŏŏns tshay kōs.*	နဝတိံသ *năwătiengthă.*
40	၄၀	လေးဆယ် *lés tshay.*	စတ္တာလီသံ *tsăttaleethăn.*

Eng. Fig.	Burm. Fig.	*Burmese Cardinals.*	*Corresponding Pali Ordinals.*
41	၄၁	လေးဆယ်တစ် *léstshay teet.*	ဧကစတ္တာလီသံ *ékătsăttaleethăn.*
42	၄၂	လေးဆယ်နှစ် *léstshay hneet.*	ဒွါစတ္တာလီသံ *dwătsăttaleethăn.*
43	၄၃	လေးဆယ်သုံး *léstshay thŏŏns.*	တေစတ္တာလီသံ *tétsăttaleethăn.*
44	၄၄	လေးဆယ်လေး *léstshay lés.*	စတုစတ္တာလီသံ *tsădŏŏtsăttaleethăn.*
45	၄၅	လေးဆယ်ငါး *léstshay gnas.*	ပဉ္စစတ္တာလီသံ *pĕgnytsătsăttaleethăn.*
46	၄၆	လေးဆယ်ခြောက် *léstshay khyouk.*	ဆစတ္တာလီသံ *tshătsăttaleethăn.*
47	၄၇	လေးဆယ်ခွံနှစ် *léstshay khwŏnhneet.*	သတ္တစတ္တာလီသံ *thăttătsăttaleethăn.*
48	၄၈	လေးဆယ်ရှစ် *léstshay sheet.*	အဋ္ဌစတ္တာလီသံ *ăhṭătsăttaleethăn.*
49	၄၉	လေးဆယ်ကိုး *léstshay kōs.*	နဝစတ္တာလီသံ *năwătsăttaleethăn.*
50	၅၀	ငါးဆယ် *gnastshay.*	ပညာသံ *pĕgnyathăn.*
51	၅၁	ငါးဆယ်တစ် *gnastshay teet.*	ဧကပညာသံ *ékăpĕgnyathăn.*
52	၅၂	ငါးဆယ်နှစ် *gnastshay hneet.*	ဒွပညာသံ *dwăpĕgnyathăn.*
53	၅၃	ငါးဆယ်သုံး *gnastshay thọŏns.*	တိပညာသံ *tiepĕgnyathăn.*
54	၅၄	ငါဆယ်လေး *gnastshhay lés.*	စတုပညာသံ *tsădŏŏpĕgnyathăn.*
55	၅၅	ငါးဆယ်ငါး *gnastshay gnas.*	ပဉ္စပညာသံ *pĕgnytsăpĕgnyathăn.*
56	၅၆	ငါးဆယ်ခြောက် *gnastshay khyouk.*	ဆပညာသံ *tshăpĕgnyathăn.*
57	၅၇	ငါးဆယ်ခွံနှစ် *gnastshay khwŏnhneet.*	သတ္တပညာသံ *thăttăpĕgnyathăn.*
58	၅၈	ငါးဆယ်ရှစ် *gnastshay sheet.*	အဋ္ဌပညာသံ *ăhṭăpĕgnyathăn.*
59	၅၉	ငါးဆယ်ကိုး *gnastshay kō.*	နဝပညာသံ *năwăpĕgnyathăn.*
60	၆၀	ခြောက်ဆယ် *khyouktshay.*	ဆဋ္ဌိ *tshăhṭie.*
61	၆၁	ခြောက်ဆယ်တစ် *khyouktshay teet.*	ဧကဆဋ္ဌိ *ékătshăhṭie.*

B B

Eng. Fig.	Burm. Fig.	Burmese Cardinals.	Corresponding Pali Ordinals.
62	၆၂	ချောက်ဆယ်နှစ် *khyouk tshay hneet.*	ဒွာသဋ္ဌိ *dwätshähṭie.*
63	၆၃	ချောက်ဆယ်သုံး *khyouk tshay thöŏns.*	တေသဋ္ဌိ *tétshähṭie*
64	၆၄	ချောက်ဆယ်လေး *khyouk tshay lés.*	စတုသဋ္ဌိ *tsädöŏtshähṭie.*
65	၆၅	ချောက်ဆယ်ငါး *khyouk tshay gnas.*	ပဉ္စသဋ္ဌိ *pĕgnytsätshähṭie.*
66	၆၆	ချောက်ဆယ်ချောက် *khyouk tshay khyouk.*	ဆသဋ္ဌိ *tshätshähṭie.*
67	၆၇	ချောက်ဆယ်ခွံနှစ် *khyouk tshay khwŏn hneet.*	သတ္တသဋ္ဌိ *thättätshähṭie.*
68	၆၈	ချောက်ဆယ်ရှစ် *khyouk tshay sheet.*	အဋ္ဌသဋ္ဌိ *ähṭätshähṭie.*
69	၆၉	ချောက်ဆယ်ကိုး *khyouk tshay kos.*	နဝသဋ္ဌိ *näwätshähṭie.*
70	၇၀	ခွံနှစ်ဆယ် *khwŏnhneet tshay.*	သတ္တတိ *thättätie.*
71	၇၁	ခွံနှစ်ဆယ်တစ် *khwŏnhneet tshay teet.*	ဧကသတ္တတိ *ékäthättätie.*
72	၇၂	ခွံနှစ်ဆယ်နှစ် *khwŏnhneet tshay hneet.*	ဒွာသတ္တတိ *dwäthättätie.*
73	၇၃	ခွံနှစ်ဆယ်သုံး *khwŏnhneet tshay thöŏns.*	တေသတ္တတိ *téthättätie.*
74	၇၄	ခွံနှစ်ဆယ်လေး *khwŏnhneet tshay lés.*	စတုသတ္တတိ *tsädöŏthättätie.*
75	၇၅	ခွံနှစ်ဆယ်ငါး *khwŏnhneet tshay gnas.*	ပဉ္စသတ္တတိ *pĕgnytsäthättätie.*
76	၇၆	ခွံနှစ်ဆယ်ချောက် *khwŏnhneet tshay khyouk.*	ဆသတ္တတိ *tshäthättätie.*
77	၇၇	ခွံနှစ်ဆယ်ခွံနှစ် *khwŏnhneet tshay khwŏn hneet.*	သတ္တသတ္တတိ *thättäthättätie.*
78	၇၈	ခွံနှစ်ဆယ်ရှစ် *khwŏnhneet tshay sheet.*	အဋ္ဌသတ္တတိ *ähṭäthättätie.*

Eng. Fig.	Burm. Fig.	*Burmese Cardinals.*	*Corresponding Pali Ordinals.*
79	၇၉	ခွံနှစ်ဆယ်ကိုး *khwŏnhneet tshay koz.*	နဝသတ္တတိ *năwăthăttatie.*
80	၈၀	ရှစ်ဆယ် *sheettshay.*	အသီတိ *ătheetie.*
81	၈၁	ရှစ်ဆယ်တစ် *sheet tshay teet.*	ဧကာသီတိ *ékatheetie.*
82	၈၂	ရှစ်ဆယ်နှစ် *sheettshay hneet.*	ဒွာသီတိ *dwatheetie.*
83	၈၃	ရှစ်ဆယ်သုံး *sheettshay thŏŏn.*	တြာသီတိ *tyatheetie.*
84	၈၄	ရှစ်ဆယ်လေး *sheettshay léz.*	စတုရာသီတိ *tsădŏŏratheetie.*
85	၈၅	ရှစ်ဆယ်ငါး *sheettshay gnaz.*	ပဉ္စာသီတိ *pĕgnytsatheetie.*
86	၈၆	ရှစ်ဆယ်ခြောက် *sheettshay khyoukz.*	ဆါသီတိ *tshatheetie.*
87	၈၇	ရှစ်ဆယ်ခွံနှစ် *sheet tshay khwŏnhneet.*	သတ္တာသီတိ *thăttatheetie.*
88	၈၈	ရှစ်ဆယ်ရှစ် *sheettshay sheet.*	အဋ္ဌာသီတိ *ăhṭatheetie.*
89	၈၉	ရှစ်ဆယ်ကိုး *sheet tshay kōz.*	နဝါသီတိ *năwatheetie.*
90	၉၀	ကိုးဆယ် *kōztshay.*	နဝုတိ *năwŏŏtie.*
91	၉၁	ကိုးဆယ်တစ် *kōztshay teet.*	ဧကနဝုတိ *ekănăwŏŏtie.*
92	၉၂	ကိုးဆယ်နှစ် *kōztshay hneet.*	ဒွနဝုတိ *dwănăwŏŏtie.*
93	၉၃	ကိုးဆယ်သုံး *kōztshay thŏŏn.*	တြိနဝုတိ *tyănăwŏŏtie.*
94	၉၄	ကိုးဆယ်လေး *kōztshay léz.*	စတ္တရိနဝုတိ *tsăttărienăwŏŏtie.*
95	၉၅	ကိုးဆယ်ငါး *kōztshay gnaz.*	ပဉ္စနဝုတိ *pĕgnytsănăwŏŏtie.*
96	၉၆	ကိုးဆယ်ခြောက် *kōztshay khyouk.*	ဆနဝုတိ *tshănăwŏŏtie.*
97	၉၇	ကိုးဆယ်ခွံနှစ် *kōztshay khwŏnhneet.*	သတ္တနဝုတိ *thăttănăwŏŏtie.*
98	၉၈	ကိုးဆယ်ရှစ် *kōztshay sheet.*	အဋ္ဌနဝုတိ *ăhṭănăwŏŏtie.*
99	၉၉	ကိုးဆယ်ကိုး *kôztshay kōz.*	နဝနဝုတိ *năwănăwŏŏtie.*

Eng. Fig.	Burm. Fig.	*Burmese Cardinals.*	*Corresponding Pali Ordinals.*
100	၁၀၀	တရာ *tăra.*	သတံ *thătăn.*
1,000	၁၀၀၀	တထောင် *tăhtoung.*	သဟါသံ *thăhathăn.*
10,000	၁၀၀၀၀	တသောင် *tăthoung.*	အသသဟါသံ *ăthăthăhathăn.*
100,000	၁၀၀၀၀၀	တသိန်း *tăthiens.*	သတံသဟါသံ *thătănthăhathăn* or လိက္ခံ *liekkhăn.*
1 Million	၁၀၀၀၀၀၀	တသံး *tăthăns.*	ဒသသတံသဟါသံ *dăthăthănthăha thăn.*
10 Millions	၁၀၀၀၀၀၀၀	တကုဋေ *tăköŏḍé.*	သတံဒသသသဟါသံ *thătăndăthăthă thăhathăn,* or ကောဋိ *kăŭḍie.*

Multiples of any of the six last numbers are expressed as follows: 200, &c., ၂၀၀ နှစ်ရာ *hneet ra,* "two *ra,*" or "hundreds;" 3,000 ၃၀၀၀ သုံးထောင် *thŏŏnshtoung,* "three *htoung,*" or "thousands;" 40,000 ၄၀၀၀၀ လေးသောင် *lésthoung,* "four *thoung,*" or "ten thousands;" 500,000 ၅၀၀၀၀၀ ငါးသိန်း *gnas thiens,* "five *thiens,*" or "hundred thousands;" 6,000,000 ၆၀၀၀၀၀၀ ခြောက်သန်း *kyoukthăns,* "six *thăn,*" or "millions;" 70,000,000 ၇၀၀၀၀၀၀၀ ခုံနှစ်ကုဋေ *khwŏhneetkŏŏḍé,* "seven *kọŏḍés,*" or "tens of millions," 70 millions.

TABLE OF PALI NUMERALS IN THE BURMESE CHARACTER.

	Cardinals.	*Ordinals.*
1	ဧက *éka,* တိ *tie,* or တြိ *tyie.*	ပဌမ *pǎhṭǎmǎ.*
2	ဒွိ *dwie.*	ဒုတိယ *döötieyǎ.*
3	တိ *tie.*	တတိယ *tǎtieyǎ.*
4	စတု *tsǎtöö.*	စတုတ္ထ *tsǎtǫöttǎ.*
5	ပဉ္စ *pěgnytsǎ.*	ပဉ္စမ *pěgnytsǎmǎ.*
6	ဆ *tshǎ.*	ဆဌမ *tshǎhṭǎmǎ.*
7	သတ္တ *thǎttǎ.*	သတ္တမ *thǎttǎmǎ.*
8	အဌ *ǎhṭǎ.*	အဌမ *ǎhṭǎmǎ.*
9	နဝ *nǎwǎ.*	နဝမ *nǎwǎmǎ.*
10	ဒသ *dǎthǎ.*	ဒသမ *dǎthǎmǎ.*
11	ဧကဒသ *ékǎdǎthǎ.*	ဧကဒသမ *ékǎdǎthǎmǎ.*
12	ဒွါဒသ *dwǎdǎthǎ.*	ဒွါဒသမ *dwǎdǎthǎmǎ.*

The remaining Cardinals are the same as their Ordinals, as may be seen in the former table from 13 downwards; as တေရသ *térǎthǎ,* is "thirteen," or "the thirteenth," and so on with the rest.

$\frac{1}{2}$. တဝက် *tǎwět,* or တချမ်း *tǎkhyǎns,* or ထက်ဝက် *htětwět,* all imply "one-half," from ဝက် *wět,* and ချမ်း *khyans,* roots implying "division into equal parts."

$\frac{1}{4}$. တစိတ် *tǎ tsiet,* "a quarter," from စိတ် *tsiet,* a root implying "division into four parts."

$\frac{3}{4}$. သုံးစိတ် *thöönstsiet,* from သုံး *thööns,* "three," and စိတ် *tsiet,* "a quarter."

$1\frac{1}{2}$. တခုနှင့်တဝက် *tăkhŏŏ hnĕng tăwĕt*, from တ *tă*, "one," ခု *khŏŏ*, numeral generic affix, နှင့် *hnĕng*, "and," and တဝက် *tăwĕt* "a half."

$1\frac{3}{4}$. တခုနှင့်သုံးစိတ် *tăkhŏŏ hnĕng thŏŏns tsiet*, as above.

ကျိပ် ***kyiet***. In enumerating rational beings the term ကျိပ် ***kyiet***, is used as a substitute for the decimal ဆယ် *tshay*, "ten;" as တကျိပ် *tă kyiet*, "one ten;" နှစ်ကျိပ် *hneet kyiet*, "two tens," or "twenty." This numeral is used before the noun, and with or without a Numeral Generic Affix; as တကျိပ်သောလူတို့သည် *tă kyiet thăŭ lōō dō thee*, "ten men;" နှစ်ကျိပ်သုံးပါးမိဘုရားတော်တို့သည် *hneet kyiet thŏŏns pa miebhŏŏras dāū dō thee*, "twenty-three Queens;" သုံးကျိပ်ငါးဦးရဟန်းတော်တို့သည် *thŏŏns kyiet gnasōōs răhăns dāū dō thee*, thirty-five rahans, or priests of Boodha.

On Compounding a Numeral with a Noun.

1. In compounding a Numeral with a Noun, the Burmese never use a simple numeral, as "one man;"—but employ, as auxiliary affixes, words or terms signifying either the class to which the name belongs, the use to which it is put, or some shape, form, or idea to which it may have some resemblance real or otherwise. These affixes may be styled generic, that is descriptive of some class or kind. The term numeral affix would be incorrect; a numeral affix being one that points out the number of the root, to which attached.

2. To form an idea of the nature and use of these affixes an example may be given in English. To render into Burmese the idea of "two oxen" it would be necessary to say, "oxen two animals;" "animal" being the head under which oxen would be classed. To render "two dollars" it would be necessary to say "dollars two flat things;"

as "flat things" is the head under which dollars, or pieces of money would be classed. "Two carriages" would be rendered—"carriages, two conveyances," as they would be classed under that head. "Two languages" would be rendered "languages two, uttered things," that being their proper class.

3. The choice of words to form these affixes is very arbitrary, even a fancied resemblance to any subject being sufficient to warrant, such word being chosen and used as a numeral generic affix.

4. It will be perceived that there are many words which would be liable to fall under more than one head, as "a horse," or "elephant," which might be classed either as *animals*, or as *conveyances*, they being beasts of burden; a "ship" likewise might be classed either as a *conveyance*, or as a *thing whose length is greater than its breadth.* The choice of affix in such cases rests with the speaker.

5. Having premised thus much, it will be necessary to state, that if the numeral does not exceed "ten," but consists of a simple unit; it is prefixed to the generic affix; as နွား *nwas*, "an ox" သုံး *thŏŏns*, "three," and ကောင် *goung*, the generic affix for animals,—forms နွားသုံးကောင် *nwas thŏŏns goung*, "three cows;" ဒင်္ဂါး *dingas*, "a dollar," လေး *lés*, "four," and ပြား *byas*, the generic affix for "flat things,"—forms ဒင်္ဂါးလေးပြား *dingas lés byas*, "four dollars;" လူ *lōō*, "a man," ကိုး *kōs*, "nine," and ယောက် *youk*, the generic affix for "rational beings," —forms လူကိုးယောက် *lōō kōs youk*, "nine men;" ပုလင်း *pălĕngs*, "a bottle," ဆယ် *tshay*, "ten," and လုံး *lŏŏns*, the affix for "round things," —forms ပုလင်းဆယ်လုံး *pălĕngs tshay lŏŏns*, "ten bottles."

6. Should the number however be "ten," or a clear multiple of it; as 20, 40, 70, then the generic affix is used in the substantive form and precedes the numeral, the noun still remaining first; as နွားအကောင်နှစ်ဆယ် *nwas ăgoung hneet tshay*, "twenty oxen;" ဒင်္ဂါးအပြားသုံးဆယ် *dingas ăbyas thŏŏns tshay*, "thirty rupees;" လူအယောက်ခြောက်ဆယ် *lōō ăyouk khyouk tshay*, "sixty men;" ပလင်းအလုံးခွံနှစ်ဆယ် *pălengs ălŏŏns khwŏnhneet tshay*, "twenty bottles."

7. But should the number exceed "ten," and not be a clear multiple of it, having units over; as 15, 45, 101, 1152, &c., then the generic affix in its *substantive* form is prefixed as the numeral auxiliary of all the numbers up to ten, and in its *radical* form, it is again affixed to the supernumerary units; as နွားအကောင်တဆယ်ငါးကောင် *nwas ăgoung tă tshay gnas goung*, "fifteen cows;" ဒင်္ဂါးအပြားလေးဆယ်ငါးပြား *dingas ăbyas lés tshay gnas bya*, "forty-five dollars;" လူအယောက်တရာတယောက် *lōō ăyouk tăra tă youk*, "one hundred and one men;" ပလင်းအလုံးတထောင်တရာငါးဆယ်နှစ်လုံး *pălĕngs ălŏŏns tă htoung tăya gnas tshay hneet lŏŏns*, "one thousand one hundred and fifty-two bottles." These distinctions, however, are only attended to in writing, as in common parlance, the generic affix is generally affixed in its radical form, and attached to the numeral, whether it be a compound or simple number, a perfect or imperfect multiple of ten; ဒင်္ဂါးနှစ်ဆယ်နှင့်နှစ်ပြား *dingas hneet tshay hnĕng hneet byas*, "twenty-two dollars;" လူငါးဆယ်ငါးယောက် *lōō gnas tshay gnas youk*, "fifty-five men."

8. Numerals with their generic affixes may be combined to nouns, either, as in the above instances, by immediately following them, or

they may precede their nouns, and be connected to them by the connective affix သော *thăü,* in which case the number is emphatically stated; as နှစ်ယောက်သောသူ *hneet youk thăü thōō,* "the two men," or "the men who are two;" တဆယ်ငါးပြားသောဒင်္ဂါး *tă tshay gnas byas thăü dingas,* "the fifteen dollars," or "the dollars that are fifteen."

9. When any numeral, exceeding one, is thus combined with a noun, the noun may have a numeral affix (that is an affix of the plural number), attached to it, or not; နှစ်ယောက်သောလူတို့ *hneet youk thăü lōō dō̤,* "the two men;" or the numeral affix တို့ *dō̤,* may be used after the numeral generic affixes; as လူနှစ်ယောက်တို့ *lōō hneet youk dō̤,* "two men."

10. Sometimes the numeral precedes, and the numeral generic affix follows the noun, the force is then more demonstrative; as နှစ်လူယောက် *hneet lōō youk,* "the two men;" လေးကျွန်းလုံး *lės kywŏns lŏŏns,* "the four Islands;" or this is more correctly, "the four round Islands:" the adjective being made to serve the place both of an attributive and a generic affix.

11. Should the noun be qualified by an adjective connected with it by သော *thăü,* the numeral with its generic affix, may precede the noun, without having any connective adjunct; as နှစ်ယောက်ကောင်းသောသူ *hneet youk koungs thăü thōō,* "the two good men;" သုံးယောက်လှသောမိန်းခလေးတို့သည် *thŏŏns youk hlă thăü miens khălé dō̤ thee,* "the three pretty little girls."

12. Should a numeral be found combined with a generic affix alone, without any other substantive, then the compound has the significa-

tion of that number of whatever the generic affix expresses; as သုံး ကောင် *thŏŏns goung*, "three animals;" တခွက် *tă khwĕt*, "a cup;" နှစ် ယောက် *hneet youk*, "two men."

13. Sometimes numerals are used, without any generic affix, with nouns implying measures of weight, capacity, or time, &c. these, however, when thus used, obey the same law as generic affixes; as အချင် ကိုးတောင်ခန့် *ăkhyĕng kōs toung khăn*, "about nine cubits in diameter;" အလုံးအတောင်သုံးဆယ်ခန့် *ălŏŏns ătoung thŏŏns tshay khăn*, "about thirty cubits in circumference;" အလျားအတောင်ငါးဆယ်ရှစ်တောင်ခန့် *ălyăs toung gnas tshay sheet toung khăn*, "about fifty-eight cubits in length;" အသက်ကိုးနှစ်ခန့် *ăthĕt kōs hneet khăn*, "about nine years old;" အသက် အနှစ်တဆယ်ခန့် *ăthĕts ăhneet tă tshay khăn*, "about 10 years of age;" အသက်အနှစ်တဆယ်လေးနှစ်ခန့် *ăthĕt ăhneet tătshay lés hneet khăn*, "about 14 years of age;" ကိုးရက်ပတ်လုံး *kōs rĕt pătlŏŏns*, "during nine days;" အရက်တဆယ်ပတ်လုံး *ărĕt tă tshay pătlŏŏns*, "during 10 days;" အရက်တ ဆယ်လေးရက်ပတ်လုံး *ărĕt tă tshay lés rĕt pătlŏŏn,s* "during 14 days."

NUMERAL GENERIC AFFIXES.

In the following list the affixes are given in their radical form accompanied by the corresponding substantives.

ဦး *ōōs*, a root implying "chief, beginning, first, &c.;" substantive အဦး *ăōōs*, is applied to nouns implying "Chief, Lord, or respectable characters;" as ဘုရားသခင်တဦး *bhōōras thăkhĕng tă ōōs*, "one Lord God;" မင်းကြီး နှစ်ဦး *mĕngs gyees hneet ōōs*, "two kings;" ဘုံးကြီးလေးဦး *bhŏŏns gyees lés ōōs*, "four Phoongies," or "Boodhist priests;" ဆရာငါးဦး *tshăra gnas ōōs*, "five teachers;" မိဘုရားအဦးလေးဆယ် *miephŏŏras ăōōs lés tshay*, "forty

Queens;" သူရဲးအဦးနှစ်ဆယ်ငါးဦး *thōōrais ăōōs hneet tshay gnas ōōs,* "twenty-five fighting men;" ဦး *ōōs,* seems also used with inanimate objects, when alluded to as agents or principals; as တဦးကိုတဦးသင်္ဘောတွေကြုံကြလျှင် *tă ōōs gō tă ōōs thĕngbhăū twę kyŏŏn kyă hlyĕng,* "should one ship meet the other."

သူ *tshōō,* a root which seems to have the meaning of "to distress, inflict pain, &c.," substantive အသူ *ătshōō,* is applied to objects of adoration, or to things belonging to, or dedicated to objects of adoration; as ဘုရားသခင်နှစ်သူ *phōōrăs thăkhĕng hneet tshōō,* "two Gods;" ဗုဒ္ဓလေးသူ *Bōōddhă lęs tshōō,* "four Boodhas;" စေတီတသူ *tsédie tă tshōō,* "one tsédyă or Pagoda."

ပါး *bas,* a root implying "being with, having," substantive အပါး *ăbas,* is applied to nouns signifying "respectable characters, Deities, objects of reverence," &c., and likewise to immaterial objects, such as, "an element, an idea," &c., ဘုရားတပါး *phōōras tă bas,* "one Phōōras," or "object of worship;" တပြည့်ဒေါ်နှစ်ပါး *tăbyęe dāū hneet bas,* "two sacred disciples;" ရဟန်းလေးပါး *răhăns lés bas,* "four Ministers of Religion;" ပုဏ္ဏားအပါးငါးဆယ်နှစ်ပါး *pŏŏnnas ăbas gnas tshay hneet bas,* "fifty-two Brahmins;" နတ်တပါး *năt tă bas,* "a Nat," or "Angel;" ဝိညာဉ်နှစ်ပါး *wie gnyee hneet bas,* "two souls" or "spirits;" မိတ်ဆွေလေးပါး *miettshwé lé bas,* "four friends;" ပါရမီဆယ်ပါး *parămee tshay bas,* "the ten virtues," or "accomplishments;" မြေကြီးနှိုတ်ဉ်ဖွယ်ခွန်နှစ်ပါး *myé gyees hnŏit ăn hpway khwŏn hneet bas,* "the seven wonders of the world." It is also sometimes used without any particular reference to respectability; as သူတပါး *thōō tă bas,* "one person;" sometimes as a recapitulating affix, with things material, or immaterial; as မုန့်။ဆန်။လက်ဖက်ချောက်။ဤသုံးပါးတို့ကိုငါ ယူပြီး *mŏŏn*॥*tshăn*॥*lĕthpĕt khyouk*॥*ee thŏŏns băs dō gō gnă yŏō byees,* "bread, rice, dried tea, these three articles I have brought."

ယောက် *youk,* from ယောက်ျား *youkyas,* "a male," substantive အယောက် *ayouk,* is affixed to the names of rational beings of any sort, inferior to Divine ones; as ယောက်ျားနှစ်ယောက် *youkyas hneet youk,* "two males;" မိန်းမသုံးယောက် *miens mă thŏŏns youk,* "three women;" သားငါးယောက် *thas gnas youk,* "five sons;" လင်တယောက် *lĕng tăyouk,* "one husband;" စစ္ဆေလေးယောက် *tsătshélés youk,* "four ghosts," or "apparitions;" နတ်ရုပ်တယောက် *năt yŏŏk tăyouk,* "one figure of a Năt;" hence when applied to အရုပ် *ăyŏŏk,* "a statue," &c., it implies; as အရုပ်တယောက် *äyŏŏk tă youk,* "a figure" or "statue of a *human* being;" giving its definitive generic meaning to the substantive အရုပ် *ărŏŏk.* This affix is not applied to human corpses.

ကောင် *goung,* substantive အကောင် *ăgoung,* "a brute beast," is affixed to the names of all irrational beings, whether birds, beasts, fishes, reptiles, &c.; as နွားတကောင် *nwas tă goung,* "an ox;" ကျားနှစ်ကောင် *kyas hneet goung,* "two tigers;" ကြံ့သုံးကောင် *kyăn thŏŏns goung,* "three rhinoceroses;" ကုလားအုတ်နှစ်ကောင် *kŏŏlas ŏŏk hneet goung,* "two camels;" ဝက်ဝံနှစ်ကောင် *wĕt wŏŏn hneet goung,* "two bears;" ပိုးတကောင် *pōs tă goung,* "an insect;" ပိုးဟပ်သုံးကောင် *pōs hăt thŏŏns goung,* "three cockroaches;" ကြမ်းပိုးတကောင် *kyăns pōs tă goung,* "a bug;" ခူယားတကောင် *khōōyas tă goung,* "a sort of caterpillar;" တောက်တဲ့နှစ်ကောင် *touktai hneet goung,* "two touktais," a species of lizard; ကျိုင်းနှစ်ကောင် *gyŏing hneet goung,* "two locusts;" ပျားလေးကောင် *pyas lés goung,* "four bees;" မြွေခြောက်ကောင် *mrwé khyouk goung*, "six serpents;" ယင်လေးကောင် *yĕng lés goung*, "four flies;" ဖားလောင်းတကောင် *hpas loungs tă goung*, "a tadpole;" ငါးမန်းတကောင် *gnasmăns tă goung*, "a shark;" ကြက်နှစ်ကောင် *krĕt hneet goung*, "two fowls;" ငှက်သုံးကောင် *gnhĕt thŏŏns goung*, "three birds;" ဆင်ရုပ်ခွန်နှစ်ကောင် *tshĕng rŏŏk khwŏnhneet goung*, "seven figures of elephants;" hence with အရုပ် *ărŏŏk*, "a statue," it implies; as အရုပ်တကောင် *ărŏŏk tă goung*, "a figure of an *animal*."

ပြား *pyas*, a root signifying "superficial extent," substantive အပြား *ăpyas*, is applied to things whose superficial extent considerably exceeds their depth; as ဒင်္ဂါးတပြား *dingas tă byas*, "a dollar," or "rupee;" ပြည်သုံးပြား *pyee thŏŏns byas*, "three countries;" ပုကန်နှစ်ပြား *păgăn hneet byas*, "two dishes;" ငါးကြေးနှစ်ပြား *gnas kyés hneet byas*, "two fish scales;" ဥယည်လေးပြား *ŏŏyeen lés byas*, "four gardens;" သက္ကလတ်ရှစ်ပြား *thăggălĕt sheet byas*, "eight blankets."

လုံး *lŏŏns*, a root signifying "rotundity," substantive အလုံး *ălŏŏns*, is affixed to the names of things that are globular, cylindrical, oval, conical, or whose circumference consists of a circle, or any part of a circle; also to some square things, such as square bottles, bricks, tiles, boxes, &c.; as အဥနှစ်လုံး *ăŏŏ hneet lŏŏns*, "two eggs;" မုံ့တလုံး *mŏṇn tă lŏŏns*, "a loaf of bread;" ပုလင်းလေးလုံး *pălĕngs lés lŏŏns*, "four bottles;" ဘူးဆို့လေးလုံး *bhōōs tshọ lés lŏŏns*, "four bottle stoppers;" ခွက်နှစ်လုံး *khwĕt hneet lŏŏns*, "two cups;" ပုကန်နှစ်လုံး *păgăn hneet lŏŏns*, "two saucers;" ခြေနှစ်လုံး *khyé hneet lŏŏns*, "two feet;" လက်နှစ်လုံး *lĕt hneet lŏŏns*, "two hands;" ချေဆန်ဆယ်လုံး *kyétshăn tshay lŏŏns*, "ten toes;" လက်ချောင်းဆယ်လုံး *lĕt khyoungs tshay lŏŏns*, "ten fingers;" မီးပေါက်တလုံး *meespouk tă lŏŏns*, "a spark of fire;" မီးတိုင်နှစ်လုံး *meeɜ dŏing hneet lŏŏnɜ*, "two candles;" မီးအိမ်တလုံး *meeɜ ieng tă lŏŏnɜ*, "a lantern;" ဆီမီးခွက်နှစ်လုံး *tshee meeɜ khwĕt hneet lŏŏnɜ*, "two cressets;" လက်စွတ်နှစ်လုံး *lĕt tsŏk hneet lŏŏnɜ*, "two finger rings;" နားတောင်းနှစ်လုံး *naɜ doungɜ hneet lŏŏnɜ*, "two nadoungs," or "ear cylinders;" တောင်းနှစ်လုံး *toungɜ hneet lŏŏnɜ*, "two baskets;" အစ်နှစ်လုံး *eet hneet lŏŏnɜ*, "two lacquered boxes;" အသီးနှစ်လုံး *ătheeɜ hneet lŏŏnɜ*, "two fruits;" ဆူးနှစ်လုံး *tshōōɜ hneet lŏŏnɜ*, "two thorns;" တက်နှစ်လုံး *tĕt hneet lŏŏnɜ*, "two oars;" ဝါးနှစ်လုံး *waɜ hneet lŏŏnɜ*, "two bamboos;" သစ်တာနှစ်လုံး *theetta hneet lŏŏnɜ*, "two boxes;" တောင်နှစ်လုံး *toung hneet lŏŏnɜ*, "two mountains;" ပတ်နှစ်လုံး *păt hneet lŏŏnɜ*, "two drums;" ပြွန်နှစ်လုံး *pywŏn hneet lŏŏnɜ*, "two water pipes;" ဖရဲသီးနှစ်လုံး *hpărai theeɜ hneet lŏŏnɜ*, "two melons;" ဘိနပ်နှစ်လုံး *bhienăt hneet lŏŏnɜ*, "two sandals;" မျက်စိနှစ်လုံး *myĕt tsie hneet lŏŏnɜ*, "two eyes;" ရေဘူးနှစ်လုံး *rébhōōɜ hneet lŏŏnɜ*, "two water goglets;" ရေဘုံးနှစ်လုံး *rébhŏŏnɜ hneet lŏŏnɜ*, "two water buckets;" တိုင်သုံးလုံး *tŏing thŏŏnɜ lŏŏnɜ*, "three masts;" အုပ်နှစ်လုံး *ŏk hneet lŏŏnɜ*, "two bricks;" အုပ်ကြွတ်နှစ်လုံး *ŏk krwĕt hneet lŏŏnɜ*, "two tiles;" အိုးနှစ်လုံး *ōɜ hneet lŏŏnɜ*, "two pots;" ဘီးနှစ်လုံး *bheeɜ hneet lŏŏnɜ*, "two wheels;" ခဲရန်နှစ်လုံး *khairăn hneet lŏŏnɜ*, "two balled cartridges."

ထွေး *htwé*, a root implying "globular," substantive အထွေး *ăhtwéɜ*, is applied somewhat in the same manner, as လုံး *lŏŏnɜ*; as မုန့်နှစ်ထွေး *mŏŏn hneet htwéɜ*, "two loaves;" ရေဘူးတထွေး *ré bhōōɜ tă htwéɜ*, "one water goglet."

ဝင်း *tsĕngɜ*, a root implying "extension in a straight line," substantive အဝင်း *ătsĕngɜ*, is applied to articles whose length considerably exceeds their breadth; as ငါးမျှားတန်နှစ်ဝင်း *gnaś hmyaś tăn hneet tsĕngś*, "two fishing rods;" ကြိုးနှစ်ဝင်း *krōś hneet tsĕngś*, "two lines," or "chains;" လှံနှစ်ဝင်း *hlăn hneet tsĕngś*, "two spears;" သင်္ဘောနှစ်ဝင်း *thĕngbhăŭ hneet tsĕngś*, "two ships;" တိုင်နှစ်ဝင်း *tŏing hneet tsĕngś*, "two masts;" ဆံနှစ်ဝင်း *tshăn hneet tsĕngś*, "two hairs;" လှေနှစ်ဝင်း *hlé hneet tsĕngś*, "two boats;" လမ်းနှစ်ဝင်း *lănś hneet tsĕngś*, "two roads;" မြောင်းနှစ်ဝင်း *myoungś hneet tsĕngś*, "two furrows;" တံတားနှစ်ဝင်း *tădăś hneet tsĕngś*, "two bridges;" ထိုးတံနှစ်ဝင်း *htōś dăn hneet tsĕngś*, "two rammers, spits, &c." မြစ်ကြီးငါးဝင်း *myeet gyeeś gnaś tsĕngś*, "the five great rivers."

တန်း *tănś*, substantive အတန်း *ătănś*, a root having the same signification, as ဝင်း *tsĕngś*, may be used in its place.

စီး *tseeś*, a root implying co-existence with, and motion with; both ideas combined; as worms in the belly, a parasite on, or conveyed in, or infesting the body, a spirit possessing a man, &c., substantive အစီး *ătseeś*, is appended to the names of animals, or articles used for the purpose of conveyance, or transportation; as မြင်းနှစ်စီး *myĕngś hneet tseeś*, "two horses;" ဆင်နှစ်စီး *tshĕng hneet tseeś*, "two elephants;" နွားနှစ်စီး *nwaś hneet tseeś*, "two carriage oxen;" သင်္ဘောနှစ်စီး *thĕngbhăŭ hneet tseeś*, "two ships;" လှေနှစ်စီး *hlé hneet tseeś*, "two boats;" ပုခက်နှစ်စီး *pŏŏkhĕt hneet tseeś*, "two swinging cradles;" ရထားနှစ်စီး *răhtaś hneet tseeś*, "two chariots;" လှည်းနှစ်စီး *hleeś hneet tseeś*, "two carts;" ဒန်းနှစ်စီး *dănś hneet tseeś*, "two swings."

ဘက် *bhĕt*, or ဖက် *hpĕt*, "a pair;" subst. အဘက် *ăbhĕt*, is applied to articles whose nature is dual, or which are naturally in pairs; as လက်နှစ်ဖက် *lĕt hneet bhĕt*, "two hands;" မျက်စိနှစ်ဖက် *myĕttsie hneet bhĕt,* "two eyes;" ခြေနှစ်ဖက် *khyé hneet bhĕt,* "two feet;" ဘိနပ်နှစ်ဘက် *bhienăt hneet bhĕt,* "two slippers;" လိန်ဥတဖက် *lien ŏŏ tă bhĕt,* "one testicle;" ပါးတဖက် *pas tă bhĕt,* "one cheek;" ကမ်းပါးတဖက် *kăns pas tă bhĕt,* "one bank," or "shore;" နါးတသက် *nas tă bhĕt,* "one ear;" ဘီးလေးဘက် *bhees lés bhĕt,* "four wheels;" ခြေလေးဘက် *khyé lés bhĕt,* "four feet."

ကြောင်း *gyoungs,* a root implying "drawn out into an extended line," substantive အကြောင်း *ăgyoungs,* is applied to words of such a nature; as လမ်းတကြောင်း *lăns tă gyoungs,* "a road;" ခရီးနှစ်ကြောင်း *khărees hneet gyoungs,* "two paths;" မြစ်နှစ်ကြောင်း *myeet hneet gyoungs,* "two rivers;" မြောင်းနှစ်ကြောင်း *myoungs hneet gyoungs,* "two gutters."

ထည် *htee,* a root from whence အထည် *ăhtee,* "a piece of cloth;" is used with nouns implying articles of clothing, or pieces of cloth; သက္ကလတ်တထည် *thăgkhălăt tă htee,* "a blanket;" ထဘီန်တထည် *htăbheen tă htee,* "a htabheen," or "Burman petticoat;" အင်္ကျီနှစ်ထည် *ăngyee hneet htee,* "two jackets;" ပဝါနှစ်ထည် *pŏŏha hneet htee,* "two handkerchiefs."

ဆောင် *tshoung,* a root implying "enduring, sustaining, containing," substantive အဆောင် *ătshoung,* is affixed to nouns which imply articles that are made to contain any thing; as "houses, &c." also any thing which has any thing in it; as a "bell with a clapper," &c.; အိမ်နှစ်ဆောင် *ieng hneet tshoung,* "two houses;" ချိုင့်နှစ်ဆောင် *khyōing hneet tshŏung,* "two cages;" ဆင်ကနှစ်ဆောင် *tshĕnggă hneet tshŏung,* "two howdahs;" တန်းနှစ်ဆောင် *tăns hneet tshŏung,* "two lock up houses," ကျောင်းနှစ်ဆောင် *kyoungs hneet tshoung,* "two monasteries;" နန်းနှစ်ဆောင် *năns hneet tshoung,* "two palaces;" အိမ်သားနှစ်ဆောင် *iengthas hneet tshoung* "two out-houses;" အခန်းနှစ်ဆောင် *ăkhăn: hneet tshoung*, "two rooms;" ခေါင်းလောင်းနှစ်ဆောင် *khoung:loung: hneet tshoung*, "two dome-shaped bells without clappers;" ဆွဲလွဲနှစ်ဆောင် *tshwailwai hneet tshoung*, "two small bells with clappers;" သစ်တာနှစ်ဆောင် *theetta hneet tshoung*, "two boxes;" and so on: as also with any word compounded of several words of which the root ဆောင် *tshoung*, is one.

စောင်း *tsoung:*, a root implying "steepness, a side, &c.," subst. အစောင်း *ătsoung:*, is applied to writings, books, &c.; as စာအုပ်နှစ်စောင်း *tsa ŏŏk hneet tsoung:*, "two bound books;" ကျမ်းစာနှစ်စောင်း *kyăn: tsa hneet tsoung:*, "two religious books;" စာထုပ်တစောင်း *tsa htŏŏk tă tsoung:*, "a bundle of written papers:" also to a punkah; as လေခံယပ်တစောင်း *lé khăn yăt tă tsoung:*, "a punkah."

ချပ် or ချတ် *khyăt*, a root implying "flatness," substantive အချပ် *ăkhyăt*, is applied to articles that are thin and flat, or laminated; as ဖျာနှစ်ချပ် *hpya hneet khyăt*; "two mats;" ပေနှစ်ချပ် *pé hneet kyăt*, "two palmyra leaves;" ငါးကြေးနှစ်ချပ် *gna: kyé: hneet khyăt*, "two fish scales;" ယပ်နှစ်ချပ် *yăt hneet khyăt*, "two fans;" မှန်နှစ်ချပ် *hmăn hneet khyăt*, "two looking-glasses."

လွှာ *hlwa*, a root signifying "laminated, split into pieces," as talc, &c. substantive အလွှာ *ăhlwa*, is applied to all articles denoting leaves, &c.; as အရွက်နှစ်လွှာ *ărwĕt hneet hlwa*, "two leaves;" ယပ်တောင်နှစ်လွှာ *yăt toung hneet hlwa*, "two priest's fans."

ရပ် *răt*, a root signifying "fixed, settled, remaining in," substantive အရပ် *arăt*, "a place," is applied to all things peculiar to any place or country; such as languages, rites, customs, habits, ceremonies, &c.; as

စကားနှစ်ရပ် *tsăgas hneet răt,* "two languages;" မင်္ဂလာတရပ် *mĕngăla tă yăt,* "one sacrament," or "religious rite."

တန် *tăn,* a root implying "separation by time, or space," substantive အတန် *ătăn,* is applied to immaterial things, events, &c. that happen at intervals, or to any things succeeding each other at intervals; as အကျိုးနှစ်တန် *ăgyōs hneet tăn,* "two rewards;" ပြစ်မှားနှစ်တန် *pyeet hmas hneet tăn,* "two sins;" ဖိုလ်လေးတန် *hpō lés tăn,* "the four attainments;" မဂ်လေးတန် *mĕt lés tăn,* "the four grand ways;" တံခါးနှစ်တန် *tănkhas hneet tăn,* "two doors occurring at intervals."

ပင် *pĕng,* a root implying "growing up from a root," as trees, &c., substantive အပင် *ăpĕng,* is applied to the names of all trees, plants, &c., likewise to anything springing from roots; as ပင်နှစ်ပင် *pĕng hneet pĕng,* "two trees;" ဝါးနှစ်ပင် *was hneet pĕng,* "two bamboo plants;" ဆံနှစ်ပင် *tshăn hneet pĕng,* "two hairs;" ကျူနှစ်ပင် *kyōō hneet pĕng,* "two reeds."

ခွန်း *khwŏns,* a root implying "sound" of any description, substantive အခွန်း *ăkhwŏns,* is applied to words implying sounds; as အက္ခရာနှစ်ခွန်း *ăkkhăra hneet khwŏns,* "two letters of the alphabet;" စကားနှစ်ခွန်း *tsăgas hneet khwŏns* "two words;" သံနှစ်ခွန်း *thăn hneet khwŏns,* "two sounds."

ချောင်း *khyoungs,* a root implying any thing like "a stiff bar of metal," or any thing straight and stiff, is applied to words of a cognate sort; as အပ်နှစ်ချောင်း *ăt hneet khyoungs,* "two needles;" ဆူးနှစ်ချောင်း *tshōōs hneet khyoungs,* "two thorns;" ခဲတံနှစ်ချောင်း *khai dăn hneet khyoungs,* "two lead pencils;" မှင်တံနှစ်ချောင်း *hmĕng tăn hneet khyoungs,* "two pens;" ထိုးတံနှစ်ချောင်း *htōs dăn hneet khyoung,* "two ramrods."

လက် *lĕt,* "the hand," substantive အလက် *ălĕt,* is applied to all things subject to be handled, or used by the hands; as သေနတ်နှစ်လက် *thénăt hneet lĕt,* "two muskets;" ဓားနှစ်လက် *dhas hneet lĕt,* "two daos," or "swords;" ဇွန်းနှစ်လက် *dzwŏns hneet lĕt,* "two spoons;" ခရာနှစ်လက် *khă-ra hneet lĕt,* "two bugles."

သွယ် *thway,* a root implying "a continuous direction," substantive အသွယ် *ăthway,* is applied to rivers, streams, &c.; as မြစ်နှစ်သွယ် *myeet hneet thway,* "two rivers."

ခင်း *khĕngs,* a root implying "spread out," substantive အခင်း *ăkhĕngs,* is applied to all articles spread out; as သက္ကလတ်နှစ်ခင်း *thăkkhălăt hneet khĕngs,* "two blankets;" ဖျာနှစ်ခင်း *hpya hneet khĕngs,* "two mats."

ချက် *khyĕt,* a root implying a "central point of motion towards," whether of thought or action, substantive အချက် *ăkhyĕt,* is applied to all radiated objects; as ဘီးနှစ်ချက် *bhees hneet khyĕt,* "two wheels;" ထီးနှစ်ချက် *htees hneet khyĕt,* "two umbrellas."

ကွင်း *kwĕngs,* a root implying "circular," substantive အကွင်း *ăkwĕngs,* is applied to all circular objects; as လက်စွပ်နှစ်ကွင်း *lĕt tswŏt hneet kwĕngs,* "two finger rings."

ကုံး *kŏŏns,* a root implying "concatenation, stringing together," is applied to all articles of such a nature; as ပုထီးနှစ်ကုံး *pădhees hneet gŏŏns,* "two necklaces."

ခွက် *khwĕt,* a root implying "concavity," substantive အခွက် *ăkhwĕt,* is applied to articles of a cup-like shape; as နာရီးနှစ်ခွက် *narees hneet khwĕt,* "two pocket watches."

ကိုယ် *kōh,* "a body," is applied to articles which have a corporeal shape;

as အရုပ်နှစ်ကိုယ် *ărŏŏk hneet kōh,* "two statues," or "figures;" ဆင်ရုပ်တကိုယ် *tshĕngrŏŏk tăkōh,* "one figure of an elephant."

ခု *khŏŏ,* a root implying "to eke out, supply deficiencies, &c." is applied to any nouns which do not fall under a particular head; as သော့နှစ်ခု *thăŭ hneet khŏŏ,* "two keys." It may also be applied to any of the above enumerated classes of words, except rational beings, and animals, or immaterial articles; as စားပွဲနှစ်ခု *tsaszbwaisz hneet khŏŏ,* "two tables;" ပုလင်းနှစ်ခု *pălĕngsz hneet khŏŏ,* "two bottles;" သေနတ်နှစ်ခု *thénăt hneet khŏŏ,* "two muskets;" and so on. It is also the affix used with numerals, when *not consisting of decades;* as သုံးခု *thŏŏnsz khŏŏ,* "three;" သက္ကရာဇ်တထောင်တခုနှစ် *thakkăreet tă htoung tă khŏŏ hneet,* "the year 1001."

ပြည့် *pyee,* "full, complete;" is the affix of *decades,* or *full tens;* as တဆယ်ပြည့် *tă tshay pyee,* "ten;" နှစ်ဆယ်ပြည့် *hneet tshay byee,* "twenty;" သက္ကရာဇ်တထောင်ပြည့်နှစ် *thăkkăreet tă htoung byee hneet,* "the year 1000."

ထပ် *htăt,* a root implying "repetition, similarity," &c., is used, as a generic affix, with the names of places or things, or their parts, in which similarity of objects recur; as a fort, its bastions, moats, gates, &c.; as အုတ်တပ်နှစ်ထပ် *ŏŏktăt hneet htăt,* "two fortified places;" ကျုံးနှစ်ထပ် *kyŏŏnsz hneet htăt,* "two moats."

ရွာ *rwa,* is used with nouns implying "aggregated dwellings," &c.; as နတ်လူပြဟ္မာဘုံးသုံးရွာ *năt lōō byămhă bhŏŏnsz thŏŏnsz rwa,* "the three mansions of the Nats, Men, and Brahmas."

Finally the noun itself is often repeated, and used as a generic affix; as ပြည်နှစ်ပြည် *pyee hneet pyee,* "two countries;" မင်းနှစ်မင်း *mĕngsz hneet mĕngsz,* "two lords."

In compound substantives the latter member of the compound often becomes the numeral generic affix; as စာ *tsa*, "any thing written," and အုပ် *ŏŏk*, "to pack together," forms စာအုပ် *tsaŏŏk*, "a bound book," စာနှစ်အုပ် *tsa hneet ŏŏk*, "two bound books;" စာ *tsa*, "a writing," and ထုပ် *htŏŏk*, "to bundle together," forms စာထုပ် *tsa htŏŏk*, "a bundle of written papers," စာနှစ်ထုပ် *tsa hneet htŏŏk*, "two bundles of written papers;" အုန်း *ŏŏns*, "a cocoa-nut," and ပင် *pěng*, "a tree," forms အုန်းပင် *ŏŏns pěng*, "a cocoa-nut tree," အုန်းနှစ်ပင် *ŏŏns hneet pěng*, "two cocoa-nut trees;" with သီး *thees*, "a fruit," forms အုန်းနှစ်သီး *ŏŏns hneet thees*, "two cocoa-nuts;" ကွမ်း *kwăns*, "betel," and ရွက် *rwět*, "a leaf," forms ကွမ်းနှစ်ရွက် *kwăns hneet rwět*, "two betel leaves." All the compound substantives of the nature mentioned in page 38, &c. are of this nature, except those implying human, or rational beings; as သံနှစ်စ *thăn hneet tsă*, "two pieces of iron;" မြေနှစ်ပုံ *myé hneet pŏŏn*, "two maps;" နွား *nwas*, "an ox," and ရှည် *shee*, "to couple," form နွားနှစ်ရှည် *nwas hneet shee*, "two yoke of oxen;" လျှပ် *hlyăt*, "lightning," and ပြက် *pyět*, "to become manifest," form လျှပ်ပြက် *hlyăt pyět*, "a flash of lightning," လျှပ်နှစ်ပြက် *hlyăt hneet pyět*, "two flashes of lightning;" ခြေစွပ် *khrétsŏk*, "a stocking," and ရန် *răn*, "a pair," form ခြေစွပ်ရန် *khrétsŏk răn*, "a pair of stockings," ခြေစွပ်နှစ်ရန် *khrétsŏk hneet răn*, "two pairs of stockings." In such a word as အိမ်ရှင် *ieng shěng*, "a master of a house," အိမ်နှစ်ရှင် *ieng hneet shěng*, would imply "two masters of one house," but အိမ်ရှင်နှစ်ဦး *ieng shěng hneet ŏŏs*, "two masters of houses." In some other compounds likewise the above rule does not hold good, and these a little attention will point out to the learner; as အိပ်ရာခင်း *iekrakhĕngs*, "a bed sheet," from ခင်း *khĕngs*, "to spread out," and အိပ်ရာ *iekra*, "a bed," would not be အိပ်ရာနှစ်ခင်း *iekra hneet khĕngs*, but အိပ်ရာခင်းနှစ်ခင်း *iekrakhĕngs hneet khĕngs*.

When a question is asked with the interrogative ဘယ်နှစ် *bhay hneet*, "how many?" the numeral generic affix must always be used; as ဒင်္ဂါးဘယ်နှစ်ပြားရှိသည်လား *dingas bhay hneet byas shie thee las*, "how many rupees are there?" ထဘိန်းဘယ်နှစ်ထည်ပေးမည်လား *htăbhiens bhay hneet tee pés mee las*, "how many petticoats will you give?" and so on with any others.

Should a question be asked in a similar way, and of which a compound substantive was the article mentioned, then the latter member of the compound would be the generic affix; as မြေဘယ်နှစ်ပုံရေးပြီးလား *myé bhay hneet pŏŏn rés byees las*, "how many maps have you drawn;" ကွမ်းဘယ်နှစ်သီးဝယ်ယူပြီးလား *kwăns bhay hneet thees way yŏŏ byees las*, "how many betel nuts have you bought;" and so on.

Combinations of the Numeral တ *tă*, "one," with various Roots.

The numeral တစ် *teet*, "one," in its contracted form of တ *tă*, is employed in connection with various roots; as

ဖက် *hpĕt*. When combined with ဖက် *hpĕt*, "a side;" the numeral generic affix of words which imply an object whose nature is dual, it often forms the term used to express "the other," of such object; as ကမ်း *kăns*, "a bank;" ကမ်းတဖက် *kăns tă hpĕt*, "the other bank;" လက် *lĕt*, "the hand;" လက်တဖက် *lĕt tă hpĕt*, "the other hand."

လုံး *lŏŏns*. In connection with လုံး *lŏŏns*, the root of the word အလုံး *ălŏŏns*, "all;" it is combined with words to express "the whole or entire substance" of such object. In such cases the တ *tă*, is prefixed, and လုံး *lŏŏns*, affixed; as တမြို့လုံး *tă myō lŏŏns*, "the whole city," or "entire city." Sometimes the substantive is found reduplicated, and တ *tă*, and လုံး *lŏŏns*, used only in connection with the last member, the compound has then a stronger and more emphatic signification; as မြို့တမြို့လုံးကိုလှည့်သွားသည် *myō tă myō lŏŏns gō hlee thwas thee*, "he wanders all over the city;" ပြည်တပြည်လုံးကိုလှည့်၍တောင်း၏ *pyee tă pyee lŏŏns gō hlee rwĕ toung ee*, "he goes begging all over, and over the country." When used with nouns in the plural number, the affix လုံး *lŏŏns*, is often omitted; as တပြည်တနိုင်ငံတို့ကိုသိမ်ဖျက်လျက်၏ *tăpyee tănŏinggnăn dō gō thien hpyĕt lyăt ee*, "he ravages and destroys whole countries, and kingdoms."

ကျွတ် *kwyăt*, "to be entire without remainder," is often used in connection with တ *tă*, and လုံး *lŏŏns*; as တအိမ်လုံးကျွတ်လဲကျသည် *tă ieng lŏŏns kwyăt lai kyă thee*, "the whole house is falling down;" the verbal affix အောင် *oung*, "so as to be," is sometimes added; as တအိမ်လုံးကျွတ်အောင်လဲကျသည် *tă ieng lŏŏns kwyăt oung lai kyă thee*, "the whole house, so as to be entirely so, is falling down."

တ *tă*, reduplicated and prefixed to each noun, is often used to convey the idea of "this and that, the one and the other;" as တအိမ်မှသည်တအိမ်သို့သွားလာသောသူ *tă ieng hmă thee tă ieng thō thwas la thăū thōō*, "the man coming, and going from one house to the other."

တ *tă*, reduplicated and combined, the first with စုံ *tsŏŏn*, a root implying "aggregation, or any aggregate quantity or number;" the second with a numeral generic affix, is used to imply "some one, a single one," of the objects of which the generic affix is the type; as တစုံတယောက်

မျှမရှိဘူ *tă tsŏŏn tă youk hmyă mă shie bhōō,* "there is not so much as a single (person);" တစုံတခုကိုမတွေ့နိုင်ဘူ *tă tsŏŏn tă khŏŏ gō mă twé hnŏing bhōō,* "(I) cannot find a single (thing)." Sometimes the compound has an indefinite meaning; as တစုံတယောက် *tă tsŏŏn tă youk,* may imply "some one, a certain person."

စု *tsŏŏ,* "to collect," is reduplicated, and used in the following manner with တ *tă,* or a numeral; ဇမ္ဗူဒိပါကျွန်းလုံးကိုဆယ်စုစု၍တစုတယောက် ဝေဘန်၍ရလေ၏—"having divided the whole island of Zamboodiba into ten aggregate parts or shares, they each got one."

တ *tă,* combined with ခု *khŏŏ,* the generic affix of inanimate things, or any other generic affix according to the signification, implies "an item, a particle or individual" of such object of which the generic affix is the type; as ထိုအမှုတခုမကျန်ဘဲ *htō ăhmŏŏ tă khŏŏ mă kyăn bhai,* "without omitting a particle of that affair;" တခုတခု *tă khŏŏ tă khŏŏ,* implies "item by item, one by one;" တယောက်တယောက် *tă youk tă youk,* "one by one," of persons.

တ *tă,* reduplicated and combined with a numeral generic affix, and လေ *lé,* a persistive particle, forms a compound implying "here and there one, a few, now and then one" of the class implied by the generic affix; as တယောက်တလေ *tă youk tă lé,* or တလေတယောက် *tă lé tă youk,* "here and there a person, now and then a person;" တကောင်တလေ *tă goung tă lé,* or တလေတကောင် *tă lé tă goung,* "here and there an animal;" တခါတလေ *tă kha tă lé,* or တလေတခါ *tă lé tă kha,* "now and then a time, sometimes."

ပါး *pa:,* or ချား *khya:.* When combined with ပါး *pa:,* or with ချား *khya:,* roots implying "separation, &c." it forms an adjective implying "another;"

လူတပါး *lōō tăbas,* or လူတချား *lōō tăkhyas,* "another man;" တချား *tă khyas,* also sometimes implies "apart;" as ယောက်ျားတချား။မိန္မတချား ခွဲထားပြီး *youkyas tă khyas॥miemmă tă khyas khwai htas byees,* "he sorted and placed the men apart, and the women apart."

တူ *tōō.* When combined with တူ *tōō,* a root implying "similarity, accompaniment," it forms a compound signifying "similar to, same as;" as ငါတတူ *gna tătōō,* "the same as I, one and the same as I."

ညီး *gnyees.* Combined with ညီး *gnyees,* a root implying "similarity," it forms a compound signifying "even as, like as, just as."

ကွ *kwă.* With ကွ *kwă,* a root implying "accompaniment," it forms a compound signifying "together with."

တကွနက် *tăkwănĕt,* တပြိုင်နက် *tăpyŏing nĕt.* Combined with ကွ *kwă,* as above, or with the addition of ပြိုင် *pyŏing,* a root implying "to pair, put together," and with နက် *nĕt,* a root implying "accumulation, mass," it forms a compound signifying "all together;" as တကွနက် *tăkwă nĕt,* or တပြိုင်နက် *tă pyŏing nĕt,* "all at once, all together, all of a heap."

တခဲနက် *tăkhainĕt.* Combined with ခဲ *khai,* a root implying "constrictedness, or solidity," and with နက် *nĕt,* as above, it forms a compound signifying; as တခဲနက် *tăkhainĕt,* "blended, mixed undistinguishably, commingled," also "all together."

တ *tă,* a generic affix, and လ *lé,* combined with a numeral generic affix followed by the persistive affix လေ *lé,* it forms a compound implying "a single one" of the objects expressed by the noun; as လူတယောက်လေ *lōōtăyŏuk lé,* "a single person;" နွားတကောင်လေ *nwas tăgoung lé,* "a single ox;" ဒင်္ဂါးတပြားလေမရှိ *dinga: tă bya: lé mă hie,* "there is not a single dollar."

တစေ့ *tătsẹ́.* Combined with စေ့ *tsẹ́,* a root implying "particularity," it forms a compound signifying "merely, nothing but, only:" the numeral generic affix intervenes; as လူတယောက်စေ့ *lōō tăyouk tsẹ́,* "merely a man, only a man."

တဖန် *tăhpăn.* Combined with ဖန် *hpăn,* a root implying "to assume, or to cause to assume an appearance, manifesting &c.," it forms a compound; as တဖန် *tăhpăn,* "again, once again, once more." When ဖန် *hpăn,* is reduplicated, or combined with a root of a cognate signification, as ပြန် *pyăn,* or တုံ့ *tŏŏn,* implying "repetition, doing again, returning," a compound is formed signifying "repeatedly;" as တဖန်ဖန် *tăhpăn hpăn,* or တဖန်ပြန် *tăhpănpyăn,* or တဖန်တုံ့ *tăhpăntŏŏn,* "repeatedly, again and again."

တထူး *tăhtōō:.* တ *tă,* when combined with ထူး *htōō:,* a root implying "separation, difference," forms a compound implying; as တထူး *tăhtŏŏ:,* "different, diverse, various."

တဝတည် *tăwătee.* တ *tă,* combined with ဝ *wă,* a root implying "kind, sort," and တည် *tee,* a root of a similar import, forms a compound; as တဝတည် *tăwătee,* "all together," in reference to *time,* "at one and the same time, keeping time as a band, &c."

တကိုယ် *tăkōh.* တ *tă,* combined with ကိုယ် *kōh,* "a body, substance," forms a compound used to express "similarity in amount;" as နှစ်ခုနှင့် သုံးခုပေါင်း။ငါးခုတကိုယ်ဖြစ်ပါသည် *hneet khŏŏ hnẹ̆ng thŏŏn: khŏŏ poung: gna: khŏŏ tăkōh hpyeet pa thee,* "two and three are equal to five."

Numeral Auxiliaries.

Various roots are found combined with numerals and express various relations of such numbers.

မြောက် *myouk,* "to be raised," being attached to a numeral generic affix, in connection with any cardinal number, expresses the corresponding ordinal of such number;" as သား၂စ်ယောက်မြောက် *thas hneet youk myouk,* "the second son." The substantive may be the last member of the compound; as နှစ်ဆယ်ရှစ်ရက်မြောက်နေ့တွင် *hneet tshay sheet rĕt myouk nẹ́ dweng,* "on the twenty-eighth day:" or the substantive may be connected by သော *thău;* as နှစ်ရက်မြောက်သောနေ့ *hneet rĕt myouk thău nẹ́,* "the second day;" လေးလမြောက်နှိုက် *lés lă myouk hnŏit,* "on the fourth month."

ကြိမ် *gyien,* a root implying "reiteration, time, &c.," when used with any cardinal number implies so many times that number. The rules para. 5, 6, 7, &c., page 99, in reference to numeral generic affixes are equally applicable to this adjunct; တကြိမ် *tă gyien,* "once;" နှစ်ကြိမ် *hneet gyien,* "twice;" သုံးကြိမ် *thŏŏns gyien,* "thrice;" အကြိမ်နှစ်ဆယ် *ăgyien hneet tshay,* "twenty-times;" အကြိမ်နှစ်ဆယ်လေးကြိမ် *ăgyien hneet tshay lés gyien,* "twenty-four times." Or should it be required to compound it with an ordinal, the ordinal adjunct မြောက် *myouk,* is the last of the compound; as နှစ်ကြိမ်မြောက် *hneet gyieng myouk,* "the second time;" အကြိမ်တစ်ဆယ်မြောက် *ăgyien tă tshay myouk,* "the tenth time;" အကြိမ်တဆယ်လေးကြိမ်မြောက် *ăgyien tă tshay lés gyien myouk,* "the twenty-fourth time." ကြိမ် *gyien,* is not used as a multiplier.

ခေါက် *khouk,* has a cognate meaning and application to the preceding.

လီ *lee,* the root of the word အလီ *ălee,* "a time, or turn," is used with cardinal numbers to form a multiplier; the multiplicand must always precede the multiplier and has often one of the numeral generic affixes ခု *khŏŏ,* or ပြည် *pyee,* appended, according as the numeral is a full multiple of ten, or otherwise; as ခုံနှစ်ခုရှစ်လီ *khwŏhneet khŏŏ sheet lee,* "eight times seven;" ကိုးခုကိုးလီ *kōs khŏŏ kōs lee,* "nine times nine;" တရာခုံနှစ်ဆယ်ချောက်ခုသုံးလီ *tă ra khwŏhneet tshay khyouk khŏŏ thŏŏns lee,* "three times one hundred and seventy-six." When required to be used in connection with ကြိမ် *kyien,* or မြောက် *myouk,* the arrangement is thus: အကြိမ်နှစ်ဆယ်ချောက်လီမြောက် *ăgyien hneet tshay khyouk lee myouk,* "the sixth time, twentieth time," လေးခုချောက်လီပေါင်းကိုနှစ်ဆယ်လေးခုပေါင်းတကိုယ်ဖြစ်ပါသည် six times four, is twenty-four, တဆယ်ပြည့်အလီတဆယ်ငါးလီ *tă tshay pyee ălee tă tshay gnas lee,* "fifteen times ten."

ပိုင်း *pŏings.* Any fractional part whatever of a number may be expressed by the word, ပိုင်း *pŏings,* (a root signifying "parcelling, or dividing into parts,") being attached both to the denominator, and numerator; the denominator thus formed always precedes the numerator. The denominator has the affix ၏ *ee,* "of," or တွင် *dwĕng,* "in, among," understood or expressed; as နှစ်ပိုင်းတပိုင်း *hneet pŏings tă pŏings,* "of two parts one part," i. e. "one half;" ဆယ်ပိုင်းခုံနှစ်ပိုင်း *tshay pŏings khwŏhneet pŏings,* "of ten parts seven parts," i. e. "seven-tenths;" အပိုင်းတဆယ်ငါးပိုင်း အပိုင်းတဆယ်လေးပိုင်း *ăpŏings tă tshay gnas pŏings ăpŏings tă tshay lés pŏings,* "of fifteen parts fourteen parts," i. e. "fourteen-fifteenths."

ဆ *tshă,* a root signifying "a portion, share, &c.," is affixed to numerals to convey the idea of so many fold; as နှစ်ဆ *hneet tshă,* "two-fold;" သုံးဆ *thŏŏns tshă,* "three-fold;" ခုနှစ်ဆ *khwŏhneet tshă,* "seven-fold;" အဆတဆယ် *ătshă tă tshay,* "ten-fold;" အဆလေးဆယ် *ătshă lés tshay,* "forty-fold;" အဆခြောက်ဆယ်လေးဆ *ătshă khyouk tshay lés tshă,* "sixty-four-fold."

It will be remarked that all these preceding numeral auxiliaries obey the same rules in composition as were laid down for numeral generic affixes, in paragraphs 5, 6, 7, &c., page 99.

ချမ်း *khyăns,* a root signifying "division into equal parts," is the most common affix used to express "one half;" as လ *lă,* "a moon," or "month," လချမ်း *lă khyăns,* "a half moon," or "half month;" or the numeral တ *tă,* "one," may be used in connection with it; as လတချမ်းသည် *lă tăkhyăns thee,* "a half moon." It is also found used in a substantive form; as လအချမ်း *lă ăkhyăns,* "a half month."

စိတ် *tsiet,* a root implying "division into four parts," breaking first length-wise and then cross-wise, is, either in its substantive form prefixed, or in its radical form, or in connection with the numeral တ *tă,* "one," affixed to nouns to express a "fourth part;" as လစိတ် *lă tsiet,* or လတစိတ် *lă tă tsiet,* "one quarter of a moon," or "of a month," i. e. a week; လမ်းခရီးအဝေးတစိတ်လောက်မျှကိုမထွက်မကုန်သေးပြီး *lăns khăreet ăwés tă-tsiet louk hmyă gō mă dwĕt mă gŏŏn thés byees,* "have not yet gone as much as about one quarter of the distance;" တုလာအစိတ် *tōōla ătsiet,* "a quarter tola."

လောက် *louk.* When the term "about a number," is to be expressed, the word လောက် *louk,* "to be about" or "sufficient," is used as an affix, the adjective မျှ *hmyă*, "to be the same in quantity," may precede it; as ငါးဂိုလောက် *gnas gō louk*, "about five;" or ငါးမျှလောက် *gnas hmyă louk*, "about as much as five;" သုံးနာရီချက်တီလောက် *thŏŏns narees khyĕt-tee louk*, "about three o'clock."

ခန့် *khặn*, "to be about so much," is affixed to words of time, or quantity, to express the same as the preceding; as တနှစ်ခန့် *tă hneet khặn*, "about a year;" တူလာခန့် *tōōla khặn*, "about a tola;" or ခန့်မျှလောက် *khặn hmyă louk*, may be used; as တနှစ်ခန့်မျှလောက် *tă hneet khặn hmyă louk*, "about a year."

လွန် *lwŏn*, "to excel," is affixed to numbers to express "more than;" မျှ *hmyă*, may likewise precede it; as သုံးနာရီးချက်တီမျှလွန်သည် *thŏŏns na-rees khyĕttee hmyă lwŏn thee*, "more than three o'clock," or "exceeding three o'clock;" တစ်ရက်လွန်သောအချိန် *tă yĕt lwŏn thăŭ ăkhyien*, "more than a day's time."

ကျော် *gyăū*, "to surpass, &c.," has the same power as the preceding; as တရာကျော် *tă ra gyăū*, "more than a hundred."

လျော့ *lyặŭ*, "to lessen," is affixed to numbers to express "less than," that number; as တရာလျော့ *tă ya lyặŭ*, "less than a hundred."

စုံ *tsŏŏn*, "to be complete," is used in connection with numerals to express the "whole of such numbers," the numeral generic affix intervenes between it, and the numeral; as လက်နှစ်ဖက်စုံ *lĕt hneetbhĕt tsŏŏn*, "both hands."

လုံး *lŏŏns*, from အလုံး *ălŏŏns*, "all," by itself or in connection with စ *tsă*, prefixed from အစ *ătsă*, "a beginning," as စလုံး *tsălŏŏn*, is used in the same manner to express the "whole of any number, or thing."

စီ *tsee,* is a particle used in connection with numerals, and the generic affixes of their nouns to express such number individually considered; as ဒင်္ဂါလေးပြားစီပေးမည် *dinga lés byas tsee pés mee,* "(I) will give four rupees each;" တယောက်စီ *tă youk tsee,* "each one person;" နှစ်ယောက်စီ *hneet youk tsee,* "each couple." Or the numeral may have စီ *tsee,* affixed, and the whole be then reduplicated; as နှစ်စီနှစ်စီယောက် *hneet tsee hneet tsee youk,* "each two persons, two and two in couples."

သာ *tha,* is an adverb affixed to numerals and their generic affixes to express "such a number only;" as လူတယောက်သာ *lōō tă youk tha,* "one man only;" ဒင်္ဂါနှစ်ပြားသာ *dinga hneet byas tha,* "two dollars only;" လူအားသာ *lōō aas tha,* "to man only."

ချင်း *khyĕngs,* is likewise used in the same way; as လူတယောက်ချင်း *lōō tă youk khyĕngs,* "one man only;" လက်ချင်း *lĕt khyĕngs,* "the hand only;" လက်ဖြင့်ချင်း *lĕt hpyẹng khyĕngs,* "by hand only."

တည်း *tees,* is also found used in the same way; as လူတယောက်တည်း *lōō tă youk tees,* "one man only;" တယောက်တည်းသောသူ *tă youk tees thău thōō,* "the person by himself;" or သာ *tha,* may be added; လူတယောက်တည်းသာ *lōō tă youk tees tha,* "only man alone." It also expresses "by one's self;" as တယောက်တည်းနေလျက်ဧ *tă youk tees né lyĕt ee,* "he usually remained alone;" ချင်း *khyĕngs,* is also found attached to it; as ငါတို့နှစ်ယောက်တည်းချင်းလျှင် *gna dō hneet youk tees khyĕngs hlyĕng,* "should we two be by ourselves;" lit. "should we be two alone;" တည်း *tees,* is also found used as an intensative to the numeral တ *tă,* "one;" as တကိုယ်တည်း *tă kōh tees,* "one and the same body, two bodies amalgamated into one;" တည်း *tees,* is also found used with other words besides numerals; as သံကိုတည်းလုပ်သည် *thăngō teet lōōk thee,* "made entirely of iron;" or သံကိုသာတည်းလုပ်သည် *thăngōtha teetlŏŏk thee,* "made entirely of only iron." Vide also infra under the head of miscellaneous verbal affixes for various applications of both these.

PART IV.

Verbs.

Verbs are formed in the Burmese language from the abstract root by the use of certain affixes. The pure root by itself, however, may be said to convey, when combined with another verbal root, the power of the infinitive mood; as ပြောလာသည် *pyău la thee,* "he comes to speak," in this case the affix of the future tense, or of the gerund is understood; as ပြောမည်လာသည် *pyău mee la thee,* or ပြောအံ့သောငှါလာသည် *pyău ąn thău gnha la thee.*

Some of the relations of verbal roots require another verb to express them; as "I can go," which is rendered ငါသွားနိုင်သည် *gna thwas hnŏing thee,* but care must be taken to distinguish between such a compound, and one consisting of two or more verbal roots combined for the purpose of conveying one homogeneous idea; as "to wander," would be rendered by the two roots လှည့် *hlęe,* "to turn, change position by turning," and သွား *thwas,* "to go," hence လှည့်သွား *hlęe thwas,* "to wander." In this latter case the two roots are often connected by the increment ၍ *rwę;* as လှည့်၍သွား *hlęerwęthwas.*

It is the genius of the Burmese language thus to combine roots, so as to express, exactly, an idea that could be rendered in English only by a circumlocution; as အုပ် *ŏŏk,* "to cover, overwhelm," and မိ *mie,* or ရ *ră,* "to obtain," form အုပ်မိ *ŏŏkmie,* or အုပ်ရ *ŏŏkră,* "to catch by overwhelming," as fish in a net; လှုပ် *hlŏŏk,* "to vibrate, shake," and သံ *thăn,* "to emit a sound," form လှုပ်သံ *hlŏŏk thăn,* "to ring as a bell;" ကြား *kyas,* "to hear," and ပြော *pyăŭ,* "to speak," form ကြားပြော *kyaspyăŭ,* "to repeat as information;" ဖြန့် *hpyăn,* "to spread out," and ချ *khyă,* "to cast down," form ဖြန့်ချ *hpyăn khyă,* "to cast," or "throw a net, &c.;" ဆွဲ *tshwai,* "to pull, or drag," and တင် *tĕng,* "to place," form ဆွဲတင် *tshwai tĕng,* "to land a net;" ပုံ *pŏŏn,* "a pattern," and ရိုက် *rŏik,* "to knock, hammer," form ပုံရိုက် *pŏŏn rŏik,* "to print, take off an impression;" ပြ *pyă,* "to show," and ပေး *pés,* "to give," form ပြပေး *pyăpés,* "to give signs of, show symptoms of;" and so on with any combinations.

Another peculiarity, in the Burmese language, is that causal affixes, or what in other languages would be styled prepositions of case, are used to express certain relations of verbal roots, such as are in general rendered by participles; as ပြော *pyăŭ,* "to speak," and မှာ *hma,* "in," make ပြောမှာ *pyăŭ hma,* "in speaking, as he was speaking;" with မှ *hmă,* "from," ပြောမှ *pyăŭ hmă,* "having spoken;" with နှင့် *hnĕng,* "together with," as အဖဖြစ်သည်နှင့် *ăhpă hpyeet thee hnĕng,* "because he was his father, being his father, in that he was his father."

Verbal roots are of only two descriptions, that is, in their original form, they convey either an idea of action, whether mental, or corporeal; as ပြု *pyŏŏ,* "to do;" ဆို *tshō,* "to speak;" ဆဲရေး *tshairés,* "to abuse;" မုန်း *mŏŏns,* "to hate;" ယူ *yōō,* "to bring;" ကူး *kōōs,* "to cross over;" မြင် *myĕng,* "to see;" or of a state of inertion, or inactive existence; as နေ

né, "to remain;" ထိုင် *htöing,* "to sit;" ကောင်း *koungs,* "to be good;" လှ *hlă,* "to be beautiful;" ကြောက် *krouk,* "to be afraid;" and so on.

The active verb can be formed at any time from the neuter root by affixing the verb စေ *tsé,* "to cause." This form is especially used with those roots expressing any state, quality, or condition of mind; as ငြိမ် *gnyien,* "to be in a state of quietness, comfort, freedom from affliction," ငြိမ်စေ *gnyien tsé,* "to soothe, to ease, cure, &c.;" သိ *thie'* "to know, beware of," သိစေ *thie tsé,* "to inform, tell;" သန့်ရှင်း *thăn shĕngs,* "to be pure," whether in mind, or body; သန့်ရှင်းစေ *thăn shĕng tsé,* "to purify." When စေ *tsé,* is thus affixed to an active root it merely implies "to cause to do," the action implied in the root; as စကားပြော *tsăgas pyăŭ,* "to speak," စကားပြောစေ *tsăgas pyăŭ tsé,* "to cause to speak."

An active verb is very often formed from a neuter root, by aspirating the initial consonant, or, if it have a corresponding aspirate, by changing it for such aspirate; as ကျ *kyă,* (neuter), "to fall down," or "become low," ချ *khyă,* (active), "to cast," or "put down;" ကြောက် *krouk,* "to be afraid," ခြောက် *khrouk,* "to frighten;" ကျား *kyas,* "to be diversified, not uniform," ချား *khyas,* "to make dissimilar, separate into compartments;" ကြွင်း *kywĕngs,* "to remain, be a remnant," ခြွင်း *khywĕngs,* "to leave behind, set aside;" ဝေ *gnă,* "to be distributed," ငှ *gnhă,* "to distribute;" ရုတ် *tsöök,* "to be torn, rent," ဆုတ် *tshöök,* "to tear, rend;" နစ် *neet,* "to be sunk, immersed," နှစ် *hneet,* "to sink, or immerse;" လှုတ် *löök,* "to shake or tremble," (neuter), လှုပ် *hlöök,* "to shake," or "tremble," (active), and so on with many others.

ထား *htas*, a root implying mental or corporeal action, but in the sense of "putting, placing," whether as "putting a question," or "placing an object," is used with many roots, as an auxiliary adjunct of action; as မှာ *hma*, "to direct, order," မှာထား *hma htas*, ditto; ကွယ် *kway* and ဖွက် *hwĕt*, to conceal, hide, ကွယ်ထား *kway htas*, and ဖွက်ထား *hwĕt htas*, ditto; မှတ် *hmăt*, "to note, mark," မှတ်ထား *hmăt htas*, "to particularize;" မြစ် *myeet*, means "to obstruct, prevent," in the sense of "being or lying in the way," but မြစ်ထား *myeet htas*, implies "to prevent, obstruct," in the sense of "putting an obstacle in the way;" in the latter case the sense is compound, the obstruction being caused by the object put, and the person putting; hence မြစ် *myeet*, by itself, is used to imply "to forbid," in the sense of a *law* forbidding; မြစ်ထား *myeet htas*, in the sense of a *lawgiver* forbidding; ရိုက်ထား *roik htas*, "to fasten by hammering;" ပုံထား *pŏŏn htas*, "to place in heaps."

လုပ် *lŏŏk*, "to do work," is likewise found used as an adjunct, with active verbs implying any manual work; as ဆောက် *tshouk*, "to build, erect," ဆောက်လုပ် *tshouk lŏŏk*, ditto; ရုပ်ပုံထုလုပ် *rŏŏk pŏŏn htō lŏŏk*, "to carve a statue," from ထု *htō*, "to carve, &c."

ပြု *pyŏŏ*, "to do," i. e. mental doing, "to act," is combined with roots in their adverbial form implying any mental quality, or action, to form a corresponding active; မုန်းစွာပြု *mŏŏns tswa pyŏŏ*, "to hate," lit. "to act hatingly;" မင်စွာပြု *mĕng tswa pyŏo*, "to love, act lovingly;" it is also found combined with the simple root; as သတိပြု *thădie pyŏŏ*, "to take care, beware;" ရန်ပြု *răn pyŏŏ*, "to quarrel."

ခံ *khăn*, "to endure, suffer, be the subject, or patient of," may be applied to roots to render them passive; as စေ *tsé*, "to order," စေခံ *tsé khăn*, "to obey, be subject;" စစ် *tseet*, "to fight," စစ်ခံ *tseet khăn*, "to be attacked;" ယပ် *yăt*, "to fan," ယပ်ခံ *yăt khăn*, "to be fanned." In such instances as the following it apparently has an active signification; as မွေခံ *mwé khăn*, "to inherit," from အမွေ *ămwé*, "an inheritance;" သက်သေခံ *thĕtthé khăn*, "to witness," lit. "to *bear* witness:" in this latter case the word "bear," gives an idea of endurance, and in the other no *action* is implied. When ခံ *khăn*, is not thus used as an auxiliary, but as an absolute verb, the root ရ *ră*, "to obtain," is generally affixed to it; as ခံရ *khăn ră*, "to suffer," ပြင်းစွာခံရသည် *pyĕngs tswa khăn yă thee*, "suffers grievously."

ရ *ră*, "to obtain, find," is also sometimes used as an auxiliary to verbs implying an emotion, or quality of the mind, or state of the body, and seems to form a sort of passive, or neuter; as ခြောက်ရသည် *khrouk yă thee*, "to be afraid," lit. "to get frightened;" ချစ်ရသည် *khyeet yă thee*, "to be loved," or "get loved;" ချရသည် *khyă yă thee*, "to fall," or "get a fall."

The passive verb is comparatively seldom found used in the Burmese language, the corresponding neuter being made use of instead;
ဖြစ် But it may be formed in the same way as in English by the use of the substantive verb ဖြစ် *hpyeet*, "to be, or become," or sometimes
ရှိ *shee*, "to be;" an instance of active, neuter, and passive is as follows; ကြောက် *krouk*, (neuter) "to fear," ခြောက် *khrouk*, (active) "to frighten," ကြောက်ဖြစ်သည် *krouk hpyeet thee*, (passive) "to be afraid." Often the participial affix သည် *thee*, intervenes between the two

roots; as စေသည်ဖြစ်သည် *tséthee hpyeet thee,* "to be sent," from စေ *tsé,* "to send." When the plural number, or any tense is required to be expressed, the *substantive* verb should be inflected with the necessary affixes.

The substantive verb is also capable of being rendered passive; as ဒေါသစိတ်ရှိသည်ဖြစ် *däŭthătsiet shie thee hpyeet,* "became malignant-minded;" ဝမ်းမြောက်သောစိတ်ရှိသည်ဖြစ် *wŏns myouk thăŭ tsiet shie thee hpyeet,* "became delighted." In this way it may be said to express the idea of "to become." In the use of this substantive verb ဖြစ် *hpyeet,* or ပြစ် *pyeet,* the word သူ *thōō,* "a person," or a cognate one is understood after the first သည် *thee,* which is only a connective affix or relative increment; as သွားဆဲသည်ဖြစ်သည် *thwas tshai thee hpyeet thee,* "(he) is just going," or written in full, သွားဆဲသောသူ *thwas tshai thăŭ thōō,* or သွားဆဲသည်သူဖြစ်သည် *thwas tshai thee thōō hpyeet thee,* "(he) is a just going person." Again ဘုရားသခင်သည်ခပ်သိမ်းသောအရပ်၌ရှိတော်မူသည်ဖြစ်၏ "God is in every place,"—or in full "God is One being in every place."

Neither the root, nor the noun, undergo any inflection or alteration on account of the persons of the nominative case. The only alteration being in the case of number, where, if the nominative case be of the plural number the root has a numeral affix appended.

Number.

There is no affix of the singular number, the root by itself being indicative of the singular number; as ငါသွားသည် *gna thwas thee,* "I go."

ကြ The plural number is expressed by affixing ကြ *kyă,* or ကုန် *gŏŏn,* or ကြကုန် *kyă gŏŏn*; as ငါတို့သွားကြသည် *gna dọ thwa: kyă thee,* or သွားကုန်သည် *thwa: gŏŏn thee,* or သွားကြကုန်သည် *thwa: kyă gŏŏn thee,* "we go." The numeral affix is always attached to the *root,* no other ever intervening.

To give some idea of a verbal root with its various affixes, the verb သွား *thwa:,* "to go," is in a measure conjugated, although all its relations are by no means given.

သွား *thwa:,* "to go."

INDICATIVE MOOD.

PRESENT TENSE.

Singular.	*Plural.*
သွားသည် *thwa: thee,* "I, thou, he, she, it goes."	သွားကြသည် *thwa: kyă thee,* "We, ye, they go."

IMPERFECT.

သွားဘူးသည် *thwa: bhōō: thee,* "I, &c. went."	သွားကြဘူးသည် *thwa: kyă bhōō: thee,* "We, &c. went."

PERFECT.

သွားပြီး *thwa: byee:,* "I, &c. have gone."	သွားကြပြီး *thwa: kyă byee:,* "We, &c. have gone."

PLUPERFECT.

သွားနှင့်ပြီး *thwa: hnẹng byee:,* "I, &c. had gone."	သွားကြနှင့်ပြီး *thwa: kyă hnẹng byee:,* "We, &c. had gone."

FUTURE.

သွားမည် *thwa: mee,* "I, &c. will go."	သွားကြမည် *thwa: kyă mee,* "We, &c. will go."

IMPERATIVE.

သွားလော့ *thwas lǎu̥*, "Go thou." သွားကြလော့ *thwas kyǎ lǎu̥*, "Go ye."

သွားစို့ *thwas tsō̥*, "Let us go."

POTENTIAL MOOD.

PRESENT TENSE.

Singular.	*Plural.*
သွားနိုင်သည် *thwas hnŏing thee*, "I, &c. can," or "am able to go."	သွားကြနိုင်သည် *thwas kyǎ hnŏing thee*, "We, &c. can go," or "are able to go."

IMPERFECT.

သွားနိုင်ဘူးသည် *thwas hnŏing bhōōs thee*, "I, &c. could go."	သွားကြနိုင်ဘူးသည် *thwas hnŏing bhōōs thee*, "We, &c. could go."

PAST.

သွားနိုင်ပြီး *thwas hnŏing byees*, "I, &c. could have gone."	သွားကြနိုင်ပြီး *thwas kyǎ hnŏing byees*, "We, &c. could have gone."

FUTURE.

သွားနိုင်မည် *thwas hnŏing mee*, "I, &c. can at some future time go."	သွားကြနိုင်မည် *thwas kyǎ hnŏing mee*, "We, &c. can at some future time go."

SUBJUNCTIVE MOOD.

PRESENT.

သွားကောင်းသည် *thwas goungs thee*, I, &c. may probably go."	သွားကြကောင်းသည် *thwas kyǎ goungs thee*, "We, &c. may probably go."

And in the same way for the other tenses.

သွားသော် *thwas thău*, or သွားလျှင် *thwas hlyĕng*, "Should I, &c. go."

သွားကြသော် *thwas kyă thāū*, or သွားကြလျှင် *thwas kyă hlyĕng*, "Should we, &c. go."

သွားအံ့သောငှါ *thwas ạn thăū gnha*, "for the purpose of going."

သွားမှာ *thwas ḥma*, "going," or "in going."

သွားမှ *thwas hmă*, "having gone."

သွားလို *thwas lō*, "about to go."

Verbal Affixes.

It is to be premised in reference to verbal affixes, that there are three assertive affixes, that is positive affixes of time; viz., သည် *thee*, the assertive affix of the present tense; ပြီး *byees*, the assertive affix of the past tense; and မည် *mee*, the assertive affix of the future tense. Whatever modal, or auxiliary affix may be used with a root, it requires an assertive affix to make the meaning complete; as သွား *thwas*, a root implying "to go," ကြ *kyă*, the numeral affix, and နိုင် *hnŏing*, "to be able, to can," forms သွားကြနိုင် *thwas kyă hnŏing*, "(they) able to go;" but it requires the assertive affix သည် *thee*, to define the meaning; as သွားကြနိုင်သည် *thwas kyă hnŏing thee*, "(they) *are* able to go," သွားကြနိုင်မည် *thwas kyă hnŏing mee*, "(they) *will be* able to go." The imperative mood and in some cases the negative mood, are the only two which dispense with an assertive affix. The assertive affix is always the last, except in the interrogative mood, where it intervenes between the interrogative affix and the root.

Though the above are assertive affixes, yet they are sometimes auxiliary affixes pointing out the relative time of some other relation of the verb; as when used with လျှင် *hlyĕng*, a suppositional affix; as

သူသွားသည်လျှင် *thōōthwas theehlyĕng,* "should he be going;" သူသွားပြီးလျှင် *thōō thwas byees hlyĕng,* "should he have gone;" သူသွားမည်လျှင် *thōōthwas meehlyĕng,* "should he hereafter go."

သည် *thee,* is the simple affix of the indicative mood present tense; as ငါပြုသည် *gnapyŏŏ thee,* "I do;" သူဆိုသည် *thōō tshōthee,* "he says;" ငါတို့လာကြသည် *gna dọ la kyă thee,* "we come;" သူတို့သွားကြသည် *thōō dọ thwas kyă thee,* "they go."

၏ *ee,* is likewise an affix of the present tense, but referring to a past time, as in English the present tense is colloquially used; as "so says I," &c. referring to something past. It may thus be styled the narrative affix; it is likewise used in the place of the affix သည် *thee,* at the close of the sentence.

ဆဲ *tshai,* is an auxiliary affix of the present tense, implying "just now;" as ငါသွားဆဲသည် *gna thwas tshai thee,* "I am just going;" သူတို့သေဆဲဖြစ်ကြသည် *thōō dọ thétshai hpyeet kyă thee,* "they are just now dead."

ဘူး *bhōōs,* is an affix used in connection with the present affix သည် *thee,* to express an indefinite past; as ငါသွားဘူးသည် *gna thwas bhōōs thee,* "I went;" သူတို့လာကြဘူးသည် *thōō dọ la kyă bhōōs thee,* "they came."

ပြီး *byees,* implying "done, past, accomplished," is the affix of the past tense; as ငါပြုပြီး *gnapyŏŏ byees,* "I have done;" သူတို့သွားကြပြီး *thōō dọ thwas kyă byees,* "they have gone."

မည် *mee,* အံ့ *ăn,* and အံ့မည် *ăn mee,* are all affixes of the future tense; as ငါသွားမည် *gna thwas mee,* or သွားအံ့ *thwas ăn,* or သွားအံ့မည် *thwas ăn mee,* "I will go;" သူတို့သွားကြမည် *thōō dọ thwas kyă mee,* or သွားကြအံ့ *thwas kyă ăn,* or သွားကြအံ့မည် *thwas kyă ăn mee,* "(they) will go."

Besides the above there are certain indefinite past affixes that may be used with an assertive affix of tense, modifying its time with their own indefinite signification; as

ဘူ *bhöö,* may be used either with the present affix သည် *thee,* or the past affix ပြီး *byee*; as ငါသွားဘူသည် *gna thwa bhöö thee,* "I have been going;" ငါသွားဘူပြီး *gna thwa bhöö byee,* "I had gone," or "had been going."

ခဲ့ *khai,* is a present past affix; as ငါသွားခဲ့သည် *gna thwa ghai thee,* "I have just gone;" သူသွားခဲ့ပြီး *thöö thwa ghai byee,* "he had just gone."

လေ *lé,* is used with a present, or a past affix; as ငါသွားလေသည် *gna thwa lé thee,* "I have been going;" ငါသွားလေပြီး *gna thwa lé byee,* "I had gone."

နှင့် *hnĕng,* and လင် *lĕng,* and ခင့် *khĕng,* are affixes that may be used either, with the present affix သည် *thee,* the past affix ပြီး *byee,* or the future affix မည် *mee;* and they infer the action to have been done prior to something alluded to; as ငါသတိပေးနှင့်သည် *gna thädie pé hnĕng thee,* "I caution you (beforehand);" ငါသွားခင့်မည် *gna thwa khĕng mee,* "I will go," i. e. "before something else referred to."

လတ္တံ့ *lättăn,* is the affix of a distant or prophetic future; as ဤသို့ဖြစ်လတ္တံ့ *ee thō hpyeet lättăn,* "thus shall it be."

The future tense is also found, as in many other languages, having a suppositional, problematical or conjectural signification, and may be variously rendered in English by "should, may, might, though, &c.;" as သူလာအံ့ငါမပြောမည် *thöö la ăn gna mă pyä ŭ mee,* "though he come I will not tell;" သင်လာမည်အခါကိုငါသိရလျှင် *thĕng la mee ăkha gō gna thie yăhlyĕng*, "had I known when you would have come" or "the time of your coming;" ထိုအခန်းမှာလူတို့သည်ငါးဆယ်ကျော်ခန့်ရှိလိမ့်မည် *htō ăkhăng hmalōō dō thee gnaitshay gyăŭ khăn shie liĕm mee*, "in that room there must have been," or "may have been upwards of fifty persons," lit. "in that room there will be more than about fifty persons;" ငွေဒင်္ဂါးတသောင်းခန့်ရှိပါလိမ့်မည် *gnwĕ dinga: tă thoungs khăn shie pa liĕm mee*, "there must have been" or "may have been about ten thousand rupees;" သင်သားဖြစ်လိမ့်မည်။မဖြစ်လိမ့်မည်ကိုငါမသိ *thĕng thaι hpyeet liĕm mee mă hpyeet liĕm mee gō gna mă thie*, "whether he is your son or not, I know not."

ရ *ră*, "to obtain, find &c.," often intervenes between the root, and the future affixes; and is then rendered in English by "must;" as ငါသွားရမည် *gna thwaι yă mee*, "I must go, I shall positively go;" ဖြစ်ရမည် *hpyeet yă mee*, "it must be;" ငါတို့သွားကြရမည် *gna dō thwa kyă yă mee*, "we must go." It is also inserted in other moods to form their future tense, as will be shewn in its proper place, also to form a future to verbal compounds; as သွားရသောအခါ *thwaι yă thăŭ ăkha*, "the time of probable going, the time of obtaining going."

Indicative Mood.

သည် *thee*, is the only proper affix of the indicative mood, but it is very seldom expressed; an assertive affix being considered sufficient to show the mood is indicative: it is however found used; as ပြောသည်မည်သူလာသည် *pyăŭ thee mee thōō la thee*, "he comes to speak," lit. "will speak, he comes:" here ပြော *pyăŭ*, is the root implying "to speak," သည် *thee*, is the modal affix of the indicative mood, and မည် *mee*, is the assertive affix of the future tense. The plural of the above would correctly, and grammatically be thus; ပြောကြသည်မည်သူတို့လာကြသည် *pyău kyă thee mee thōō dō la kyă thee.*

ရ *ră*, "to obtain," is often very frequently used as an indicative affix; as ငါတို့သွားကြရသည် *gna dō thwas kyă ră thee*, "we go," or "are going;" သူသွားရပြီး *thōō thwas ră byees*, "he has gone;" သူသွားရမည် *thōō thwas ră mee*, "he will go," likewise "must go," as above.

Imperative and Precative Mood.

The root by itself is sometimes used imperatively, but never precatively; as သွား *thwas*, "go thou;" သွားကြ *thwa kyă*, "go ye;" but more commonly certain imperative affixes are made use of.

လော *lău*, တော့ *dău*, လည်း *lees*, ခြည် *khyee*, are the only true imperative affixes, and would be used when commanding; as သွားလော *thwas lău*, "go thou;" သွားကြတော့ *thwas kyă dău*, "go ye."

လှန်းလှည် *hlăns hlee*, is likewise an imperative termination.

ဦး pronounced အုံး *ŏŏns*, ပါ *pa*, ခဲ *khai*, ချေ *khyé*, ပါစေ *patsé*, စင် *tsăn*, စင်ပါ *tsănba*, ပေ *pé*, ရစ် *reet*, ရော *răŭ*, လေ *lé*, လိုက် *lŏik*, သိ *thie*, are all precative, and imperative affixes; as နေဦး *néŏŏns*, "stay;" ကြည့်စင် *kyee tsăn*, "look;" ခေါ်ခဲ *khău khai*, "call."

စေသော *tsé thău*, စေလို *tse lō*, စေသတည်း *tsé thă tees*, စေပါ *tséba*, ပါစေ *ba tsé*, ပါလေစေ *balé tsé*, are all compounds of the verb စေ *tsé*, "to cause," and imply "let, pray let;" သွားပါစေ *thwas ba tsé*, "let (me) go;" သွားစေလို *thwas tsé lō*, ditto.

စို့ *tsō*, is chiefly used in writing, and implies the first person plural imperative mood; as သွားစို့ *thwas tsō*, "let us go."

In conversation the future tense forms a sort of imperative; ငါတို့သွား

ကြအံ့ *gna dŏ thwaa kyă ăn,* or သွားကြမည် *thwaa kyă mee,* "let us go," or "we'll be going."

ရာ *ra.* This form when combined with the narrative affix ၏ *ee,* has the power of an injunction; as တရားဆင်သောအမှုသည်နှစ်ဖက်သားတို့၏စကား ကိုကောင်းစွါနားဦး၍ဟုတ်မှန်သောအတိုင်းဆုံးဖြတ်ရာ၏ "listen well to the statements of both parties in a suit, aud then let your decision be in conformity to truth and justice."

Auxiliary verbal affixes are of two kinds: 1st, those that express a modal relation of a verb; as နိုင် *hnŏing,* "to be able," which expresses the potential mood "can;" as သွားနိုင်သည် *thwaa hnŏing thee,* "can go;" and 2dly, those that express an extraneous relation of the verb; as သွားလွယ်သည် *thwaa lway thee,* "easy to go." In the first instance the original root remains the principal verb, the other root being merely a modal affix; in the second, the original root becomes a dependent verb in the infinitive mood, and does not admit of any affix. The distinction between these two classes of affixes is fully pointed out at page 30, para. 4.

Subjunctive Mood.

လျှင် *hlyĕng,* လျက် *lyĕt,* လည်း *lees,* မှု *mōō,* မှုကား *mōōgas,* တမှုကား *tămōō gas,* are all subjunctive affixes. The three first are the most common. They are varied in their significations, expressing a *contingency;* as ငါသွားလျှင် *gna thwaa hlyĕng,* "should I go," or "if I go;" ငါသွားပြီးလျှင် *gna thwaa byees hlyĕng,* "if I have gone," or "should I have gone." If the contingency be not future (as implied by the word "should") but continuative, then လျက် *lyĕt,* would be used; as ငါအမှာအတိုင်းပြုလျက်

gna ăhma ădŏing: pyŏŏ lyĕt, "if (he) were acting according to my order;" ငါအမှာအထိုင်းပြုသည်လျက် *gna ăhma ădŏing: pyŏŏ thee lyĕt,* "if (he) acts according to my order;" ငါသွားနိုင်လျက် *nga thwa: hnŏing lyĕt,* "if I were able to go;" ငါသွားနိုင်လျှင် *gna thwa: hnŏing hlyĕng,* "should I be able to go." ရ *ră,* is inserted in this mood to form a *positive* (in contradiction to a *suppositional)* future; as ငါသွားရလျှင် *gna thwa: ră hlyĕng,* "should I hereafter go," lit. "should I obtain going;" ငါသွား နိုင်ရလျှင် *gna thwa: hnŏing ră hlyĕng,* "should I hereafter be able to go," lit. "should I obtain ability to go."

လျှင် *hlyĕng,* may be styled the suppositional affix; as မတွေ့လျှင်ပြန်မလာရဘူး *mă twę hlyĕng pyăn mă la yă bhōō:,* "should (you) not find (it) (you) must not return." In this way it is found attached to any part of speech giving its suppositional power to the clause, the substantive verb being understood; as ထိုသို့လျှင် *htō thọ hlyĕng,* "should (it be) thus;" ငါ၏သားလျှင် *gna ee tha: hlyĕng,* "should (it be) my son:" sometimes its suppositional power is nearly lost; as တတောင်လျှင်ထွာပေါင်းနှစ်ထွာရှိပါသည် *tă htoung hlyĕng htwa poung: hneet htwa shie pa thee,* "the total of spans in a cubit is two," lit. "should (it be) a cubit, (then) the total of spans is two spans;" တလလျှင်တတင် *tă lă hlyĕng tă tĕng,* "a *tĕng* (basket measure) per month," lit. "should (it be) a month, (then) a *teng.*"

For a further application of both these affixes လျက် *lyĕt,* and လျှင် *hlyĕng,* vide infra. Past participial affixes, and in addition for လျက် *lyĕt,* vide infra. Auxiliary affixes.

အောင် *oung,* a root implying "to be complete, to have attained to," is used as a subjunctive affix; as သွားအောင် *thwa: oung,* "that (he) may go;" သွားကြအောင် *thwatkyăoung*, "that (they) may go;" သွားရအောင် *thwatrăoung*, "that he may hereafter go."

ကောင်း *koungt*, a root implying "to be good, proper, fit," is also used as a subjunctive affix; as သွားကောင်းသည် *thwat koungt thee*, "(he) may be going;" သွားကြကောင်းသည် *thwat kyă koungt thee*, "they may be going;" သွားနိုင်ကြကောင်းမည် *thwat hnŏing kyă goungt mee*, "they) will probably be able to go," or "they may hereafter be able to go; here နိုင် *hnŏing*, is not a modal affix, but an auxiliary one, expressing an extraneous relation of the verb သွား *thwat*, &c., and therefore has the plural increment ကြ *kyă*, attached to it; သွားကြကောင်းပြီး *thwat kyă koungt byeet*, "(they) have probably gone." N. B. The use of ကောင်း *koungt*, in forming a compound verb must not be confounded with the above; as မသွားကောင်း *măthwat koung*, "it is not right to go," therefore used to express the phrase "don't go," lit. "not to go, is good;" also thus သွားကောင်းလျှင်သွားမည် *thwat koungt hlyĕng thwat mee*, "should it be right to go I will go," i. e. "when it is proper (I) will go." In both these two last cases ကောင်း *koungt*, is an auxiliary verb, and not a modal affix.

Potential Mood.

နိုင် *hnŏing*, "to be able, to overcome, to be powerful," is the most common affix of the Potential Mood; as သွားနိုင်သည် *thwat hnŏing thee*, "(he) can go;" သွားကြနိုင်သည် *thwat kyă hnŏing thee*, "(they) are able to go," i. e. "can go;" သွားနိုင်မည် *thwat hnŏing mee*, "(he) will be able to go, he hereafter can go;" သွားကြနိုင်ပြီး *thwatkyă hnŏing byeet*, "(they) have been able to go."

နှိင် *nŏing*, the neuter form of the preceding is also similarly used. ဆောက် *tsouk*, is also so used, but more rarely.

OPTATIVE MOOD.

There is no *Modal* affix (similar to the preceding) to express this mood, but the verbs ချင် *khyĕng*, and လို *lō*, both implying "to wish, to want, to desire," are used as principals, and the original verb, whose relation is to be expressed, becomes in the Infinitive Mood. In other words the affixes of this mood do not admit of the plural increment preceding them; thus ငါတို့သွားချင်ကြသည် *gna dō thwas khyĕng kyă thee*, "we wish to go," i. e. "we would go;" ငါသွားလိုလိမ့်မည် *gna thwas lō liẹmmee*, "I will wish to go;" သွားလိုကြလေပြီး *thwas lō kyă lé byees*, "(we), wished to go."

The other auxiliary affixes not being modal are not given here, but below after the MOODS.

THE INFINITIVE MOOD.

The root by itself, as has been remarked page 125, is properly an infinitive, that is, if it be combined, or governed as one; as သွားခွင့်ပေးပါ *thwas khwẹng pés ba*, "give permission to go:" but most generally it is expressed by the future tense; either by one of the future temporal affixes alone, or by one in connection with a causal affix; as ပြောမည်လာသည် *pyăŭ mee la thee*, "(he) comes to speak," lit. "will speak (he) comes;" အမိန့်တော်ခံမည်ကျွန်တော်လာပါသည်ဘုရား *ămiẹn dăŭ khăn mee kywŏn dăŭ la pă thee hpŏŏras*, "to receive your excellency's order, I come my Lord." Sometimes the connective affix ဟု *hŏŏ*, "to wit," intervenes between the two clauses; as ငါပြန်သွားမည်ဟုအလိုရှိသည် *gnă pyănthwaымee hŏŏ ălō shie thee,* "I will return, to wit, is (my) wish," i. e. "(my) wish is to return;" ငါအိမ်သို့သွားမည်ဟုကျံသည်ကိုသူသိလေသော် *gna ieng thọ thwaымee hŏŏ kyăn thee gọ thōō thie lé thăū,* "I will go to house, to wit, intention, he having known," i. e. "he having known of my intention to go to my house." Likewise either of the future affixes မည် *mee,* and အံ *ăn,* may be used in connection with the causal affixes ငှါ *gnha,* "for, in order to," or ကြောင့် *gyoụng,* "because of, on account of," to express the Infinitive mood, and generally connected by the increment သော *thăū;* အံ့ *ặn,* being generally used with ငှါ *gnha,* and မည် *mee,* with ကြောင့် *gyoụng;* as သွားအံ့သောငှါအလိုရှိပါသည် *thwaы ặn thăū gnha ălō shie pa thee,* "to go, is (my) wish;" ပြောမည်သောကြောင့် လာပြီး *pyăū mee thăū gyoụng la byeeы,* "(he) has come to speak, for the purpose of speaking."

This mode, and that with the addition of အကြောင်း *ăgyoungы,* a noun implying "matter, affair," and which perhaps is the more common, is the only way in which the English idiom "may" or "might," in connection with "that," can be rendered in Burmese; as in the last example, "he has come to speak," or "that he might speak;" သင်လာမည်အကြောင်း။ငါစေလွှတ်သည်ဖြစ် *thĕng la mee ăgyoungы॥gna tsé hlwăt thee hpyeet,* "that, you may, or might come, I have sent;" သတိခံမည်အကြောင်း။ငါစေ &c., *thădie khăn mee ăgyoungы॥gna tsé, &c.,* "I have sent that (you) might be warned." The peculiar use here of the stop is to be noted.

လို့ *lŏŏ,* and လို့နီးပြီး *lŏŏneeы byeeы,* both express an infinitive mood, future tense; (the latter is only used with the substantive verb); သွားလို့ *thwaы lŏŏ*, "about to go;" ရှိလိမ့်နိုးပြီး *shie lŏŏneeː byeeː*, "about to be;" လို *lŏŏ*, does not alter its meaning whatever affixes of time may be superadded; as သွားလိုသည် *thwaː lŏŏ thee*, သွားလိုပြီး *thwaː lŏŏː byeeː*, and သွား လိုမည် *thwaː lŏŏ mee*, are all equally "about to go." Another, or more imperfect future tense infinitive mood is expressed by the use of a future temporal affix (as အံ့ *ăn*,) in connection with the causal affix သို့ *thō*, implying "motion to;" as မင်းကြီးသည်ပုဂါန်အံ့သို့ထင် *mengː gyeeː thee pŏŏgan ăn thō htĕng*, "the king thinking (he) was about to rebel;" here we have ပုဂါန် *pŏŏgăn*, "to rebel," with အံ့ *ăn*, shows that it is a *future state* of rebellion, with သို့ *thō*, superadded, shows that this future state of rebellion, is still further modified by *progression towards it.*

PARTICIPLES.

သည် *thee*, သော *thău*. The connective affixes သည် *thee*, and သော *thău*, may be said to be the two proper participial terminations; as သွားသည်ကို *thwaː thee gō*, "the going," (objective); သွားသည်ကြောင့် *thwaː thee gyoung*, "because of the going."

သဖွယ် *thăhpway*, လိ *lie*, လိလိ *lie lie*, are all participial affixes, as also are ဂမန်း *gămănː*, ဘနန်း *bhănănː*, မတတ် *mătăt*, denoting "similarity, likeness, resemblance."

ရာ *ra*, is a participial termination that abounds in narrative discourse; it generally closes the clause, and never takes any affixes: it implies that the action implied in the root is in the act of being done; as ကျောက်ဆွဲရပ်နေရာ *kyouk tswai răt né ra*, "(we) cast anchor, and remain," or "as (we) are anchoring;" ကျောက်နှုတ်ရွက်ရွက်တိုက်သွားရာ *kyouk hnŏŏk rwę rwĕt tŏik thwaː ra*, "(we) weigh anchor, spread sail, and go off;" မင်းကြီးကိုအစီရင်ခံရာ *mĕngː gyeeː gō ătsee rĕng khăn ra,* "having asked of the king," perfect present.

It remains to show how the time of participles are expressed. This is by the use of causal affixes attached to the root; the connective သည် *thee,* may be said to be understood.

Present Participles.

ကား *gaː,* the nominative affix, or မှာ *hma,* "in" the locative affix, both imply the time to be present; as သွားကားပြောသည် *thwaː gaː pyăü thee,* or သွားမှာပြောသည် *thwaː hma pyăü thee,* "(he) speaks as he goes, going, or while going he speaks."

နှင့် *hnĕng,* "together with," is also a present affix; as အမိဖြစ်သည်နှင့် သူကိုနှစ်သက်သည် *ămie hpyeet thee hnĕng thōō gō hneet thĕt thee,* "being the mother," or "in that she is the mother, she loves him."

Past Participles.

မှ *hmă,* and က *gă,* the affixes of the ablative case express the time to be past; as လာရောက်မှ *la rouk hmă,* လာရောက်က *la rouk gă,* "having arrived, when he arrived." They may be affixed after the past affixes ပြီး *byeeː,* or လျှင် *hlyĕng,* and then the compound has a signification of "after having;" as လာရောက်ပြီးမှ *la rouk byeeː hmă,* or လာရောက်လျှင် မှ *la rouk hlyĕng hmă,* "after having arrived."

သဖြင့် *thăhpyĕng,* "by means of," is also past, and rendered by "having;" as ဟုမိန့်တော်မူသဖြင့် *hō mieṇ dăü mōō thă hpyĕng,* "having thus said;" တကာကိုထက်ကောင်းသဖြင့်ရွေးကောက်သည် *tăga gō htĕt koungː thă hpyĕng rwéː gouk thee hpyeet thee,* "having been the best (it) was selected."

လျှင် *hlyĕng,* is a common past participial affix; as သွားလျှင် *thwa: hlyĕng,* "having gone, when (he) had gone, after that (he) had gone," the past affix ပြီး *byee:,* may be used before it; as သွားပြီးလျှင် *thwă: byee: hlyĕng,* "when (he) had gone, &c."

လျှက် *lyĕt,* is the same in signification and application as the preceding; သွားလျှက် *thwa: lyĕt,* "having gone, when (he) had gone."

မှု *mōō,* မှုကား *mōōga:,* and တမှုကား *tămōōga,* are the same as the preceding, but less common.

When participles are compounded with a substantive their terminations are generally omitted, and the imitial အ *ă,* of the substantive is dropped; as သွားသည် *thwa: thee,* "going," and အခါ *ăkha,* "time," or more fully သွားသည့်၏အခါ *thwa: thee ee ăkha,* becomes သွားခါ *thwa: kha,* "the time of going;" again သွားသဉ် *thwa: thee,* and အစဉ် *ătsee,* "continuance, duration," becomes သွားစဉ် *thwa: tsee,* "during the going, while going;" with အစ *ătsă,* "a beginning," forms သွားစ *thwa: tsă,* "the beginning of going;" with အဆုံး *ăsthŏŏn:,* "an end," forms သွားဆုံး *thwa: tshŏŏn:,* "the end of going."

Again, when it is necessary to couple a personal pronoun with a participle, instead of the pronoun being in the genitive, it is in the nominative case; as ငါသွားသဉ်ကောင်းလျှင် *gna thwa: thee koung: hlyĕng,* "if my going be good," or lit. "I going if it be good."

Honorific Mood.

The Honorific Mode of expression is by the use of the Honorific Increment တော် *daū,* (v. p. 46,) in connection with the verb မှု *mōō,* "to do, perform." That is when speaking of any exalted personage instead of saying "the king spake," it would be necessary to say "the king did sacred," or "royal speaking," and so on; as မင်းကြီးလည်မိန့်တော်မူလေ၏ *mĕngː gyeeː lee mien dāū mōō lé ce,* "and the king spake;" ဘုရားသခင်မြင်တော်မူလျှင် *hpōōraːthăkhĕng myĕng dāū mōō hlyĕng,* "God having seen," i. e. "having done sacred seeing."

In reference to these honorific increments, viz. တော် *dāū,* and မူ *mōō,* they are never used separately, and they always intervene between the original verb, and its affixes, or in other words, the original verb becomes dependent on the verb မူ *mōō,* which in all cases has the affixes of number, mood, and time attached, except in the case of the optative modal affix, and the second kind of auxiliary verbal affixes, (p. 101,) which form a compound verb with the original verb; but even in this last case the verb မူ *mōō,* takes the other affixes, viz., of number, and time; as 1st. Ex. မင်းကြီးတို့လာတော်မူကြလေ၏ *mĕng gyeeː dọladāūmōōkyălé ee,* "the kings came;" here, the original root being simple, and the tense assertive, the mood the same, and therefore indicative; the verb မူ *mōō,* takes the numeral, and temporal affixes; 2nd. Ex. မင်းကြီးတို့လာတော်မူကြနိုင်လေ၏ *mĕngː gyeeːdọla dāū mōō kyă hnōing lé ee,* "the kings can come," here the original root is still simple, but the verb မူ *mōō,* takes the numeral, the modal, and temporal affixes; 3rd. Ex. မင်းကြီးတို့လာချင်တော်မူကြလေ၏ *mĕngː gyeeː dọ la khyĕng dāū mōō kyă lé ee,* "the kings would come," here the verb ချင် *khyĕng,* expressing the Optative Mood is compounded with the original root, which is thus no longer simple, but still the verb မူ *mōō,* takes all the other affixes; 4th. Ex. မင်းကြီးတို့လာမြဲတော်မူကြနိုင်သည် *mĕngː gyee dọ la myai dãũ mõõ kyă hnŏing thee,* "the kings continue to come," the original verb is here a compound of လာ *la,* "to come," and မြဲ *myai,* "to continue permanent." The negative way of expressing this mood will be treated of under the head of the Negative Mood.

Interrogative Mood.

The Interrogative Mode of expression is formed by the use of certain affixes which are always placed after the assertive affixes of time. In conversation the assertive affix of the present tense is frequently omitted.

The Interrogative affixes are,

လာ *la,* the most common in use; ထမင်းစားပြီးလာ *htămĕngs tsăs byees la,* "have (you) eat dinner;" ထမင်းစားကြမည်လာ *htămĕngs tsăs kyă mee la,* "shall (we) eat dinner;" ဘယ်မှာရှိသည်လာ *bhay hma shie thee la,* "where is (it)?" မာအေလာ *ma ee la,* "are (you) well?"

လဲ *lai,* and လည်း *lees,* are used similar to the above; ဘယ်နှယ်ဟာလဲ *bhay hnay ha lai,* or ဘယ်နှယ်ဟာလည်း *bhay hnay ha lees,* ရှိသည် *shie thee,* understood, "What (is) the matter?"

ထုံ *dŏŏn,* used chiefly in conversation, when a question is asked by an interrogative pronoun; as ဘာဆိုသည်ထုံ *bha tshō thee dŏŏn,* "what do (you) say.?"

စင် *tsĕng,* and စံ *tsăn,* are used chiefly in simple clauses, and without an assertive affix; as သွားစံ *thwas tsăn,* "does (he) go?"

The above are colloquial.

လော *lăŭ,* is used in writing, or formal conversation.

နည်း *nees,* is likewise used in formal writing, or colloquially, but when the question is asked by an interrogative pronoun, or its compounds.

ရ *ră*, is sometimes used as the assertive affix of the future tense with these affixes; as သွားရသလော *thwas ră thă lău*, "Wilt (thou) go?" ဘယ်သို့သွားကြရသနည်း *bhay thō thwas kyă yă thă nees*, "Whither will ye go?" The above two being used in a formal manner necessarily imply the asking an indefinite question.

Sometimes when နည်း *nees*, is used; the interrogative pronominal, and the future affix, are used combined in a peculiar manner, the pronominal being in an abbreviated and nearly obsolete form; as သွားနိုင်ပချိန်နည်း *thwas hnŏing pă khyien nees*, "What, i. e. person, or thing (then) can go," "what will be able to go;" သွားစေပချိန်နည်း *thwas tsé pă khyien nees*, "What, (person or thing) will cause to go:" here ပချိန် *pă khyien*, is a compound of ပ *pă*, an abbreviation of ဘယ် *bhay*, and ချိန် *khyien*, a combination of the euphonic affix ချေ *khyé*, with the future affix အံ့ *ăn*.

နော် *nău*, is an affix having a precative, together with an interrogative signification, that is, asking a question so as to solicit acquiescence. It is more of the nature of an interrogative exclamation, similar to the English ey? but more respectful; as သူသွားသည်နော် *thōō thwas thee nău*, "he goes, ey?" i. e. "he may go, mayn't he." But it is chiefly used with the future tense in connection with the affix တော့ *dău*, implying "necessity;" as ပွဲလမ်းကိုကြည့်သွားတော့မည်နော် *bwai lăns gō kyee thwas dău nău*, "I shall go to see the festival, ey? mayn't I."

An interrogative in the future tense sometimes implies a wavering opinion; as ရာဇာသားဖြစ်လိမ့်မည်လော *raza thas hpyeet liem mee lău*, "he'll be the son of a king?" i. e. "Is he the son of a king do you think?"

Interrogative affixes are found attached to any part of speech, the substantive verb being understood; as ငါလား *gnala,* "I?"; လူဘယ်နှစ်ယောက်လဲ *lōō bhay hneet youk lai,* "how many men?"; အိမ်မှလား *ieng hmă la,* "from the house?".

In the honorific form of this mood, the interrogative affixes are attached in the usual way to the verb မူ *mōō*; as သွားတော်မူကြပြီးလော *thwas dāū mōō kyă byees lău,* "have (ye) gone?".

The interrogative mood is also found used in a simple assertive manner; as "the reason why he laughs is this," would be rendered အဘယ်ကြောင့်ရယ်သနည်းဟူမူကား *ăbhay gyoungs ray thă nees hōō mōō gas,* "why does he laugh? for this reason, viz.;" or rather "the reason why he laughs? why for this reason, viz."

For the negative form of this mood, vide Negative Mood.

Negative Mood.

The Negative Mood is formed by prefixing မ *mă,* the particle of negation to the root; as မလာသည် *mă la thee,* "comes not;" မသေပြီး *mă thé byees,* "has not died;" မပြောလျှင် *mă pyău hlyĕng,* "should (I), not speak, if (I) do not speak, not having spoke;" မပြောနိုင်သည် *mă pyău hnŏing thee,* "can't say."

The negative mood often dispenses with an assertive affix of time; as ငါသွားချင်သည် *nga thwas khyĕng thee,* "I wish to go;" ငါမသွားချင် *nga mă thwas khyĕng,* "I do not wish to go;" သင်လာမည်လား *thĕng la mee la,* "wilt thou come?", ငါမလာ *nga mă la,* "I won't come;" ငါမသွားဝံ့ *nga mă thwas wŏn,* "I dare not go;" သူတို့မလာကြ *thōō dŏ mă la kyă,* "they come not," or "will not come."

ရ *ră*, is an affix employed in this mood to express the future "shall;" as သင်တို့မသွားကြရ *thĕng dō mă thwas kyăyă*, "ye shall not go."

နှင့် လင့် When the negative is prohibitory, that is imperative, the affix နှင့် *hnĕng*, or လင့် *lĕng*, is appended to the root; as မသွားလင့် *mă thwa lĕng*, "go not;" မလာကြနှင့် *mălakyăhnĕng*, "come not," (plural): also a precative affix may be added; as မသွားပါနှင့် *măthwas ba hnĕng*, "please don't go."

ဘူး *bhōōs*, is often used in the place of an assertive affix; as မလာဘူး *măla bhōōs*, "comes not;" မသွားသေးဘူး *măthwas thés bhōōs*, "goes not yet;" မသွားရဘူး *măthwas yă bhōōs*, "shall not go," i. e. "must not go."

ဘဲ *bhai*, is an affix used in connection with the negative prefix to express "without;" မစားဘဲ *mă tsas bhai*, or မစားဘဲနှင့်သွားသည် *mă tsas bhai hnŏit thwas thee*, "he goes without eating."

ခင် *khĕng*, and မှီ *hmee*, are also auxiliary negative affixes, used in connection with the negative prefix to express "before;" as မစားခင်သွားသည် *mă tsas khĕng thwas thee*, or မစားမှီသွားသည် *mă tsas hmee thwas thee*, "(he) goes before having eat;" နှိုက် *hnŏit*, "in," or a similar locative causal affix expressing *present* time may be used; as မစားမှီနှိုက် *mătsas hmee hnŏit*, "before eating;" မမြင်ခင် *mă myĕng khĕng*, "before long, shortly afterwards."

မှု *mōō*. When a compound relation of the verb is to be negatived then the verb မှု *mōō*, "to do, perform," is used as an auxiliary, and the negative prefix is attached to it; as သွားအံ့သောငှါ *thwas ăn thău gnha*, "for the purpose of going," သွားအံ့သောငှါမမှု *thwas ăn thău gnha mă mōō*, "not for the purpose of going," lit. "does not act, or do, for the purpose of going." This is the only case where the verb မူ *mōō,* is thus used as an auxiliary without the honorific increment.

စဘူး *tsăbhōōs,* from စ *tsă,* "to begin," is affixed to the root, in connection with the negative prefix, to imply "*never;*" as မသွားစဘူး *măthwas tsă bhōōs,* "(he) never goes;" မသွားမပြန်နိုင်စဘူး *măthwasmăpyănhnŏing tsă bhōōs,* "(he) never can go again."

Compound roots are generally negatived in each member of the compound; as ဆင်ရင် *tshĕngrĕng,* "to put in order," မဆင်မရင်နှင့် *mă tshĕng mă rĕng hnĕng,* "put not in order;" ယူသွား *yōōthwas,* "to take away," မယူမသွားလင့် *măyōō măthwaslĕng,* "take not away."

But when the original verb is compounded with the auxiliary verbal affixes of the second Class, (v. p. 138 and infra,) the particle of negation is generally only once prefixed; as သွားအပ် *thwasăt,* "fit to go;" would be negatived thus, မသွားအပ် *mă thwas ăt,* "not fit to go," lit. "fit not to go;" မသွားဝံ့သည် *mă thwas wŏn thee,* "does not dare to go," lit. "dares not go." Sometimes with the auxiliary Optative affix ချင် *khyĕng,* two negatives are used; as မတိုင်မချင်လျှင်မသွားနှင့် *mătŏing mă khyĕng hlyĕng mă thwas hnĕng,* "if (you) do not wish to ask leave, do not go," i. e. "go not without asking leave."

In some cases of compound roots not being negatived in both members of the compound, the apparent exception will disappear when examined; as in the clause နားမလည် *nas mălee,* "don't understand," compounded of နား *nas,* "to hear," and လည် *lee,* "to comprehend;" when negatived in the above manner the word လည် *lee,* being alone negatived, it implies "that though one hears, one does not comprehend," i. e. "don't understand;" again နောင်တရ *noungtără*, "to repent," from နောင် *noung*, "after," တ *tă*, "to regret," and ရ *ră*, "to obtain, find," becomes နောင်တမရ *noungtămără*, "not to repent," i. e. "not to find after-regret."

ရာ *ra*. When roots terminating in the participial termination ရာ *ra*, are negatived, the compound has a future or an injunctive future signification; as မနေရာ *mănéra*, "would not remain;" မနိုင်ရာ *măhnŏingra*, "shall not overcome;" တံဒိုးသုံးပါးတို့ကိုမငဲ့ရာ *tădzōsthŏŏns bas dōgō ma gnaira*, "incline not to the three evil influences."

မဲ့ *mai*, affixed to any noun implies deficient in the quality, &c. implied by such noun; as အကြိုးမဲ့ *ăkyōs mai*, "without respect;" အချားမဲ့ *ăkhyăs mai*, "without an interval;" သတိမဲ့ပြောသည် *thădiemaipyăŭthee*, "(he) speaks without caution." When affixed to a root in connection with the negative prefix မ *mă*, it become a stronger negative; as မပြောမဲ့သွားပါ *măpyăŭ mai thwas ba*, "go without speaking;" မပြောမဲ့မသွားနှင့် *mă pyăŭmaimăthwas hnĕng*, "go not without speaking."

မှုတုံး *mōdŏŏns*, is likewise a negative affix, and is used by itself *after* the assertive affixes; as သွားသည်မှုတုံး *thwastheemōdŏŏn*, "(he) goes not."

The honorific mood is negatived in the same manner; as လာတော်မမူသည် *ladăŭ mămōōthee*, "does not come," (honorific); သွားတော်မမူကြနိုင်လေဪ *thwas dăŭ mă mōō kyă hnŏing léee*, "(they) cannot go," (honorific).

The interrogative mood is generally negatived, or a negative question is usually asked, by forming a compound sentence, the simple fact being stated in the first clause and the negative question put in the next; ငါသွားပြီးမဟုတ်လော *gna thwaး byeeး mă hō lău*, "I went, was it not so?" သင်တို့သိကြသည်မဟုတ်လော *thĕng dō thie kyă thee mă hō lău*, "ye perceive, is it not so?" i. e. "do ye not perceive?"

Auxiliary Affixes.

The Auxiliary Affixes are those that do not express a modal relation of a verb, but become incorporated with the root and form a compound verb. They are numerous.

ပြု *pyŏŏ*, "to do;" as သွားပြုသည် *thwaး pyŏŏ thee*, "(he) continues to go," lit. "he does going."

ပြန် *pyăn*, "again;" သွားပြန်ကြသည် *thwaး pyăn kyă thee*, "(they) go again."

ပြင်း *pyĕngး*, "to dislike;" as သွားပြင်းသည် *thwaး pyĕngး thee*, "dislikes going."

ဝံ့ *wŏŏn*, "to dare;" as သွားဝံ့သည် *thwaး wŏŏn thee*, "dares to go."

နေ *né*, "to remain;" as သွားနေသည် *thwaး né thee*, "remains going;" ဖြစ်နေသည် *hpyeet né thee*, "exists."

တတ် *tăt*, "to be skilled in, to know," implies "to be accustomed to;" as သွားတတ်သည် *thwăး tăt thee*, "accustomed to go, usually goes." It expresses what is naturally the quality or habit of any animal or thing; as ခွေးတို့ဟောင်တတ်ကြသည် *khwéး dō houng tăt kyă thee*, "dogs bark."

ရ *ră*, "to obtain;" as ဝင်ရသည် *wĕng ră thee*, "obtains admittance;" ငါတို့မြင်ရကြသည် *gna dō myĕng ră kyă thee*, "we got a sight."

ရစ် *reet*, "to remain behind; as ပြုရစ်သည် *pyŏŏ reet thee*, "remaining behind, (he) did it;" နေရစ်သည် *né reet thee*, "remains behind."

မိ *mie*, or မှိ *hmie*, "accidentally, of a chance," from မိ *mie*, "to obtain;" as သွားမိသည် *thwas mie thee*, "(he) happens to go."

ခဲ *khai*, or ခက် *khĕt*, "to be difficult;" as သွားခဲသည် *thwas khai thee*, or သွားခက်သည် *thwas khĕt thee*, "(he) goes with difficulty, (his) going is affected by some difficulty," i. e. "(he) is delayed in going."

လွယ် *lway*, "to be easy;" as သွားလွယ်သည် *thwas lway thee*, "(he) goes easily."

အပ် *ăt*, "to be fit;" as သွားအပ်သည် *thwas ăt thee*, "(he) is fit to go."

ရာ *ra*, the same as preceding.

ထိုက် *htŏik*, "worthy;" as သွားထိုက်သည် *thwas htŏik thee*, "worthy to go."

သင့် *thĕng*, "to be ready, agree with;" as သွားသင့်သည် *thwas thĕng thee*, "ready to go," vulg. "agreeable to go."

စေ *tsé*, "to cause;" as သွားစေသည် *thwas tsé thee*, "causes to go:" စိမ့် *tsiẹn*, is the corresponding future, compounded of စေ *tsé*, and အံ့ *ặn*; as သွားစိမ့် *thwas tsiẹn*, "will cause to go."

စမ် *tsăn*, "to try;" as သွားစမ်သည် *thwas tsăn thee*, "tries to go."

မြဲ *myai*, "to continue, be permanent;" as သွားမြဲသည် *thwas myai thee*, "still goes;" ကုန်သွယ်မြဲသည် *kŏŏn thway myai thee*, "(he) still carries on trade, continues to trade."

လေ့ *lẹ́*, "to be accustomed to, acquainted with;" ယောကျာ်းတို့သည်မိန္မတို့၏အဝတ်ကိုမဝတ်လေ့ကြ၏ *youkyas dọ̄ thee miemmă dọ̄ ee ăwĕt gō mă wẹ̆t lẹ́ ee*, "men are not in the custom of wearing women's apparel."

ဦး pronounced *ōōns*, from အုန်း *ŏŏns*, "to be many, numerous," implies "more;" as ပေးဦးမည် *pés ōōns mee*, "(he) will give more."

တုံ့ *dŏọn*, "to reciprocate;" as ချစ်တုံ့သည် *khyeet dŏọn thee*, "(he) loves in return, mutual love."

စ *tsă*, "to begin;" as မသွားစသည် *mă thwas tsă thee*, or သွားစမပြုသည် *thwas tsă mă pyŏŏ thee*, "(he) does not begin to go."

ပိုင် *pŏing*, "to own, possess, have power or right to;" as ပေးပိုင်သည် *peś pŏing thee*, "has right, or authority to give;" ဆိုပိုင်သည် *tshō pŏing thee*, "has authority to say."

ရက် *rĕt*, "to be unmerciful, void of feeling;" as သွားရက်သည် *thwas rĕt thee*, "unfeeling enough to go."

နိုး *nōs*, နိုးနိုး *nōs nōs*, စနိုး *tsănōs*, followed by a verb expressive of opinion denotes what is likely to take place; as သင်္ဘောရောက်မည်နိုးနိုးထင်သည် *thĕngbhău rouk mee nọs nōs htĕng thee*, "(he) thinks that the ship will probably arrive." (Judson.)

လျက် *lyĕt*, it is to be remarked, that besides being a subjunctive affix, p. 138, and a participial affix, p. 145, is also used as an auxiliary affix to imply "continuation, a continued or customary action;" as တယောက်တည်းနေလျက်၏ *tă youk tees né lyĕt ee*, "usually remains by himself;" ပြောလျက်နေကြဦး *pyău lyĕt né kyă ōōns*, "keep (ye) on talking;" စကားပြောလျက်ရှိသည် *tsăgas pyău lyĕt shie thee*, "is one that keeps talking." This affix may be used with the assertive affix of any tense; but being properly a *past* affix, when used without any assertive affix, it has a *past* signification; thus ထိုခုတင်မှာအိပ်လျက်သည် *htō khădĕng hma iet lyĕt thee*, "(he) usually sleeps in that bed;" ထိုခုတင်မှာအိပ်လျက် *htō khădĕng hma iet lyĕt*, "(he) used to sleep in that bed;" ထိုခုတင်မှာအိပ်လျက်မည် *htō khădĕng hma iet lyet mee*, "(he) will usually sleep in that bed."

It's use as a suppositional and subjunctive affix, may be easily distinguished from it's use as above, by the often repeated rule pointed out in p. 30, and elsewhere, viz., by the positions of the assertive, or of the numeral affixes; thus in the clause သွားနိုင်သည်လျက် *thwaꞌhnŏing thee lyĕt,* လျက် *lyĕt,* is a *modal* affix, and the meaning is "if (he) be able to go;" but the clause သွားနိုင်လျက်သည် *thwaꞌ hnŏing lyĕt thee,* implies "(he) usually is able to go."

Connective Affixes.

သည် *thee,* and သော *thăü;* the use of these connective affixes have been treated of already in various places; vide Index.

ရော *răü,* used sometimes for သော *thăü,* before words of time; as ထိုရော အခါ *htō răü ăkha,* "at that time."

ရွေ့ *rwę̄,* generally found in its contracted form of (၍) is chiefly used to connect verbal roots, the last only being inflected with affixes, thus the sense may be carried through a number of clauses.

ဟု *hŏŏ,* may be styled a *quotative* affix, it is in very common use, and of a connective nature; its use will be best illustrated by examples; လာမည်ဟုဆိုသည် *la mee hŏŏ tshō thee,* "(I) will come, thus" or "to wit, quoth he;" မင်းရှင်စောဟုဘွဲ့ကိုပေးသည် "Mengꞌshengzauꞌ, to wit, he gives him the title," i. e. "he gives a title, viz., Mengꞌshengzau;" မိုးကြိုး၍ လျှပ်ပြက် သောအခါ၌မိုးရွာချင်းနီးသည်ဟုငါသိသည်မဟုတ်လော *mōghꞌkyōꞌrwę̄ hlyĕt pyĕt thăü ăkha hnŏit mōghꞌ rwa khyĕngꞌ neeꞌ thee hŏŏ gna thie thee mă hō lăü,* "In the time of thunder, and lightning, rain, to wit, is near I know, don't I?" i. e. "When it thunders and lightens, don't I know that rain is near?"

ဟူ *hōō,* is the verbal form of the preceding, and is used like any other verbal root. It is connected to the subsequent clause by သော *thăŭ,* or ၍ *rwę́,* and is used always when it is necessary to inflect the subsequent clause; as ငါမသိဟူသောစကားရှန်ပြောသောကြောင့် *gnamă thie hōō thăŭ tsăgas shăn pyăŭ thăŭ gyoung,* "on account of telling the lie, viz. I don't know," i. e. "on account of the lie you have told in saying you did not know;" ငါမသိဟူ၍ပြောသည် *gna mă thie hōō rwę́ pyăŭ thee,* "I do not know, this to wit, says he;" မင်းကြီးသားကား။သာဂရ။ ဥပသာဂရ။ဟူ၍နှစ်ယောက်ဖြစ်၏ *mĕngs gyees thas gas*॥ *thagără ŏŏpăthagără hōō rwę́ hneet youk hpyeet ee,* "the king's sons were two, viz. Thagără and Opăthagără;" in this example, ဟူသောနှစ်ယောက် *hōō thăŭ hneet youk,* might have been used. ဟူ *hōō,* has sometimes the particularizing causal affix မူကား *mōōgas,* appended to it, and becomes adverbial, implying "for this reason, namely, &c."

Miscellaneous Affixes.

Under this head are classed some that are of an adverbial nature, some that are indiscriminately affixed to any part of speech; as likewise two or three prefixes.

တကား *tăgas,* is an emphatic affix and always closes a sentence or clause, it implies "regret, surprise;" as ဤသို့ဆိုသည်တကား *ee thō̤ tshō thee tăgas,* "thus he says!"

ချင်း *khyĕngs,* is applied in the same manner, as the preceding, but not so frequent.

ရှာ *sha,* is an affix implying "severe sorrow and affliction," and is affixed to the root itself; as ငါ၏တယောက်တည်းသောသားသေရှာပြီး *nga ee tăyouk teeз thăŭ thaзthésha byeeз,* "ah me! alas, alas! my son, my only one is dead!"

ပင် *pĕng*, "even," an emphatic affix, may be attached to any part of speech, and throws an emphasis on such word, is best rendered by an emphatic intonation of the voice; as ငါပင်အားဆိုခဲ့ပြီး *nga pĕng aaз tshō khai byeeз,* "to *me* (he) spoke;" ငါအားဆိုပင်ခဲ့ပြီး *gna aaз tshō pĕng khai byeeз,* "(he) *spoke* to me;" ငါပင်ဖြစ်၏ *gna pĕng hpyeet ee,* "I even I, am;" အိမ်ထဲမှာပင် *ieng htai hma pĕng,* "actually *in* the house."

စင် *tsĕng*, and စင်စစ် *tsĕng tseet,* have the same power and application as the preceding, but are not so frequent.

ကစား *gătsaз,* "though, notwithstanding;" as သွားကစား *thwaз gătsaз,* "though he goes, notwithstanding he goes."

ကတည်းက *găteeз gă,* "from the first of;" as သွားကတည်းက *thwaз găteeз gă,* "from the first of his going."

တောင်း *toungз,* "indeed," generally connected to the root by an euphonic affix; as လှလေတောင်း *hlă lé toungз,* "(she) is indeed beautiful;" သွားသည်တောင်း *thwaз thee toungз,* "does indeed go."

စွ *tswă,* the same as preceding.

ချည်း *khyeeз,* "only, nothing but;" as သွားသည်ချည်း *thwaз thee khyeeз,* "(he) merely goes, does nothing but go:" it can be attached to substantives; as လူတို့ချည်း *lōō dō khyeeз,* "men only, merely men."

စဉ် *tsee,* "while;" as သွားစဉ် *thwaз tsee,* "while (he) goes," or သွားစဉ်တွင် *thwaз tsee dwĕng,* ditto, ditto. Vide Participles.

တော့ *dău̧,* implies, "necessity;" as သွားသည်တော့ *thwaз thee dău̧,* "(he) of a necessity goes," used as an imperative affix.

မကာ *măgă,* "to exceed," is affixed to any part of speech to imply "more than," and generally in connexion with the adverbial increment မျှ *hmyă,* "as much as," expressed or understood; as ထိုမျှမကာ *htō hmyă măgă,* "what's more than that;" အသိန်းမကာ *ăthiens măgă,* "more than 100,000." This construction is found often used in connection with negative questions; as ထိုမျှမကာပေးမည်မဟုတ်လော *htō hmyă măgă péi mee măhōlău,* "more than that (he) will give, wo'nt (he);" သာ *tha,* "to increase," is used to strengthen the force of the comparison; as ထိုမျှမကာသာ၍ပေးမည် *htō hmyă măgă tharwę péi mee,* "far more than that (he) will give."

စိုး *tsōs,* "to be concerned about," is used in connection with လို *lō,* "similarity," or with သော့ကြောင့် *thău gyoung,* "on account of," to imply, "lest;" as သွားစိုးလို *thwas tsōs lō,* or သွားစိုးသော့ကြောင့် *thwas tsōs thău gyoung,* "for fear (he) should go, lest (he) go."

စိတ် *tsiet,* "mind, inclination;" as သွားစိတ် *thwas tsiet,* "has a mind to go, willing to go."

သော်လည်း *thăū lee,* "though, notwithstanding that;" as သွားသော်လည်း *thwas thăū lee,* "though (he) goes, notwithstanding (he) goes."

သေး *théi,* "still, yet, continuance;" as သွားသေးသည် *thwas théi thee,* "still goes, is yet going;" မတွေ့ဘူးသေး *mă twę bhōōs théi,* "has never yet met with."

ရင်း *rěngs,* "as, while;" as သွားရင်း *thwas rěngs,* "as (he) goes, while (he) goes."

ကြောင့် *gyoung,* the causal affix, from အကြောင်း *ăgyoungs* "reason, affair," expresses "on account of;" it is sometimes connected to the root by the connective သော *thăŭ;* and always, when used with verbal roots, both words take the light accent; as သွားသော့ကြောင့် *thwas thăŭ gyoung,* "on account of the going."

လို့ *lō*, လို့လည်း *lō lee,* and မို့ *mō,* all imply, "because;" as သွားလို့ *thwas lō,* သွားလို့လည်း *thwas lō lees,* or သွားမို့ *thwas mō,* "because of (his) going."

ရန် *răn,* "for the sake of, for the purpose of;" as သွားရန် *thwa răn,* "for the sake of going;" ပြင်ဆင်ရန်လို့လျှင် *pyĕng tshĕng rănlōhlyĕng,* "should (he) require (it) for the purpose of repair."

ဂမန်း *gămăns,* ဘနန်း *bhănăns,* and မတတ် *măttăt,* all imply "likeness, resemblance," as also "almost," *(Carey;)* as သွားဂမန်း *thwas gămăns,* သွားဘနန်း *thwas bhănăns,* သွားမတတ် *thwas măttăt,* "like going, resembling going, as if going, almost going or gone."

ဟန် *hăn,* "an appearance," denotes "*probably;*" as ကြောက်ဟန် *kyouk hăn,* "probably is afraid, seems to be afraid."

ရုပ်နှံ *rŏŏpnăn,* the same as ဟန် *hăn.*

ရုံ *rŏŏn,* "just, and no more," used in connection with သာ *tha,* "only;" as သွားရုံ *thwas rŏŏn,* or သွားရုံသာ *thwas rŏŏn tha,* "only just gone;" or သွားရုံရှိသည်သာ *thwasrŏŏn shie thee tha,* "is only just gone." *(Carey.)*

လေ *lé,* persistive affix; as သွားသည်လေ *thwas theelé,* "(he) *does* go."

လောက် *louk,* "nearly, about as much;" as သွားလောက် *thwaslouk,* "nearly going;" သင့်လောက် *thĕng louk,* "nearly ready."

လို *lō,* "like, similarity;" သွားလို *thwas lō,* "like going."

လိုလို *lōlō,* "a little like;" as သွားသည်လိုလို *thwas thee lōlō,* "a little like going."

လင့်ကစား *lęnggătsaː*, "though;" as သွားလင့်ကစား *thwaːlęnggătsaː*, "though (he) goes."

လျှင်း *hlyĕngː*, "as, while;" သွားလျှင်း *thwaːhlyĕngː*, "as (he) goes, while (he) goes."

ရော့ *răụ*, denotes "uncertainty;" as သွားရော့ *thwaːrăụ*, "(he) *may* go," i. e. "probably go."

ဆန်း *tshănː*, "nothing more than," used with the root reduplicated; as သွားဆန်းသွားသည် *thwaː tshănː thwaː thee*, "(he) goes and nothing more, (he) goes and that's all;" လှဆန်းလှသည် *hlă tshănː hlă thee*, "is beautiful and nothing more."

သာ *tha*, "only;" as သွားသာသည် *thwaː tha thee*, or သွား၍သာသည် *thwaː rwę tha thee*, "only goes:" is applied to any part of speech, and in any position.

တည်း *teeː*, is somewhat emphatic and is variously used: 1st. It is a kind of positive assertive affix, supplying the place of a common assertive one, especially when the nominative has a particularizing causal affix, as ကား *gaː* attached; as ငါကားကောင်းတည်း *gna gaː koungː teeː*, "I am good, as for me I am good;" အမည်ကားရွှေမောင်တည်း *ămee gaː shwémoung teeː*, "as to his name, it is Shwémoung;" 2ndly. It is used in recapitulation in connection with ဟူ *hōō;* as ငါး။မုံ့။ လဖက်။သကြား။နို့။တည်းဟူသောအလုံးစုံကိုဝယ်သဖြင့် *gnaː*॥ *mŏŏn*॥ *lăphĕt thăkyă*॥ *nō teeː hōō ălŏŏnː tsŏŏn gŏ way thăhpyĕngː*, "fish, bread, tea, sugar, milk, all these to wit, having brought." 3rdly. It is used at the end of a clause, to shew that it is either a quotation, or the idea or opinion of another, in such cases it is connected to the temporal, or other affixes by သ *thă,* and precedes the quotative ဟု *hŏŏ;* as သေလတ္တန္သတည္းဟုဆိုးဗေသောကြောင့် *thé lăttănthă tees hŏŏ tshōs bé thăŭ gyoung,* "that (he) would die, on account of this evil prediction," i. e. "on account of the evil prediction that (he) would die." 4thly. It is used, (especially in conversation,) to shew that on the clause, to which attached, the question turns, and is strongly intonated; as ငါကိုပေးမည်လာတည်းဟုဆိုသည် *gna gō peś mee la tees hŏŏ tshō thee,* "will you give me? says he;" it is to be remarked that this word is sometimes found written တည့် *teę,* with the light accent.

လားလား *laslas,* is a prefix with negative sentences, and implies "not at all;" as လားလားမသွား *las las mă thwas,* "(he) goes not at all."

တပ် *tăt,* a verb implying "to be certain," is prefixed and connected by ၍ *rwę́,* and implies "certainly;" as တပ်၍ပေးမည် *tăt rwę́ peśs mee,* "(he) will certainly give."

ကြောင်း *gyoungs,* "a reason, cause, affair," is used as an affix with verbs to express "why;" as ပြုရမည်ကြောင်းကိုငါမသိ *pyŏŏ yă mee gyoungs gō gna mă thie,* "I don't see why I should do (it);" it expresses likewise "that," in such a sentence; as သူသေပြီးကြောင်းကိုကြားရလျှင် *thōō thé byees gyoungs gō kyas ră hlyeng,* "should (you) hear that he has died," lit. "he has died affair, should you hear."

Euphonic, and Expletive Affixes.

In the application of these, attention is somewhat paid to alliteration.

ချိန့် *khyięn,* (compounded of ချေ *khyé,* and အံ့ *ăn,* the future affix,) is used in the future tense; as ငါခေါ်ချိန့်မည် *gna khăŭ khyięn mee,* "I will call (him)."

ပိမ့် *piem,* (compounded of ပေ *pé,* and အံ့ *ạn,*) is used in the same manner; as ငါပေးပိမ့်မည် *gna pés pięm mee,* "I will give."

လိမ့် *lięm,* (compounded of လေ *lé,* and အံ့ *ạn;*) as ငါလာလိမ့်မည် *gna la lięm mee,* "I will go."

ငြား or ညား *gnyat,* or လတ် *lăt,* are chiefly used before a suppositional affix, such as သော် *thāū,* လျှင် *hlyĕng,* သော်လည် *thāū lee, &c.*

ပါ *pa,* မိ *mie,* မူ *mōō,* ကဲ့ *gại,* ခဲ့ *khại,* ချေ *khyé,* ခြေ *khré,* စွာ *tswa,* လုံ *dŏŏn,* ထ *htă,* စ *tsă,* ပေါ *păŭ,* လေ *lé,* လှာ *hla,* ဘိ *bhie,* သိ *thie,* are all euphonic, and expletive.

လိုက် *lŏik,* much used with active verbs.

တမုံ *tămŏọn,* and တမူ *tămōō,* are both expletive; as သွားသည်တမူ *thwat thee tă mōō,* "(he) goes."

Adverbs

Are of two kinds: 1st, such as are so originally; as ဧကန် *ékăn,* "truly;" သာ *tha,* "only," &c.: and 2ndly, those that are derived. Derived adverbs are formed in various ways.

စွာ *tswa.* By affixing စွာ *tswa,* which is a very common adverbial termination; as ကောင်း *koungs,* "good," ကောင်းစွာ *koungs tswa,* "well."

တ *tă,* is a very common formative adverbial prefix, and is used; 1st, either prefixed to the root by itself, in which case the compound is generally used in connexion with some word of a cognate signification; as အလျှင်တဆော *ăhlyĕng tătshăŭ,* "speedily," from လျှင် *hlyĕng,* a root implying "speed," and ဆော *tshăŭ,* a root signifying "to be quick:" or 2ndly, prefixed to the root with the intensative တည်း *tees,* affixed; as တဟုန်တည်း *tă hŏŏn tees,* "speedily," from ဟုန် *hŏŏn,* "to be quick;" တချက်တည်း *tăkhyĕt tees*, "immediately," from ချက် *khyĕt*, "the instant time:" or 3dly, the root is reduplicated, and it is affixed to each member; as တကဲ့တကဲ့ *tă gḁi tă gḁi*, "by degrees," from ကဲ့ *gḁi*, "progressive:" or 4thly, it is only prefixed to the first member of the reduplicated root; as တလဲလဲ *tă lai lai*, "by turns," from လဲ *lai*, "turns:" and 5thly, it is found used as in the 1st instance, but having a peculiar power; as in the sentence မျက်စိတဆုံးခန့် *myĕt tsie tă tshŏŏns khăn̤*, "about as far as the reach of the eye," here တဆုံး *tă tshŏŏns*, is a compound of အဆုံး *ătshŏŏns*, "an end;" တနေ့သ၌ *tă nḛ thă hnŏit*, "on a certain day, once upon a time," the indefinite signification is given in this sentence by the use of the connective affix သ *thă*, with ၌ *hnŏit*, a causal affix which does not imply any substantive quality, Conf. p. 65. In all these, (especially the last,) its value as numeral may be traced.

အ *ă*. Or by affixing အ *ă*; as လွန် *lwŏn*, "to excel," အလွန် *ălwŏn*, "exceedingly;" လျင် *hlyĕng*, "to be quick," အလျင် *ăhlyĕng*, "quickly."

Or by reduplicating the root; as ကောင်း *koungs*, "good," ကောင်းကောင်း *koungs koungs*, "well."

Or by prefixing ပ *pă*, or က *gă*, to each member of compound words; as ပရုန်းပရင်း *pă rŏŏns pă rĕngs*, "confusedly, riotously," from ရုန်းရင်း *rŏŏns rĕngs*, "to be noisy;" ကရောက်ကရက် *gă rouk gă rĕt*, "heedlessly," &c. The above, and various combinations of them, are the usual form of adverbs, but besides these;

နှင့် *hnḛng*. The present participle in သည် *thee*, with the causal affix in နှင့် *hnḛng*, can render any root into an adverb; as ကောင်းသည်နှင့်

koungs thee hnēng, "well:" the same occurs when applied to some substantives; as အစု *ătsöö,* "a collection," အစုနှင့် *ătsöö hnēng,* "collectively."

ဆောင် *oung.* The verbal affix ဆောင် *oung,* is also found converting a root into an adverb; as လှပဆောင်ဆင်ထားသည် *hlă pă oung tshĕng htas thee,* "beautifully arranged," lit. "arranged (so as to be) attaining to beauty."

Conjunctions.

The various connective affixes in some cases perform the functions of conjunctions, besides those, however, are the following.

သည်မဟုတ် *thee mă hōh,* "this not the case;" ထိုမဟုတ် *htō mă hōh,* "that not the case;" သို့မဟုတ် *thō mă hōh,* "such not the case;" according to the context, all express the idea of "or, or else."

လည်း *lees,* "but, and, also," with nouns; as ထိုပြည်၌လည်း *htō pyee hnŏit lees,* "in that country also:" it conveys likewise the idea of "besides;" as ဤလူလည်းနှစ်ယောက်လူတို့လာကြပြီး *ee lōō lees hneet youk lōō dō la kyă byees,* "besides this man, two men came."

လည်းကောင်း *lees goungs,* "and also," is used to connect sentences and clauses. It is occasionally found used at the end of each clause. Sometimes it is also found as an adjective to express, "*same;*" as လည်းကောင်းနေ့၌ *lees goungs nē hnŏit,* "on the same day;" လည်းကောင်းနည်း *lees goungs nees,* "in the same manner."

ပြင် *pyĕng,* "besides;" as သည်ပြင် *thee pyĕng,* "besides this."

INTERJECTIONS.

ဪ *ōh,* "oh! holloa!"

အောမယ် *ăümay,* "how strange!"

အော် *āū,* or အော်အော် *āū āū,* "very well! that's it is it!"

အဲ *ai,* "well!"

ဟဲ *hai,* contemptuous; as ဟဲခွေး *hai khwé,* "hey! you dog!"

သယ် *thay,* သယ်လေ *thay lé,* surprise, "dear!"

စောက်ဖက် *tsoukhpĕt,* "vulva," vulgar and abusive, common among the lower order of females when startled, &c.

လေ *lé,* affix of distress, and interrogative; as ဪအဘ။အဘလေ *ōh ăbhă ăbhă lé,* "oh Father, Father oh!"

PART V.

Measures.

On the mode of compounding the names of measures with numerals, vide p. 102, para. 13.

Measures of Distance.

			Miles.	Furls.	Yards.	Feet.	Inches.
10 ဆံချည် *tshăn khyee*, "hair's breadth,"	=	1 နှမ်း *hnăn*, Sesamum seed.					
6 နှမ်း *hnăn*,	=	1 မုယော *mööyăŭ*, a species of esculent seed.					
4 မုယော *mööyăŭ*,	=	1 အသစ် *ătheet*, "finger's breadth."	..	..	..	..	nearly.
5 သစ် *theet*,	=	1 အမုတ် *ămöök*, the width of the hand with the thumb close to the fingers.	..	..	..	..	6
8 သစ် *theet*,	=	1 အမိုက် *ămŏik*, the width of the fist and thumb extended.	..	..	..	..	—
12 သစ် *theet*,	=	1 ထွာ *htwa*, "span."	..	..	..	..	9
2 ထွာ *htwa*, or 3 မိုက် *mŏik*,	=	1 တောင် *toung*, "cubit."	..	..	..	1	6
4 တောင် *toung*,	=	1 လံ *lăn*, "fathom."	..	..	..	6	—
7 တောင် *toung*,	=	1 တာ *tă*.	..	..	3	1	6
20 တာ *tă*,	=	1 ဥဿဘ *ööththăbhă*.	..	..	70	—	—

Measure		Equivalent	Miles.	Furls.	Yards.	Feet.	Inches.
20 ဥသဘာ *ŏŏththăbhă*	=	1 ကောသာ *găŭthă.*	..	6	80	—	—
4 ကောသာ *găŭthă,*	=	1 ဂါဝုတ် *gawŏŏk.*	3	1	100	—	—
4 ဂါဝုတ် *gawŏŏk,*	=	1 ယူဇနာ *yŏŏdzănă.*	12	5	180	—	—
1000 တာ *tă,*	=	တိုင် *tŏing*, "post."	1	7	200	—	—
7000 တောင် *toung,*			2, nearly				

The above is what is called "the common measure," and is the one in general use. The other measure is styled the "chief's measure," in which the cubit is styled သံတောင် *thăntoung*, or မင်းတောင် *mĕngːtoung*, both implying "Royal Cubit;" and its length is according to some accounts $19\frac{1}{10}$ English inches, according to others $22\frac{1}{8}$ English inches—but it is most usually styled "three fingers'" breadth longer than the common cubit. If the first be considered correct, according to it then, the corresponding သစ် *theet*, of the measure, would be $\frac{99}{100}$ of an inch. The လံ *lăn*, "fathom," would be $760\frac{4}{10}$ inches. The တာ *tă*, $133\frac{1}{10}$ inches: and the တိုင် *tŏing*, 2 miles, 193 yards, 2 feet, 8 inches. This is the Government measure used for assessment, &c.*

Some of the above when used with numerals are thus abbreviated. 1 သစ် *theet*, is written ၁ံ — 1 မိုက် *mŏik*, is written ဗ — 1 တာ *ta*, is

* A corresponding difference of measure is mentioned by Herodotus, L. 1. C. 178, as having obtained among the antient Babylonians; ὁ δὲ βασιλήϊος πῆχυς τοῦ μετρίου ἐστὶ πήχεος μίζων τρισὶ δακτύλοισι. "The Royal cubit, exceeds the common (moderate) cubit by three fingers' breadth." It may be, that the nations of the East, were as much indebted to the ancient Babylonians for their Metrological system, as Boeckh, has shewn those of the West were.

written ၁ါ — 1 တောင် *toung*, is written ၆ — and in the same way with numerals, as ၄ါ — "four *ta*."

တာ *tă*, implies "measure" in general, and is used as an auxiliary with measures of length; as တောင်တာ *toungta*, "a cubit."

တိုင် *tŏing*, "a post," is also a generic term for any measure approaching it in length, such as "a league, a kos, a mile, &c.;" as အင်္ဂလိတ်တိုင် *ăngăliet tŏing*, "an English mile."

Measures of Weight.

36 ပရမဏုမြူ *părămăṇŏŏmyōō*, "particle of a subtile fluid," invisible to men, but visible to Nats and Angels, ... = 1 အဏုမြူ *ăṇŏŏmyōō*, "a minute, mote, seen playing in a sunbeam."

36 အဏုမြူ *ăṇŏŏmyōō*, ... = 1 မြူ *myōō*, "a particle of fine dust," raised aloft in hot weather by the feet of men, wheels of waggons, &c.

36 မှူ *hmōō*, ... = 1 အမှုန် *ăhmŏṇ*, "particle of dust," the size of fine flour.

36 မှုန် *hmŏṇ*, ... = 1 ကညစ်ခြေး *kăgnyeet khyés*, "the minute particle that falls to the ground from an iron style when writing on a palmyra leaf."

7 ကညစ်ခြေး *kăgnyeet khyés*,.... = 1 သန်ဥက္ခေါင်း *thănŏŏkkhoungs*, "louse's head."

7 သန်ဥက္ခောင် *thănöökkhoung,* = 1 မုံညင်းစေ့ *mŏŏngnyĕngs tsé,* "a grain of mustard seed."

3 မုံညင်းစေ့ *mŏŏngnyĕngs tsé,* = 1 နှမ်စေ့ *hnăn tsé,* "sesamum seed."

4 နှမ်စေ့ *hnăn tsé,* .... = 1 ဆံစေ့ *tshăntsé,* "grain of husked rice."

4 ဆံစေ့ *tshăntsé,* .... = 1 ချင်ရွေး *khyĕng rwés,* "the seed of Abrus precatorius." *(Carey.)*

2 ချင်ရွေး *khyĕng rwés,* .... = 1 ရွေးကြီး *rwai gyees,* a species of seed.

4 ရွေးကြီး *rwai gyees,*............ = 1 ပဲး *bais.*

2 ပဲး *bais,* .... = 1 မူး *mōōs.*

2 မူး *mōōs,* .... = 1 မတ် *măt.*

4 မတ် *măt,* .... = 1 ကျပ် *kyăt,* Tickal.

5 ကျပ် *kyăt,* .... = 1 ဗိုလ် *bōh.*

20 ဗိုလ် *bōh,* or 100 ကျပ် *kyăt,* = 1 ပိဿာ *bieththa,* or *viss.*

The term အခွက် *ăkhwĕt,* is substituted for ပိဿာ *viss,* in connexion with any capital number; as အခွက်တဆယ် *ăkhwĕt tă tshay,* "ten piektha, or viss."

The weight of a ကျပ် *kyăt,* or tickal, is 252.75 grs. troy exactly. *(Low.)*

Some of the above weights are thus abbreviated with numerals, 1 ရွေး *rwés,* is written ၁ွေး sometimes ၌ ; 1 ပဲး *bais,* is written ၁ဲး— 1 မူး *mōōs,* is written ၁ူး— 1 မတ် *măt,* is written ၁ံ ; and 1 ကျပ် *kyăt,* is written ၁ —. One *viss,* or 100 *kyăt,* is written ၁॥— or ၁ါ ; and so on with other numerals

The Burmese in the English dominions also use the term ရွေး *rwés,* to express "pice;" and ပဲး *bais,* to express "anna ;" as တပဲး *tă bais* "one anna ;" နှစ်ပဲ *hneet baiꞋ*, "two *bai* or annas :" မူး *mōōꞋ*, to express "two annas ;" တမူး *tă mōōꞋ*, one *mōōꞋ*, "two annas :" မတ် *măt*, to express a four anna piece ; as တမတ် *tă măt*, one *măt*, or "four annas."

The မူး *mōōꞋ*, and ပဲ *baiꞋ*, in the above table severally equal $\frac{1}{8}$th and $\frac{1}{16}$th of a Tickal. But another denomination of these weights called the smaller or lesser *mōōꞋ* and *baiꞋ*, severally are the $\frac{1}{10}$th and $\frac{1}{20}$th of a Tickal.

The Government of Ava send, from the capital, sets of standard weights (အလေး *ăléꞋ*,) for the use of the provinces. The present are called ထိုးအလေး *tōꞋăléꞋ*, being surmounted by the figure of a ထိုး *tōꞋ*, the mythical Lion of Boodhism, and the present cognisance of Burma ; the former were styled ဟင်းသာအလေး *hĕngꞋtha ălé*, from having been surmounted with a figure of a ဟင်းသာ *hĕngꞋtha*, the famous *hansa*, or Brahminee duck, the cognisance of the kingdom of Pegu.

MEASURES OF CAPACITY.

	Cubic Inches.	Weight of distilled water in lbs. avoirdupois.	English measure.
2 လက် *lĕt*, or "handful," = 1 လက်ခုပ် *lĕtkhŏŏk*, "the two hands full."			
2 လက်ခုပ် *lĕtkhŏŏk*, ... = 1 စလယ် *tsălay*.	$34\frac{1}{3}$	$1\frac{1}{4}$ nearly	1 Pint.
4 စလယ် *tsălay*, ... = 1 ပြည် *pyee*.	$145\frac{1}{4}$	5	$\frac{1}{2}$ Gall.
2 ပြည် *pyee*, ... = 1 စရွတ် *tsărwŏt*.			
2 စရွတ် *tsărwŏt*,........ = 1 စိတ် *tsiet*.	$564\frac{1}{2}$	20	2 Galls.
2 စိတ် *tsiet*,............ = 1 ခွဲ *khwai*.			

2 ခွဲ *khwai*, or 16 ပြည် *pyee*, = 1 တင်း *tĕngs*, commonly styled "Basket," = 4493½ cub. inch. 160 lbs. av. 2 Bushels.

ကျွန်စား the fifth part of a ပြည် *pyee*, is called ကျွန်စား *kywŏn tsas*, "a meal for one person"

Some of the above measures are abbreviated with numerals; thus 1 တင်း *tĕngs*, is written ၁; 1 စိတ် *tsiet*, is written ၆; 1 ပြည် *pyee*, is written ၈; 1 စလယ် *tsălay*, is written ၆; and so on with any other numeral.

Measures of Time.

The minuter divisions of Time are somewhat various, the following table is compiled from the best procurable information:—

10 ခဏ *khăṇă*, "instant," .... = 1 ခရာ *khăra*.
10 ခရာ *khăra*, ... = 1 ပြန် *pyăn*.
6 ပြန် *pyăn*, ... = 1 ဗီဇနာ *beedzăna*.
15 ဗီဇနာ *beedzăna*, ... = 1 ပါဒ် *pad*.
4 ပါဒ် *pad*, ... = 1 နာရီ *naree*.
60 နာရီ *naree*, ... = 1 ရက် *rĕt*, or "day of 24 hours."
15 ရက် *rĕt*, ... = 1 ပက္ခ *păkkhă*, "½ of the month."
2 ပက္ခ *păkkhă*, ... = 1 လ *lă*, "moon, or month."
12 လ *lă*, ... = 1 နှစ် *hneet*, or "year."

The ရက် *rĕt*, consists of two parts: "from sunrise" နေထွက် *né dwĕt*, "to sunset" နေဝင် *né wĕng*, is called နေ့ *nẹ́*, or the "day proper;" and from sunset to sunrise again is styled ညဉ့် *gnyeen*, or "night." These are again divided into four watches each, the first from about 6 A. M. to 9 A. M., is called "the first watch," or တချက်တီး *tă khyĕttees*; from 9 A. M.

to 12 is styled the second watch, or နှစ်ချက်တီး *hneetkhyĕttees*; from 12 to 3 P. M. is styled the third watch, or သုံးချက်တီး *thŏŏnskhyĕttees*; from 3 to 6 P. M. is called the fourth watch, or လေးချက်တီး *lé khyĕttees*. Taking the 60 နာရီ *naree*, to equal 24 hours of our time, 1 *naree* would amount to 24 minutes; at the end of each နာရီ *naree*, the မောင်း *moung*, or "gong" is sounded, hence the two terms are synonymously used. The *watch* varies from 8 to 9 *naree*, according to the length of the day. The term နာရီ *naree*, is likewise used to express the English "hour;" as နံနက်ကိုးနာရီအချိန်တွင် *nännĕt kōs naree ăkhyien dwĕng*, "at 9 o'clock in the morning." ညည့်ကိုးနာရီအချိန်တွင် *gnyeen kōs naree ăkhyien dwĕng*, "at 9 o'clock at night." ပြန် *pyăn*, "again," is used to express the hours corresponding with our P. M.; thus နာရီပြန်နှစ်နာရီအချိန်တွင် *naree pyăn hneet naree ăkhyien dwĕng*, "at 2 o'clock P. M." When the night hours, however, are referred to, the word ပြန် *pyăn*, is superceded by သည့် *gnyeen*, "night;" as ညည့်တဆယ်တစ်နာရီအချိန်တွင် *gnyeen tă tshay tă naree ăkhyien dwĕng*, "at 11 o'clock at night."

Sometimes ချက်တီး *khyĕttees*, is used as a sort of numeral generic adjunct in questions; as နာရီဘယ်နှစ်ချက်တီးလာ *naree bhay hneet khyĕttees la*, "what o'clock is it?" တဆယ်နှစ်ချက်တီးလာ *tă tshay hneet khyĕttees la*, "twelve o'clock?"

"Noon," is styled မွန်း *mwŏns*; and "midnight," သံးခေါင် *thănskhoung*.

The first ပက္ခ *päkkhă*, or "half of the month," that is, from the new moon လသစ် *lă theet*, to the full moon လပြည့် *lă byee*, is styled လဆန်းပက္ခ *lă tshäns păkkhă*, or "the *păkkhă*, of the waxing or increasing moon;" from the full moon to the change again is styled လဆုတ်ပက္ခ

lă tshŏŏk păkkhă, or "the *păkkhă,* of the receding or waning moon." But the most usual term in dates for the waning of the moon is လပြည့်ကျော် *lă byẹe gyāū,* or "beyond the full moon," lit. "passing the full moon." From the disappearing of the moon to the change, is called လကွယ် *lăgway,* or "the hiding of the moon." The last day of the month is called လငယ် *lă gnay,* or "the little moon."

The Burmese date their correspondence, &c. &c., as from the 1st, 2nd, 3rd, 4th, 5th, 6th, 7th, 8th, 9th, 10th, 11th, 12th, 13th, 14th or 15th, day of the waxing, or the waning moon; thus ဝါဆိုလဆန်း လေးရက် *watshō lătshăns lés rĕt,* "the fourth day of the waxing moon Wātshō;" နတ်တော်လပြည့်ကျော်တဆယ်သုံးရက် *nătdāū lă byẹe gyāū tă tshay thŏŏns rĕt,* "the 13th day of the waning moon Nătdāū."

The day of the new moon, the 8th day of the waxing moon, the day of the full, and the 8th day of the wane, are set apart for the performance of religious duties, and are styled either ဥပုသ်နေ့ *ŏŏpŏŏth nẹ́,* or သီတင်းနေ့ *thiedĕngs nẹ́,* or အဖြိးနေ့ *ăbyees nẹ́,* all implying the "day of religious observance." On these sabbaths no public or private business is transacted, and the more strict observers of the law abstain from tasting food between the rising and setting of the sun.

The week consists of seven days, named after the Sun, Moon, and Planets.

Sunday, ..	တနင်္ဂနွေ *tănĕnggănwé,* ..	Pali	ရဝိ *răbie,* "the Sun."
Monday, ..	တနင်္လာ *tă nĕng la,*	do.	စန္ဒ *tsăndă,* "the Moon."
Tuesday, ..	အင်္ဂါ *ănga,*	do.	အင်္ဂါ *ănga,* "Mars."
Wednesday,	ဗုဒ္ဓဟူး *bŏŏddhăhōōs,*	do.	ဗုဒ္ဓ *bŏŏddhă,* "Mercury."

Thursday,. .ကြာသပတေ *kyathăpăté,* Pali ဗြဿပတိ *priethpătie,* "Jupiter."

Friday,.... သောက်ကြာ *thoukya,*....do. သောကြာ *thoukya,* "Venus."

Saturday,.. စနေ *tsăné,* .... do. သောရီ *thăŭrie,* "Saturn."

The Names of the 12 months which consist alternately of 29 and 30 days, together with their Zodiacal Signs are :—

Days.	Months.				
29	April	တံကူး *Tăgōōs,*	.... မိဿ *Miethā,*	Aries	Vulgo, သိုး *thōs,* "the Goat."
30	May	ကဆုံ *Kătshŏŏn,*	.... ဗြိဿ *Pyietha,*	Taurus	နွားလျှည်သာပ *nwas hlee thăhpă,* "the Bull."
29	June	နယုံ *Năyŏŏn,*	.... မေထုန် *Médŏŏn,*	Gemini	ပူးခေါင် *pōōskhoung,* "the full time of union of Male and Female."
30	July	ဝါဆို *Watshō,*	.... ကရကဋ် *Kărăgăt,*	Cancer..	ဂနန်း *gănăns,* "the Crab."
29	Aug.	ဝါခေါင် *Wagoung,..*	သိန် *Thien,*	Leo	ချင်သေ့ *khyĕngthé,* "the Lion."
30	Sept.	တော်သလင်း *Tāūthălĕngs,* abb. to သလင်း *thălĕngs,*	ကန် *Kăn,*	Virgo......	ကညာ *kăgnya,* "the Virgin."
29	Oct.	သတင်းကျွတ် *Thădĕngskywĕt* or ဝါကျွတ် *Wakywĕt,*	ဒူ *Dōō,*	Libra	ချိန် *khyien,* "the Scales."
30	Nov.	တန်ဆောင်မုန်း *Tătshoungmŏŏns,*	ဗြိစ္ဆာ *Pyietstsha,*	Scorpio	ကင်းခြေမြှား *kĕngskhyémyas,* "a Scorpion."

29 Dec. နတ်တော် *Nătdāū,* ...... ဓနု *Dănŏŏ,* Sagittarius Vulgo, လင်းလေး *lĕngslés,* "the Bow."

30 Jan. ပြာသိုလ် *Pyathō,* .... မကာရ *Măgară,* Capricornus .... ငါးမန်း *gnasmăns,* any "Sea Monster."

29 Feb. တပို့တွဲ *Tăbōdwai,* .... ကုံ *Gŏŏn,* Aquarius.. ရေခွက်ဒို *rérwĕtō,* "the Water Pot."

30 Mar တပေါင်း *Tăboungs,* .... မိန် *Mien,* Pisces...... ငါး *gnas,* "the Fish."

The year commences on the 18th of April, and, as shown above, consists of but 354 days, being a lunar year, but, to make it conform to the true solar year, the month ဝါဆို *watshō,* is intercalated by the Burmans on every third year; and is then called ဒုတိယဝါဆို *dătieyă watshō,* or the "second Watshō." In Arracan Proper, they intercalate the month တံကူး *tăgōōs,* calling the one တံကူးလဟောင် *tăgōōs lă houng,* or "the old month Tăgōō," and the intercalated one တံကူးလသစ် *tăgōōs lă theet,* or "the new month Tăgōōs." But, as still with these alterations the year would not coincide properly with the true solar one, at certain intervals when the irregularity has accumulated so as to be inconvenient, the king, on the advice of the Brahmin astrologers, makes an arbitrary alteration.

The year is likewise divided into three ဥတု *ŏŏtŏŏ,* "seasons," or ကာလ *kală,* "times," viz., ဆောင်ကာလ *tshoung kală,* or "cold season," which commences on the day of the full moon of တံဆောင်မုံး *tădzoungmŏŏns,* or "November," and continues up to the day of the full moon of တပေါင်း *tăboungs,* or "March:" the နွေးကာလ *nwés kală,* or "hot season," which commences on the day of the full moon of March, and continues to the day of the full moon of ဝါဆို *watshō*, or "July:" and the မိုဃ်းကာလ *mōghskală*, or "rainy season," which begins on the day of the full moon of July, and continues to the beginning of the cold season.

These seasons are explained by the courses of the Sun, and Planets around the mythological mount မြင်းမိုရ် *myĕngs mō*. The cold season corresponding to the ဗာဟိရဝိထိ *baheeră wiemie*, "the outer," or "more distant course." The hot season corresponds to the အန္တောဝိထိ *ăndău wiemie*, "the inner," or "nearer course." And the rainy season corresponds to the မဇ္ဈေဝိထိ *mătstshé wiemie*, or "middle course." Besides this there is a season called the ဝါတွင်း *wa dwĕngs*, "fast season, or lent," consisting of three months of the year, viz. from the beginning of ဝါဆို *watshō*, "July," including ဝါခေါင် *wa khoung*, "August," and တော်သလင်း *dăŭthălĕngs*, "September," and ending at the beginning of October, which is hence called ဝါကျွတ် *wakywĕt* or "lent finished."

The Era of Burmah.

There are two epochs from which the Burmese date. The one called the sacred Era, being the date that Găŭdămă entered Nieban, or "Annihilation," viz. B. C. 543; the other the vulgar epoch, A. D. 639, established by king Puppachan Rahan. Vide Prinsep's Tables.

Orthography.

It may almost be stated that there is no such thing as *Orthography* in the Burmese language; the mode of spelling varying in a most arbitrary manner and that too in every writing from an imperial edict down to a peasant's letter.

But it may be given as a summary rule, "That all letters having in any way a cognate power are found interchangeably written for each other;" thus in all those cases given in the tables of the permutations of the powers of final consonants, at p. 18, those consonants are found interchangeably written; likewise the "Linguals," and the letters ဇ and ဈ which are borrowed from the Pali language, are often found expressed by the corresponding dentals, and by the letters စ and ဆ; as ပထမ *păhtămă*, for ပဌမ *păhṭămă*, "the first;" စရပ် *tsărat*, for ဇရပ် *dzărăt*, a kind of "serai," or halting place. The following variations will hence be more easily understood ဗေထင် for ဗေဒင် the Védas; တပ် for တတ် "to be skilled in;" ဆိပ် for ဆိတ် "to be silent;" and ဆိတ် for ဆိပ် "a landing place;" ခုနှစ် for ခွနှစ် "seven;" ခြီး for ခရီး "a way." The Burmese cannot pronounce an "r," but as a "y," thus ရုံ, ရုန်, or ရုမ် and ယုံ, ယုန်, or ယုမ် "a hall of justice," are found interchangeably written. ံ, န်, မ် final are very frequently written for one another. When the character ° *thés thés těng*, terminates a word bearing the း, *shépouk*, or heavy accent, frequently a final မ်း *m*, with an additional heavy accent is superadded; thus ပတ်လုံးမ်း for ပတ်လုံး this occurs often in inscriptions. တဝတ် for တဝက် "a half;" ရွှန်း, or ရွှံး and ညွှန်း "mud, mire," are found written ဗွန်း and နွံး; ဝလွှန် for သလွှန် "a couch;" the vowel ` and ့ with the heavy accent, are found changed; as ဆွဲ for တွဲ "to hang, suspend." မယ် *may*, and လယ် *lay*, &c., are found in place of မည် *mee*, and လည် *lee*.

BURMESE INDEX.

အ *ă*.

အ *ă*, vowel; p. 1. has no symbol; p. 2. its class; p. 3. its power, inherent, permuted; p. 4. its permutations with finals; pp. 17, 18, 19. when takes accents; p. 20. privative; p. 33.

အ *ă*, mute consonant; p. 1. symbols of vowels combined with it; p. 2 and 14. presided over by the Sun; p. 25. its equivalent in *d. g.* system; p. 28.

အ *ă*, format prefix for verbals; p. 32. sometimes omitted; pp. 33. 145. format. pref. for adverbs; p. 164.

အကျွန် *ăkywŏn*, pers. pron. and comp. p. 67.

အကြောင်း *ăgyoung:*, idiomat. use of with fut. aff. p. 142.

အကြင် *ăgyĕng*, pron. adj. p. 72.

အချား *ăkhya:*, "an interval," critically expl. p. xiii. pron. adj. p. 72. its adv. comp. p. 77.

အခွက် *ăkhwĕt*, measure of weight; p. 170.

အင်္ဂါ *ănga*, "Mars, Tuesday;" p. 174.

အညီး *ăgnyee:*, comp. caus. aff. p. 62.

အဏုမြူ *ănŏŏmyŏŏ*, measure of weight; p. 169.

အတိ *ădie*, pron. interrog. p. 77.

အထိုင်း *ădŏing:*, comp. caus. aff. p. 62.

အနည် *ănee*, dem. pron. p. 70.

အန္တောဝိဓိ *ăntău wiedhie* "inner course," p. 177.

အစ် *ăt*, aux. verb. aff. p. 154.

အပြီးနေ့ *ăbyee:nĕ*, "Sabbath;" p. 174.

အဘယ် *ăbhay*, pron. interrog. and comp. p. 71.

အမုတ် *ămŏŏk*, } measure of distance; p. 167.
အမိုက် *ămŏik*, }

အရင် *ărĕng*, comp. caus. aff. p. 64.

အလျောက် *ălyouk*, comp. caus. aff. p. 64.

အလွန် *ăhlwŏn*, pref. of superlat. deg. p. 86.

အသူ *ăthŏŏ*, } contract. p. 71.
အသို *ăthŏ*, }

အံ *ăn*, } fut. temp. aff. p. 134. with dat. caus. aff. expresses infinit. mood, p. 142.
အံမည် *ănmee*, }

အံမြစ် *ăn myeet*, light accent; p. 20.

အာ *a*.

အာ *a*, vowel; p. 1. its symbol; p. 2. its class; p. 3. power; p. 4. takes accents; p. 20. equival. in *k. t.* system; p. 32.

အား *aa:*, critically expl. p. xv. caus. aff. p. 48.

အိင် *ieng*, format. aff. for comp. subst. p. 41.

အေးအေး *é: é:*, } interject. p. 166.
အဲ *ai*, }

အောက် *ouk*, comp. caus aff. p. 58. aff. of inferior degree of compar. p. 83.

အောက်မြစ် *ouk myeet*, light accent; p. 20.

အောင် *oung*, mod. aff. subj. p. 139. forms adverbs; p. 165.

အောမယ် *ăŭmay*, interj. p. 166.

အော် *ăă*, } interj. p. 166.
အော်အော် *ăăăă*, } interj. p. 166.

အို *ō*, tripthong, power, symbol, and permutation; p. 3. equiv. in *k. t.* system; p. 26. vocative; p. 57. dem. pron. p. 70. interj. p. 166.

ဣ *ie.*

ဣ *ie*, vowel; p. 1. symbol; p. 2. class; p. 3. power, and variations; p. 4. when takes accents; p. 20. equiv. in *k. g.* system; p. 25.

ဤ *ee.*

ဤ *ee*, vowel; p. 1. symbol; p. 2. class; p. 3. power, and variations; p. 4. equivalent in *k. g.* system; p. 25. takes accents; p. 20.

ဤ *ee*, dem. pron. p. 70. its adv. comp. p. 73.

ဤမည် *ee mee*, pron. adj. p. 72.

ဥ *ŏŏ.*

ဥ *ŏŏ*, vowel; p. 1. symbol; p. 2. class; p. 3. power, permutation, variation; p. 5. takes accents; p. 20. equiv. in *k. g.* system; p. 26.

ဥတု *ŏŏtŏŏ*, "season;" p. 176.

ဥပုသ်နေ့ *ŏŏpŏŏthnė*, "Sabbath;" p. 174.

ဥသဘာ *ŏŏthăbhă*, measure of distance; p. 167.

ဦ *ōō.*

ဦ *ōō*, vowel; p. 1. symbol; p. 2. class; p. 3. power, permut. and variat. p. 5. takes accents; p. 20. equiv. in *k. g.* system; p. 26.

ဦး *ōō:*, comp. caus. aff. p. 59. gener. aff. p. 102. mod. aff. imperat. p. 137. aux. verb. aff. p. 154.

ဧ *é.*

ဧ *é*, vowel p. 1. symbol p. 2. class p. 3. power, and variat. p. 5. takes accents; p. 20. equiv. in *k. g.* system; p. 26. equiv. in *d. g.* system; p. 28.

ဧည် *éee*, nature of expl. p. xviii. abbr. p. 23. caus. aff. p. 48. pron. adj. p. 69. narrat. verb. aff. 134.

အဲ *ai.*

အဲ *ai*, vowel; p. 1. symbol; p. 2. class; p. 3. power, variat. p. 5. takes accents; p. 20.

ဩ *ăŭ.*

ဩ *ăŭ*, vowel; p. 1. symbol; p. 2. class; p. 3. power, and permut. p. 5. takes accent; p. 20. equiv. in *k. g.* system; p. 26.

ဩဋ္ဌဇ *ăŭthțădză*, "labial;" pp. 3. and 5.

ဪ *ăă.*

ဪ *ăă*, vowel; p. 1. symbol; p. 2. class; p. 3. power, and permut. p. 5.

က *kă.*

က *kă*, consonant; p. 1. class; p. 5. name; p. 6. power, and permut. p. 16. other permut. p. 16. presided over by the Moon; p. 24. equiv. in *d. g.* system; p. 27. format. pref. in adverbs; p. 164.

က *gă*, caus. aff. pp. 45 and 56. expresses "time;" p. xxiii. past. aff. p. 144.

က် *k*, permutes power of preceding tripth. p. 3. item inherent vowel; p. 4. and

17. item vowel *ăü*; p. 5. permut. pp. 8 and 17. abbr. p. 23.

ကင်းခြေများ *kĕngःkhrĕ myaः*, "the Scorpion;" p. 175.

ကစား *gătsaः*, miscell. aff. p. 158.

ကဆုံ *kătshŏŏn*, "May;" p. 175.

ကတည်းက *găteeःgă*, miscell. aff. p. 158.

ကတ် *kăt*, "hard," used with names of measures, &c. to express "a *full* measure; ကတ်တောင် *kăt toung*, "a full stretched cubit."

ကညစ်ခြေ *kăgnyeet khyĕ*, measure of weight; p. 169.

ကညာ *kăgnya*, "the Virgin;" p. 175.

ကဏ္ဌဇ *kăṇṭhṭădză*, "guttural; pp. 3 and 5.

ကန် *kăn*, "Virgo;" p. 175.

ကလေ *kălĕ*, aff. of diminutives; p. 38.

ကရကတ် *kărăgăt*, "Cancer;" p. 175.

ကား *gaः*, caus. aff. p. 44. referred to; p. xxiii. pres. part. aff. p. 144.

ကာလ *kală*, "seasons;" p. 176. deriv. given; p. xii.

ကုန် *gŏŏn*, num. aff. for verbs; p. 131.

ကုန်း *gŏŏnः*, gener. aff. p. 111.

ကုံ *gŏŏn*, "Aquarius;" p. 176.

ကဲ့ *kại*, euph. aff. p. 163.

ကဲ့သို့ *gạithọ̄*, caus. aff. p. 56. dem. pron. p. 71.

ကော *găü*, ကောလေ *găülĕ*, } euph. explet. aff. p. 163.

ကောင် *young*, gen. aff. p. 104.

ကောင်း *goungः*, root expl. p. xiii. mod. aff. subj. p. 140. abbr. p. 23.

ကောသ *găüthă*, measure of distance; p. 168.

ကို *gō*, caus. aff. p. 46.

ကိုရှင် *kōshĕng*, term of compellation; p. 63.

ကိုယ် *kōh*, pron. subst. corrupt. and abbrev. p. 67. gen. aff. p. 111. comb. with တ *tă*; p. 118.

ကိုယ်ကြပ် *kōh gyăt*, pron. p. 68.

ကိုယ်တော် *kōhdāū*, pron. subst. p. 68.

ကိုယ်ရို *kōhrō*, corrupt. p. 67.

ကိုယ်ရှင် *kōhshĕng*, pron. p. 68.

ကိုး *kō:*, numeral, its meaning explained; p. 89.

ကျွန်ုပ် *kyănŏŏk*, pron. subst. p. 66.

ကျား *kyaः*, root analysed; p. xiv. implies a "Tiger," and is used as a generic prefix to names of all large beasts of prey.

ကျိပ် *kyiet*, used to express "decades" of rational beings; p. 98.

ကျုပ် *kyŏŏk*, abbr. p. 67.

ကျေ *kyĕ*, comp. caus. aff. p. 61.

ကျောက်စာဂဏန်း *kyouktsagăṇănः*, a numerical mode of writing the Alphabet, explained; p. 25.

ကျော် *gyāū*, num. aux. p. 122.

ကြ *kyă*, ကြကုံန် *kyăgŏŏn*, } num. aff. of verbs; p. 131.

ကြပ် *kyăt*, measure of weight; p. 170.

ကြာသပတေး *kyathăbădĕः*, "Thursday;" p. 175. "Jupiter," referred to p. xxxviii.

ကြိမ် *gyien*, num. aux. p. 119.

ကြောင်း *gyoungः*, abbr. p. 23. comp.

caus. aff. p. 64. gener. aff. p. 108. miscell. aff. p. 162.

ကြောင့် *gyoụng*, abbr. p. 23. caus. aff. p. 50. expresses "time;" p. xxiii. miscell. aff. p. 159.

ကွ *kwă*, compounded with a dat. caus. aff. p. 51. use with တ *tă*; p. 117.

ကွင်း *kwĕng:*, gen. aff. p. 111.

ကွယ် *kway*, pron. subst. comp. and abbr. p. 68.

ကျွတ် *kywăt*, num. adjunct. its use with တ *tă*; p. 115.

ကျွန်စား *kywŏn tsa:*, measure of capacity; p. 172.

ကျွန်တော် *kywŏndău*, pron. subst. and comp. p. 67.

ကျွန်နုပ် *kywŏnnŏŏk*, pron. subst. and comp. pp. 66 and 67.

ခ *khă*.

ခ *khă*, consonant; p. 1. takes 2d symbol of 2d vowel; p. 3. its class; p. 5. name; p. 6. power, and variat. p. 8. permuted; p. 16. presided over by Moon; p. 24. equiv. in *d. g.* system; p. 27.

ခ် *kh*, how permuted; p. 20.

ခတ် *khăt*, v. ကတ် *kăt*. item aux. verb. aff. p. 154.

ခင် *khĕng*, aux. aff. negat. mood; p. 150.

ခင့် *khẹ̆ng*, aux. aff. of indef. time; p. 135.

ခင်း *khĕng:*, gen. aff. p. 111.

ခဏ *khăṇă*, measure of time; p. 172.

ခန့် *khặn*, num. aux. p. 122.

ခမန်း *khămăn:*, part. term; pp. 37 and 143.

ခလေ *khălé*, aff. of diminutives; p. 34.

ခရာ *khăra*, measure of time; p. 172.

ခံ *khăn*, aux. adjunct. with intrans. verbs; p. 128.

ခု *khŏŏ*, gen. aff. p. 112. used with တ *tă*; p. 116.

ခဲ *khai*, aux. verb. aff. p. 154.

ခဲ့ *khại*, aux. aff. of indef. time; p. 135. mod. aff. imperat. p. 137. euph. aff. p. 163.

ခေါက် *khouk*, num. aux. p. 120.

ခိုက် *khŏik*, form. aff. for comp. subst. p. 39.

ချက် *khyĕt*, form. aff. for verbals, p. 36. gen. aff. p. 111.

ချက်တီ *khyĕttee*, term of "time," p. 172; used as. gen. aff. p. 173.

ချင် *khyĕng*, mod. aff. optat. p. 141.

ချင်ရွေး *khyĕngrwé:*, measure of weight; p. 170.

ချင်သေ့ *khyĕng thẹ́*, "the Lion;" p. 175.

ချင်း *khyĕng:*, format. term. for verbals, p. 33. for comp. subst. p. 39. pers. pron. p. 69. num. aux. p. 123. miscell. aff. p. 157.

ချည်း *khyee:*, miscell. aff. p. 158.

ချပ် *khyăt*, gen. aff. p. 109.

ချမ်း *khyăn:*, num. aux. pp. 97. 121.

ချား *khya:*, critically analysed; p. xii. use with တ *tă*; p. 116. [p. 162.

ချိန့် *khyiẹn*, euphon. and explet. aff.

ချိန် *khyeen*, used explet. with words of time; p. 40.

ချိန် *khyien*, "the Scales;" p. 175.

ချိန့် *khyiẹn*, euph. aff. p. 162.

ချေ *khyé*, mod. aff. imperat. p. 137. euph. aff. p. 63.

ချောင်း *khyoung:*, gen. aff. p. 110.

ခြင်း *khrĕng:*, format. term. for verbals; p. 33.

ခြည် *khree*, mod. aff. imperat. p. 137.

ခြေ *khré*, euph. aff. p. 163.

ခွက် *khwĕt*. gen. aff. p. 111.

ခွန်း *khwŏn:*, gen. aff. p. 110.

ခွဲ *khwai*, measure of capacity; p. 171.

ဂ *gă*.

ဂ *gă*, consonant; p. 1. takes 2d symbol of 2d vowel; p. 3. its class; p. 5. its name; p. 6 power; p. 8. presided over by Moon; p. 24.

ဂ် *g*, how permuted; p. 20.

ဂနန်း *gănăn:*, "the Crab;" p. 175.

ဂမန်း *gămăn:*, part. term; p. 37 and 143. miscell. aff. p. 160.

ဂါဝုတ် *găwŏŏk*, measure of distance; p. 168.

ဃ *ghă*.

ဃ *ghă*, consonant; p. 1. class; p. 5. name; p. 6. power, and variat. p. 8. presided over by Moon; p. 24.

ဃ် *gh*, how permuted; p. 20.

င *gnă*.

င *gnă*, consonant; p. 1. takes 2d symbol of 2d vowel; p. 3. its class; p. 5. and 7. power; p. 8. presided over by Moon; p. 24. equiv. in *d. g.* system; p. 27.

င် *ng*, permutes power of preceding triphth; p. 3. item of inherent vowel; p. 18. item vowel *ăŭ*; p. 5 and p. 9. superior. abbr. p. 23.

ငါ *gna*, pers. pron. ref. to; p. xxiii. pron. subst. p. 66.

ငါး *gna:*, "the Fish;" p. 176.

ငါးမန်း *gna:măn:*, "the Sea Monster;" p. 176.

ငြား *gnra:*, euph. aff. p. 163.

ငှါ *gnha*, caus. aff. p. 49. expresses "time;" p. xxiii. used with fut. aff. to form Infinitive; p. 142.

စ *tsă*.

စ *tsă*, consonant; p. 1. class; p. 5. name; p. 6. power; p. 9. permut. p. 16. presided over by Mars; p. 24. equiv. in *d. g.* system; p. 27.

စ *tsă*, format. aff. for comp. subst. p. 38. aux. verb. aff. p. 155. euph. aff. p. 163.

စ် *ts*, permut. of inherent vowel before; pp. 4 and 18. own power permut. p. 9.

စက် *tsĕt*, deriv. given; p. xii.

စကြဝတိ *tsĕkyă wătie*, epithet expl. p. xxix.

စင် *tsĕng*, } miscell. aff. p. 158.
စင်စစ် *tsĕngtseet*, }

စင်း *tsĕng:*, num. gen. aff. p. 106.

စင် *tsĕng*, interrog. aff. p. 147.

စည် *tsee*, abbr. p. 23. miscell. aff. p. 158.

စန္ဒ *tsăndă*, "Moon;" p. 174.

စနေ *tsăné*, "Saturday;" p. 175.

စနိုး *tsănō:*, aux. verb. aff. p. 155.

စဖွယ် *tsăphway*, format. and particip. aff. p. 37. and 143.

စဘူး *tsăbhōō:*, aux. aff. of negation; p. 151.

စမ် *tsăn*, mod. aff. imperat. p. 137. aux. verb aff. p. 154.

စမ်ပါ *tsănba*, mod. aff. imperat. p. 137.

စရာ *tsăra*, format. term for verbals; p. 34.

စရွတ် *tsărwŏt*, measure of capacity; p. 171.

စရွေ့ *tsărwé̤*, its use with ablative caus. aff. pp. 55 and 56.

စလယ် *tsălay*, measure of capacity; p. 171.

စလိ *tsălie*, format. aff. p. 37.

စလုံး *tsălōōn:*, num. aux. p. 122.

စံ့ *tsạn*, interrog. aff. p. 147.

စာငှက် *tsa gnhĕt*, "sparrow," referred to; p. xxvii.

စား *tsa:*, format. aff. for comp. subst. p. 39.

စိတ် *tsiet*, "mind," deriv. given; p. xii. miscell. aff. p. 159.

စိတ် *tsiet*, fract. num. p. 97. num. aux. p. 121. measure of capacity; p. 171.

စိမ့် *tsiẹn*, fut. of စေ *tsé*, q. v.

စီ *tsee*, num. aux. p. 123.

စီး *tsee:*, gen. aff. p. 107.

စီးရွေ့ *tsee:rwé̤*, aux. adjunct. of comparison; p. 82. may be omitted; p. 84.

စု *tsŏŏ*, used with numerals; p. 116.

စုံ *tsŏŏn*, used with တ *tă*, redupl. p. 115. num. aux. p. 122.

စေ *tsé*, aff. of action; p. 127. aux. verb. aff. p. 154.

စေတံ *tsétăn*, Pali, referred to; p. xii.

စေပါ *tséba*, စေလို *tsélō*, စေသော *tséthău*, စေသတည်း *tséthătee:*, mod. aff. imperat. p. 137.

စေ့ *tsẹ́*, comb. with တ *tă*; p. 118.

စောက် *tsouk*, mod. aff. potent. p. 141.

စောက်ဖတ် *tsoukhpăt*, interject. p. 166.

စောင်း *tsoung:*, gen. aff. p. 109.

စိုးလို *tsō:lō*, miscell. aff. p. 159.

စို့ *tsō̤*, mod. aff. imperat. p. 137.

စွ *tswă*, miscell. aff. p. 158.

စွန်း *tswŏn:*, superlat. aff. p. 87.

စွာ *tswa*, expresses superlativeness; p. 87. adv. term. p. 163. euphon. aff. p. 163.

ဆ *tshă*.

ဆ *tshă*, consonant; p. 1. class; p. 5. name; p. 6. power and variat. p. 9. permut. p. 16. presid. over by Mars; p. 24. equiv. in *d. g.* system; p. 28.

ဆ *tshă*, num. aux. p. 121.

ဆန်း *tshăn:*, miscell. aff. p. 161.

ဆံချည် *tshănkhyee*, measure of distance; p. 167.

ဆံစေ့ *tshăntsẹ́*, measure of weight; p. 170.

ဆီ *tshee*, comp. caus. aff. p. 60.

ဆုံး *tshŏŏn:*, comp. caus. aff. p. 61. aff. of superlat. deg. p. 86.

ဆူ *tshōō*, gen. aff. p. 103.

ဆဲ *tshai*, aux. aff. of pres. tense; p. 134.

ဆောင် *tshoung*, gen. aff. p. 108.

ဆောင်းကာလ *tshoung kală*, "cold season; p. 176.

ဇ *dză*.

ဇ *dză*, consonant; p. 1. class; p. 5. name; p. 6. power, and variat. p. 9. presided over by Mars; p. 24.

ဇာ *dză*, corrupt of ဘာ *bha*, p. 71.

ဈ *dzhă*.

ဈ *dzhă*, consonant; p. 1. class; p. 5. name; p. 6. power, and variat. p. 9. presided over by Mars; p. 24.

ဉ gnyă.

ဉ gnyă, consonant; p. 1. class; pp. 5 and 7. power, and variat. p. 9. presided over by Mars; p. 24. equiv. in d. g. syst. p. 28.

ဉ် gny. permut. of inherent vowel with; pp. 4 and 18. quiescent; pp. 9 and 18. abbr. p. 23.

ညဉ့် gnyeen, "night," measure of time; p. 172.

ညာ gnya, comp. caus. aff. p. 61.

ညား gnyaː, euph. aff. p. 163.

ညီ gnyee, comp. with caus. aff. p. 84. use with တ tă; p. 117.

ဋ ṭă.

ဋ ṭă, consonant; p. 1. class; p. 5. name; p. 6. power and variat. p. 10. permut. p, 16. how written when comp. with ဌ hṭă; p. 34. presided over by Saturn; p. 24.

ဌ hṭă,

ဌ hṭă, consonant; p. 1. class; p. 5. name; p. 6. power, and variar. p. 10. permut. p. 16. how written when comp. with ဋ ṭă; p. 24. presided over by Saturn; p. 24.

ဍ ḍă.

ဍ ḍă, consonant; p. 1. class; p. 5. name; p. 6. power, and variat. p. 10. inf. how abbrev. p. 24. with ဎ ḍhă, under it, how written; p. 24. presided over by Saturn; p. 24.

ဎ ḍhă.

ဎ ḍhă, consonant; p. 1. class; p. 5. name; p. 6. power and variat. p. 10 with ဍ ḍă, over it how written; p. 24. presided over by Saturn; p. 24.

ဏ ṇă.

ဏ ṇă, consonant; p. 1. class; p. 5. name; p. 6. power and variat. p. 10. presided over by Saturn; p. 24.

ဏ် ṇ, sometimes permutes power of inherent vowel; p. 4.

တ tă.

တ tă, consonant; p. 1. class; p. 5. name; p. 6. permut. p. 16. presided over by Saturn; p. 24. equiv. in d. g. system; p. 28.

တ tă, numeral; p. 90. combined with various roots; p. 114. et seq.

တ tă, format pref. for adv. p. 163.

တ် t, permut. p. 10.

တကာ tăga, used as pronoun; p. 68.

တကား tăgaː, miscell. aff. p. 157.

တကွဲနက် tăkwănĕt, meaning of; p. 117.

တခဲနက် tăkhainĕt, meaning of; p. 117.

တချား tăkhyaː, "another," analysed; p. xiii.

တင်း tĕngː, measure of capacity; p. 172.

တည်း teeː, num. aux. p. 123. miscell. aff. p. 161 and 162.

တဦ့ tẹe, abbr. p. 23.

တတ် tăt, format. aff. for comp. subst. p. 39. aux. verb. aff. p. 153.

တနင်္ဂနွေ tănĕnggănwé, "Sunday;" p. 174.

တနင်္လာ tănĕngla, "Monday;" 174.

တန် tan, gener. aff. p. 110.

တန်ဆောင်မုန်း *tădzoungmŏŏn:,* "November;" p. 175.

တန်း *tăn:,* gener. aff. 107.

တပေါင် *tăboung,* "March;" p. 176.

တပို့တွဲ *tăbọ̆dwai,* "February;" p. 176.

တပြိုင်နက် *tăpyŏingnĕt,* meaning of; p. 117.

တပ် *tăt,* miscell, pref. p. 162.

တပြည့်တော် *tăbyẹe dāū,* pron. p. 67.

တမုံ့ *tămŏọn,* explet. aff. p. 163.

တမူ *tămŏŏ,* explet. aff. p. 163.

တမူကား *tămŏŏga:,* subj. or supposit. aff. p. 138. past. part. aff. p. 145.

တယ် *tay,* superl. pref. p. 86.

တဝတည် *tăwătee,* meaning of. p. 118.

တံကူ *tăgŏŏ,* "April;" p. 175. intercal. in Arracan; p. 176.

တာ *ta,* measure of distance; p. 167.

တာလုဇ *tălŏŏdză,* "palatal;" 3 and 5.

တုံ *tŏŏn,* interrog. aff. p. 147. explet. aff. p. 163.

တုံ့ *dŏọn,* aux. verb. aff. p. 155.

တူ *tŏŏ,* root explained; p. xvii. comp. with နှင့် *hnẹng;* p. 52 and 84. with တ *tă;* p. 117.

တောင် *toung,* measure of distance; p. 167.

တောင်း *toung:,* miscell. aff. p. 158.

တော့ *dạū,* mod. aff. imperat. p. 137. miscell. aff. p. 158.

တော် *dāū,* honor. increm. origin of; p. xlii. its use with nouns; p. 65. comp. caus. aff. how used with it; p. 66. with pronoun adj. p. 69. with verbs; p. 145.

တော်သလင် *tāūthălĕng,* "September;" p. 175.

တိုင် *tŏing,* measure of distance; p. 168.

တိုင်အောင် *tŏingoung,* comp. caus. aff. p. 62.

တိုင်တိုင် *tŏingtŏing,* comp. caus. aff. p. 63.

တိုးအလေး *tŏ:ălé,* "a weight;" p. 171.

တိုးရွေ *tŏ: rwé,* adjunct. of comparison; p. 82.

တို့ *dŏ,* deriv. given; p. xix. aff. of plur. num. p. 41. abbr. of pers. pron. plur. p. 66.

တွင် *dwĕng,* caus. aff. p. 53.

တွင်း *dwịng:,* comp. cans. aff. p. 61.

ထ *htă.*

ထ *htă,* consonant; p. 1. class; p. 5. name; p. 6. power; p. 10. permut. p. 16. pres. over by Saturn; p. 24. equiv. in *k. g.* system; p. 28.

ထ *htă,* euph. aff. p. 163.

ထက် *htĕt,* comp. caus. aff. p. 58. aff. of comparison; p. 82. its meaning when used alone; p. 86.

ထည် *htee,* gener. aff. p. 108.

ထတ် *htăt,* assertive aff. used at close of a para.

ထပ် *htăt,* gener. aff. p. 112.

ထံ *htăn,* comp. caus. aff. p. 60.

ထား *hta:,* aux. adjunct. with act. verbs; p. 128.

ထီး *htee:,* aff. of mas. gend. p. 42.

ထူး *htŏŏ:,* root explained; p. xvii. comb. with တ *tă;* p. 118.

ထဲ *htai*, comp. caus. aff. p. 60.

ထို *htō*, dem. pron. p. 70. compd. p. 74.

ထိုမဟုတ် *htōmăhō*, conjunct. p. 165.

ထိုက် *htōik*, aux. verb. aff. p. 154.

ထွာ *htwa*, measure of distance; p. 167.

ထွေး *htwé:*, gener. aff. p. 106.

ဒ *dă.*

ဒ *dă*, consonant; p. 1. takes 2d symb. of 2d vowel; p. 3. class; p. 5. name; p. 6. power and variat. p. 11. pres. over by Saturn; p. 24.

ဒန္တဇ *dăntădză*, "dentals;" p. 5.

ဒူ *dōō*, "Libra;" p. 175.

ဒူးဂဏန်း *dōō:gănăn:*, system of occult writing expl. p. 27.

ဓ *dhă.*

ဓ *dhă*, consonant; p. 1. class; p. 5. name; p. 6. power and variat. p. 11. pres. over by Saturn; p. 24.

ဓနု *dhănōō*, "Sagittarius;" p. 176.

န *nă.*

န *nă*, consonant; p. 1. class; pp. 5 and 7. name; p. 6. power; p. 11. pres. over by Saturn; p. 24. equiv. in *d. g.* system; p. 28.

န် *n*, when permutes power of inher. vowel p. 4. own permut. pp. 11 and 19.

နင် *nēng*, pers. pron. p. 68.

နည်း *nee:*, interrog. aff. p. 147.

နတ်တော် *nătdāū*, "December;" p. 176.

နယုန် *năyōōn*, "June;" p. 175.

နံ *năn*, format. aff. with nouns; p. 71.

နာရီ *naree*, a measure of time; pp. 172 and 173.

နား *na:*, comp. caus. aff. p. 60.

နိဗ္ဗာန် *niebbhan*, "annihilation;" referred to; pp. xxx. and xlix.

နီး *nee:*, comp. caus. aff. p. 60.

နေ *né*, aux. verb. aff. p. 153.

နေဝင် *néwēng*, "Sunset;" p. 172.

နေထွက် *nédwēt*, "Sunrise;" p. 172.

နေ့ *né*, "a day," measure of time; p. 172.

နောက် *nouk*, comp. caus. aff. p. 59.

နော် *nāū*, interrog. and precat. aff. p. 148.

နိုင် *nōing*, mod. aff. potent. p. 141.

နိုး *nō:*, aux. verb. aff. p. 155.

နို့ *nō*, corrupt. p. 73.

နွားလှည်ဿဘ *nwa:hleeththăbhă*, "the Bull;" p. 175.

နွေးကာလ *nwé:kală*, "hot season;" pp. 176 and 177.

နှန် *hnăn*, measure of distance; p. 167.

နှင့် *hnēng*, caus. aff. p. 50. aff. of similar degree of comparison; p. 84. aux. aff. of indef. time; p. 135. aff. of pres. part. p. 144. aux. aff. of negat. mood; p. 150. forms adverbs; 164.

နှစ် *hneet*, numeral, used in questions; p. 71. measure of time, "year;" p. 172.

နှစ်လုံး *hneetlōōn:*, "heart," referred to; p. xxvii.

နှံစေ့ *hnăntsé*, measure of weight; p. 170.

နှာလဒနီ *hnalădănie*, "nasals;" p. 7.

နှိုက် *hnōit*, aff. of pres. part. time; p. xxiii. abbr. p. 23. caus. aff. p. 52.

နှိုင် *hnōing*, mod. aff. potent. p. 140.

ပ *pă.*

ပ *pă*, consonant; p. 1. takes 2d symb. of 2d vowel; p. 3. class; p. 5. name; p. 7. power; p. 11. permut. p. 16. pres. over by Jupiter; p. 25. equiv. in *d. g.* system; p. 28.

ပ *pă*, comp. caus. aff. p. 59. prefix for adv. p. 164.

ပ *pă*, abbrev. for ဘယ် *bhay*, p. 71.

ပ် *p*, permut. with inherent and other vowels; pp. 11 and 19.

ပက္ခ *păkkha*, measure of time; p. 172.

ပချင် *păkhyien*, interrog. comb. explained; p. 148.

ပင် *pĕng*, gener. aff. p. 110.

ပင် *pĕng*, miscell. aff. p. 158.

ပဉ္စ *pĕgnytsă*, numb. "five" analysed; p. x. referred to; p. 90.

ပတ်လည် *pătlee*, comp. caus. aff. p. 63.

တတ်လုံး *pătlŏŏn:*, comp. caus. aff. p. 63.

ပန်လုံး *pănlŏŏn:*, comp. caus. aff. p. 63.

ပရမာဏုမြို *părămănŏŏmyŏŏ*, measure of distance; p. 169.

ပယ် *pay*, measure used in assessment of land; 560 cubits square (Judson.)

ပါ *pa*, ⎫
ပါစေ *patsé*, ⎭ mod. aff. imperat. p. 137.

ပါ *pa*, euph. aff. may be styled aff. of respect; from ပါ *pa*, "to obtain," i. e., by being given or allowed.

ပါဒ် *pad*, measure of time; p. 172.

ပါး *pa:*, comp. caus. aff. p. 59. gener. aff. p. 103. use with တ *tă*; p. 116.

ပိန် *pien*, euph. and explet. aff. p. 163.

ပိဿာ *piekththa*, measure of weight; p. 170.

ပုံးခေါင် *pŏŏ:khoung*, "Union of male and female;" p. 175.

ပေ *pé*, mod. aff. imperat. p. 137. euph. aff. p. 163.

ပဲး *pai:*, measure of weight; p. 170. expr. "one anna;" p. 170.

ပေါ *păŭ*, explet. aff. p. 163.

ပေါ် *păŭ*, comp. caus. aff. p. 58. euph. aff. p. 163.

ပို *pŏ*, "to exceed, heap up," aux. used in compos. as ပိုအိပ်သည် *pŏ iet thee*, "sleeps excessively."

ပိုင် *pŏing*, aux. verb. aff. p. 155.

ပိုင်း *pŏing:*, num. aux. to express, "fractions;" p. 120.

ပြ *pyă*, format. aff. for comp. subst; p. 40.

ပြင် *pyĕng*, comp. caus. aff. p. 59. conjunct. p. 163.

ပြင်း *pyĕng:*, aux. verb. aff. p. 153.

ပြစ် *pyeet*, format. of pass. voice; p. 130.

ပြည် *pyee*, measure of capacity; p. 171.

ပြည့် *pyee*, gener. aff. p. 112.

ပြန် *pyăn*, aux. verb. aff. p. 153. measure of time; p. 172. expresses "afternoon;" p. 173.

ပြာသိုလ် *pyathŏ*, "January;" p. 176.

ပြား *pya:*, gen. aff. p. 105.

ပြိစ္ဆာ *pyietstsha*, "Scorpio;" p. 175.

ပြိသာ *pyietha*, "Taurus;" p. 175.

ပြဟ်ပတိ *pyiethpătie*, "Jupiter;" p. 175.

ပြီး *pyee:*, temp. aff. critically explained;

p. xv. aff. of castrat. animals; p. 43. of past tense; p. 134.

ပြို *pyŏŏ*, aux. adjunct. with verbs; p. 128. aux. verb. aff. p. 153.

ပွားရွေ့ *pwa:rwé*, aux. adjunct. of comparison; p. 82. may be omitted; p. 84.

ဖ *hpă*.

ဖ *hpă*, consonant; p. 5. name; p. 7. power; p. 11. permut. p. 16. pres. over by Jupiter; p. 24. equiv. in *d. g.* syst. p. 28.

ဖ *hpă*, masc. aff. for birds; p. 43.

ဖက် *hpĕt*, gener. aff. p. 107. used with တ *tă*; p. 114.

ဖန် *hpăn*, comb. with တ *tă*; p. 118.

ဖားလောင်း *hpa:loung:*, "tadpole," referred to; p. xxxvii.

ဖုတ် *hpŏŏk*, format. aff. for comp. subst. p. 38.

ဖိုလ် *hpō*, aff. of masc. gen. p. 43.

ဖို *hpọ̄*, format. aff. for verbals; p. 36. caus. aff. p. 57.

ဖိုရာ *hpọ̄ra*, format. aff. for verbals; p. 36.

ဖြင့် *hpyęng*, critically expl. p. xv. refer. to; p. xvi. caus. aff. p. 52.

ဖြစ် *hpyeet*, subst. verb used to form pass. voice; pp. 129 and 130.

ဖွယ် *hpway*. format. term. p. 37.

ဗ *bă*.

ဗ *bă*, consonant; p. 1. class; p. 5. name; p. 7. power; p. 11. pres. over by Jupiter; p. 24.

ဗည်ဇနာ *beedzăna*, measure of time; p. 172.

ဗာဟိရဝိဓိ *baheerăwiedhie*, "outer course;" p. 177.

ဗုဒ္ဓ *bŏŏdhă*, root analysed; p. xxxvi. "Mercury;" p. 174.

ဗုဒ္ဓဟူး *bŏŏdhăhŏŏ:* "Wednesday;" p. 174.

ဗိုလ် *bŏh*, measure of "weight;" p. 170.

ဘ *bhă*.

ဘ *bhă*, consonant; p. 1. class; p. 5. name; p. 7. power; p. 12. pres. over by Jupeter; p. 24.

ဘက် *bhĕt*, gener. aff. p. 107.

ဘနှန်း *bhănąn:*, particip. term. p. 143. miscell. aff. p. 160.

ဘယ် *bhay*, pron. interrog. p. 71. its compounds; p. 74. its use with နှင့် *hneet*; p. 72. with မျှ *hmyă*; p. 72. with မျှ *hmyă*, and a negat. p. 77.

ဘယ်နှင့် *bhayhneet*, used in asking questions; p. 71. gen. aff. must be used with it; p. 114.

ဘာ *bha*, contract. p. 71.

ဘိ *bhie*, euph. aff. p. 163.

ဘု *bhŏŏ*, aux. aff. of indef. time; p. 135.

ဘုရား *bhŏŏra:*, analysed, and deriv. given; p. xxxiv.

ဘုရားလောင်း *bhŏŏra:loung*, term analysed; p. xxxvii.

ဘူး *bhŏŏ:*, indef. past aff. p. 134. aux. aff. negat. mood; p. 150.

ဘ *bhai*, aux. aff. negat. mood; p. 150.

ဘွယ် *bhway*, format. and particip. term with subst. p. 37.

မ *mă.*

မ *mă*, consonant; p. 1. class; pp. 5 and 7. power and permut. p. 12. when inf. how abbr. p. 23. pres. over by Jupiter; p. 24. symb. in *d. g.* syst. p. 28.

မ *mă*, format. aff. for comp. subst. p. 40. aff. of fem. gen. p. 43.

မ *mă*, particle of negation, peculiarly used; p. 77. use with verbs; p. 149.

မ် *m*, its permut. with certain vowels; pp. 12 and 19.

မဂ *măgă*, miscell. aff. p. 159.

မကာရ *măkară*, "Capricornus;" p. 176.

မင်း *mĕng*. pres. pron. p. 68.

မင်းတောင် *mĕng:toung*, measure of length; p. 168.

မဇ္ဈေဝိဓိ *mătstshé wiedhie*, "middle course;" p. 177.

မည် *mee*, pron. adj. p. 72. and comp. p. 76.

မည်သည် *meethee*, used for ဘယ် *bhay*; p. 77.

မည် *mee*, fut. aff. critically expl. p. xv. abbr. p. 23. aff. of fut. tens. p. 134. expresses Inf. mood; pp. 125 and 141.

မတ် *măt*, measure of weight; p. 170. expr. "four anna piece;" p. 171.

မတာတ် *mătăt*, particip. term. p. 143. miscell. aff. p. 160.

မိ *mie*, aux. verb. aff. p. 154. euph. aff. p. 163.

မိန် *mien*, "Pisces;" p. 176.

မိမိ *miemie*, pron. p. 68.

မိမ္မ *miemmă*, fem. adjunct; p. 42.

မိဿ *mietha*, "Aries;" p. 175.

မုဒ္ဓဇ *mŏŏddhăză*, "linguals;" p. 5.

မုယော *mŏŏyău*, measure of distance; p. 167.

မုံညင်းစေ *mŏŏngnyĕng:tsé*, measure of weight; p. 170.

မူ *mŏŏ*, aux. aff. honorif. mood; p. 145. takes all affixes; p. 146. interrog. aff. attached to it; p. 149. aux. in negat. of comp. relat. of verbs; p. 150.

မူ *mŏŏ*, မူကား *mŏŏga*, } caus. aff. p. 45. mod. aff. subj. p. 138. past. particip. aff. p. 145.

မူ *mŏŏ*, euph. aff. p. 163.

မူး *mŏŏ:*, measure of weight; p. 170. expr. "two anna piece;" p. 171.

မေထုန် *médŏŏn*, "Gemini;" p. 175.

မို့ *mọi*, aff. of negation; p. 152. referred to; p. xvi.

မောင်မင်း *moungmĕng*, pers. pron. p. 68.

မောင်ရှင် *moungshĕng*, pers. pron. p. 68.

မောင် *moung*, "gong;" p. 173.

မိုဃ်းကာလ *mŏghkală*, rainy season; p. 177.

မို *mọ̆*, miscell. aff. p. 160.

မိုတုံး *mọ̆dŏŏn:*, aff. of negation; p. 152.

များ *mya:*, aff. of indef. plur. p. 41. superlat. aff. p. 87.

မြင်းမိုရ် *myĕng:mŏ*, mytholog. mount mentioned; p. 177.

မြိတ် *myeet*, "stops," nature of expl. p. xxxiii.

မြိတ် *myeet*, မြိတ်လား *myeethla:*, } analysed; p. 128.

မြတ် *myăt*, sometimes aff. to express superlat. p. 88.

မြဲ *myai,* aux. verb. aff. p. 154.

မြူ *myōō,* measure of weight; p. 169.

မြောက် *myouk,* num. aux. p. 119. referred to; p. xxx.

မှ *hmă,* referred to; p. xxi and xxiii. caus. aff. p. 54. aff. of past. part. p. 144.

မှန် *hmăn,* referred to; p. xvii.

မှာ *hma,* referred to; p. xxi and xxiii. caus aff. p. 54. aff. of pres. particip. p. 144.

မှိ *hmie,* aux. verb. aff. p. 154.

မှိး *hmee:,* aux. aff. negat. mood; p. 150.

မှုန် *hmōŏn,* measure of weight; p. 169.

မှု *hmōō,* measure of weight; p. 169.

မှုး *hmōō:,* format. aff. for comp. subst. p. 40.

မျှ *hmyă,* used for indef. questions; p. 72. peculiarly used pp. 77 and 78.

မွန်း *mwŏn:,* "noon;" p. 173.

ယ *yă.*

ယ *yă,* consonant; p. 1. its class; p. 5. name; p. 7. power; p. 12. symb. when vocal; p. 15. pres. over by Mercury; p. 25. equiv. in *k. g.* syst. p. 26. ditto in *d. g.* syst. p. 28.

ယ် *y,* p. 12.

ယင် *yĕng,* dem. pron. p. 70. its comp. p. 74.

ယံ *yăn,* used explet. with words of time; p. 40.

ယူဇနာ *yōōdzăna,* measure of distance; p. 168.

ယောက် *youk,* gener. aff. p. 104.

ယောက်ျား *youkya:,* masc. adjunct. p. 42.

ရ *ră.*

ရ *ră,* consonant; p. 1. class; p. 6. name; p. 7. power and variat. p. 12. symb. when vocal; p. 15. pres. over by Mercury; p. 25. equiv. in *k. g.* syst. p. 26. ditto in *d. g.* syst. p. 28.

ရ *ră,* aux. adjunct. with certain verbs; p. 129. intervenes between root and fut. aff. p. 136. mod. aff. indicat. p. 137. expresses fut. tense in subj. mood; p. 139. item in interrog. mood; p. 148. item in negat. mood; p. 150. aux. verb. aff. p. 153.

ရ် *r,* p. 12.

ရကား *răga:,* caus. aff. p. 45.

ရက် *rĕt,* aux. verb. aff. p. 155.

ရက် *rĕt,* measure of time; p. 172.

ရင် *rĕng,* comp. caus. aff. p. 60. pron. adj. p. 70.

ရင်း *rĕng:,* miscell. aff. p. 159.

ရည် *ree,* format. aff. for comp. subst. p. 41.

ရစ် *reet,* mod. aff. imperat. p. 137.

ရစ် *reet,* aux. verb. aff. p. 153.

ရန် *răn,* / ရံ့ *răn,* } format. term. for verbals; p. 34. miscell. aff. p. 160.

ရဝ် *răt,* gen. aff. p. 109.

ရဝိ *răwie,* "Sun;" p. 174.

ရံ့ *răn,* used explet. with nouns of time; p. 40.

ရာ *ra,* format. aff. for verbals; p. 35. preceded by explet. p. 36.

ရာ *ra,* pecul. use of; p. 138. part. term. p. 143. roots term. in when negat. have fut. signif. p. 152. aux. verb. aff. p. 154.

ရုပ်နံ *rōōpnan,* miscell. aff. p. 160.

ရုံ *rŏŏn*, miscell. aff. p. 160.

ရေရွက်အိုး *rérwĕtō*, "the Waterpot;" p. 176.

ရော *răŭ*. mod. aff. imperat. p. 137. connect. aff. p. 156.

ရောက် *rouk*, comp. caus. aff. p. 64.

ရော့ *ră̦ŭ*, miscell. aff. p. 161.

ရွာ *rwa*, gen. aff. p. 112.

ရွေး *rwé:*, measure of weight; p. 170.

ရွေးကောက် *rwé:gouk*, "to choose," analysed; p. xxviii.

ရွေ့ *rwé̦*, abbr. p. 23. comp. caus. aff. p. 63. connect. aff. p. 156.

ရွဲကြီး *rwai gyee:*, measure of weight; p. 170.

ရှ *hr*, how pronounced; p. 12.

ရှင် *shĕng*, format. aff. for comp. subst. p. 40.

ရှာ *sha*, miscell. aff. p. 157.

ရှိ *shie*, subst. verb. format. aff. for comp. subst. p. 40. forms passive; p. 129.

ရှိရာ *shiera*, comp. caus. aff. p. 61.

ရှေ့ *shé̦*, comp. caus. aff. p. 58.

ရှေး *shé:*, "before," referred to; p. xlviii.

ရှေ့ပေါက် *shé̦pouk*, heavy accent; p. 20.

ရှောက် *shouk*, comp. caus. aff. p. 64.

ရွှေ *shwé*, analysed; p. xlii.

လ *lă*,

လ *lă*, consonant; p. 1. its class; p. 6. power and permut. p. 13. pres. over by Mercury; p. 25. equiv. in *d. g.* syst. p. 28.

လ *lă*, "month," measure of time; p. 172.

လက် *lĕt*, gen. aff. p. 111. measure of capacity; p. 171.

လက်သီး *lĕt thee:*, "the fist," referred to; p. xxviii.

လက်ခုပ် *lĕt khŏŏk*, measure of capacity; p. 171.

လကွယ် *lăkway*, "hiding of moon;" p. 174.

လငယ် *lăgnay*, "little moon;" p. 174.

လင် *lĕng*, "husband," deriv. given; p. xii.

လင့် *lĕ̦ng*, aux. aff. of indef. time; p. 135. and aff. of negat. mood; p. 150.

လင့်ကစား *lĕ̦nggătsa:*, miscell. aff. p. 161.

လင်းလေး *lĕng:lé:*, "the Bow;" p. 176.

လဆန်း *lă tshăn:*, "waxing moon;" p. 173.

လဆုတ် *lă tshŏŏk*, "waning moon;" p. 173.

လည် *lee*, abbr. p. 23.

လည်း *lee:*, mod. aff. imperat. p. 137. mod. aff. subj. p. 138. mod. aff. interrog. p. 147.

လည်း *lee:*, conjunction; p. 165.

လည်းကောင်း *lee:goung:*, abbr. p. 23. conj. p. 165.

လတ္တံ့ *lăttă̦n*, aff. of dist. fut. p. 135.

လတ် *lăt*, euph. and explet. aff. p. 163.

လပြည့် *lăbyee̦*, "full moon;" p. 173.

လပြည့်ကျော် *lăbyee̦gyău*, "past full moon;" p. 174.

လသစ် *lătheet*, "new moon;" p. 173.

လယ် *lay*, comp. caus. aff. p. 59.

လံ *lăn*, "fathom," measure of distance; p. 167.

လာ *la*, interrog. aff. p. 147.

လားလား *la:la:*, miscell. pref. p. 162.

လား *la:*, aff. of mas. gend. p. 43.

လိ *lie*, particip. term. p. 143.

လိင်္ဂ *lienggăn*, Pali. referred to ; p. xii.

လိဉ် *lien*, euph. and explet. aff. p. 163.

လိလိ *lielie*, particip. term. p. 143.

လိ *lee*, num. aux. p. 120.

လု *lŏŏ*, } aff. fut. tens. inf.
လုနီးပြီး *lŏŏnee: byee:*, } p. 142.

လုပ် *lŏŏk*, aux. adjunct. with act. verbs; p. 128.

လုလင် *lŏŏlĕng*, abbr. p. 23.

လုံး *lŏŏn:*, gen. aff. p. 105. use with တ p. 114. num. aux. p. 122.

လေ *lé*, aux. aff. of indef. time; p. 135. mod. aff. imperat. p. 137.

လေ *lé*, vocat. p. 47. use with gen. aff. and တ *tă*; pp. 116 and 117. (persist); p. 160. euphon. aff. p. 163. interject. p. 166.

လေ့ *lé*, aux. verb aff. p. 154.

လဲ *lai*, interrog. aff. p. 149.

လော *lău*, mod. aff. imperat p. 137. interrog. aff. p. 147.

လောက် *louk*, num. aux. p. 121. miscell. aff. p. 160.

လို *lo*, mod. aff. optat. p. 141. miscell. aff. p. 160. euphony. aff. p. 163.

လိုလို *lōlō*, miscell. aff. p. 160.

လို *lō*, } miscell. aff. p. 160.
လိုလည် *lōlee*, }

လိုက် *lōik*, mod. aff. imperat. p. 137.

လျက် *lyĕt*, mod. aff. subj. p. 138. past. part. aff. p. 145. aux. verb. aff. p. 155.

လျာ *lya*, caus. aff. p. 57.

လျား *lya:*, comp. caus. aff. p. 63.

လျော့ *lyău*, num. aux. p. 122.

လွှန် *lwŏn*, num. aux. p. 122.

လွန်ရွှေ *lwŏnrwé*, aux. adjunct. of comparison; p. 82. may be omitted; p. 84.

လွယ် *lway*, aux. verb. aff. p. 154.

လှန်လှည် *hlăn:hlee*, mod. aff. imperat. p. 137.

လှာ *hla*, euphon. aff. p. 163.

လျှ *hlyă*, how pronounced; p. 163.

လျှင် *hlyĕng*, mod. aff. subj. p. 138. supposit. aff. p. 139. past. part. aff. p. 145.

လျှင်း *hlyĕng:*, miscell. aff. p. 161.

လျှာ *hlya*, caus. aff. p. 57.

လျှား *hlya:* comp. caus. aff. p. 63.

လွှာ *hlwa*, gen. aff. p. 109.

ဝ *wă.*

ဝ *wă*, consonant; p. 1. takes 2d symb. of 2d. vowel; p. 3. inherent. vowel with, when permut. p. 4. class; p. 6. power and permut. p. 13. power when vocal; p. 13. symb. when a vowel; p. 15. pres. over by Mercury; p. 25. equiv. of symb. in *k. g.* syst. p. 26. equiv. in *d. g.* syst. p. 28.

ဝ် *w*, use and applicat. p. 13.

ဝက် *wĕt*, fract. numb. p. 97.

ဝန် *wŏn*, format. aff. for comp. subst. p. 40.

ဝန်းကြင် *wŏn:kyĕng*, comp. caus. aff. p. 63.

ဝန်းပတ် *wŏn:păt,* comp. caus. aff. p. 63.

ဝမ်းမြောက် *wŏn:myouk,* "to be glad," analysed; p. xxx.

ဝယ် *way,* caus. aff. p. 54.

ဝံ့ *wŏn,* aux. verb. aff. p. 153.

ဝါကျွတ် *wakywăt,* "October;" p. 175. explained; p. 177.

ဝါခေါင် *wakhoung,* "August;" p. 175. means "the height of Lent."

ဝါဆို *watshō,* "July;" p. 175. means "observance of Lent." intercalated; p. 176.

ဝါတွင်း *wadwĕng:,* "Lent;" p. 177.

ဝီထိ *wiedhie,* "(Sun's) path;" p. 177.

ဝေး *wé:,* comp. caus. aff. p. 60.

သ *thă.*

သ *thă,* consonant; p. 1. class; p. 6. power; p. 13. double how written; p. 24. pres. over by Venus; p. 25. equiv. in *d. g.* p. 28.

သင် *thĕng,* pres. pron. p. 68.

သင်း *thĕng:,* dem. pron. p. 71.

သင့် *thĕ̤ng,* aux. verb. aff. p. 154.

သစ် *theet,* measure of distance; p. 167.

သည် *thee,* connect. aff. nature of expl. p. xvii. abb. p. 23. format. aff. for comp. subst. p. 38. caus. aff. p. 44. expresses "time;" p. xxiii. connect. aff. p. 65. dem. pron. p. 70. relat. increm. p. 78. use in format. of adject. p. 79. aff. of pres. tense; p. 134. mod. aff. indicat. p. 136. referred to; p. xxxi. part. term. p. 143. connect. aff. p. 156.

သည်မဟုတ် *theemăhōh,* conjunct. p. 165.

သတင်းကျွတ် *thădĕng:kywăt,* "October;" p. 175. means "the observance completed."

သတ် *thăt,* its sign and use; p. 7. symb. in *k. g.* syst. p. 26.

သန္ဒူချောင် *thănŏŏkhoung,* measure of weight; p. 169.

သဖြင့် *thăpyĕ̤ng,* expresses "time;" p. xxiii. past. part. aff. p. 144.

သဖွယ် *thăhpway,* part. term. p. 143.

သမား *thăma:,* format. aff. for comp. subst. p. 39.

သလင်း *thălĕng:,* abbr. "September;" p. 175.

သယ် *thay,* format. aff. for comp. subst. p. 38.

သယ် *thay,* သယ်လေ *thaylé,* interject. p. 166.

သရွေ့ *thărwḙ,* abbr. p. 24. use; p. 63.

သံခေါင် *thănkhoung,* "midnight; p. 173.

သံတောင် *thăntoung,* measure of distance; p. 168.

သာ *tha,* num. aux. p. 123. miscell. aff. p. 161.

သာ၍ *tharwḙ,* aux. adjunct. for compar. p. 82. may be omitted; p. 84.

သား *tha:,* format. aff. for comp. subst. p. 38.

သိ *thie,* mod. aff. imperat. p. 137. euph. aff. p. 163.

သိတင်း *thiedĕng,* analysed; p. xi.

သိတင်းနေ့ *thiedĕngnḙ,* "Sabbath;" p. 174.

သိဟ် *thien,* "Leo;" p. 175.

သီး *thee:,* format. aff. for comp. subst. p. 40.

သု *thŏŏ,* pron. adj. p. 69.

သုံး *thŏŏn,* numeral, meaning explained; p. 89.

သူ *thōō,* format. pref. for comp. subst. p. 41. pers. pron. p. 69.

သေသည် *théthee,* abbr. p. 24.

သေး *thé;,* miscell. aff. p. 159.

သေးသေးတင် *thé;thé;tĕng,* nasal mark; p. 14.

သော *thău,* connect. aff. nature of expl. p. xviii. abbr. p. 23. connect aff. pp. 65 and 156. may be used with pron. adj. pp. 69 and 70. relat. increm. p. 78. use in form. adject. p. 79. particip. term. p. 143.

သောကြာ *thoukra.* "Friday, Venus;" p. 175.

သောရိ *thăurie,* "Saturn;" p. 175.

သော် *thău,* abbr. p. 24.

သော်လည် *thăulee,* miscell. aff. p. 159.

သိုး *thō;,* deriv. given; p. xix. aff. masc. gend. p. 43. "the Goat;" p. 175.

သို့ *thọ,* true meaning of; p. 36. caus. aff. p. 47. referred to; p. xxiii. pron. adj. p. 72. and comp. p. 75.

သို့မဟုတ် *thọmăhōh,* conjunct. p. 165.

သွယ် *thway,* gen. aff. p. 111.

သွား *thwa;,* "to go;" part. conjugat. p. 131.

သွေသောက် *thwéthouk,* how abb. p. 24.

သျ *thya,* how pronounced; p. 13.

ဟ *hă.*

ဟ *hă,* consonant; p. 1. its class; p. 6. power; p. 13. symb. when a vowel, and with what letters so combined p. 15. pres. over. by Venus; p. 25. equiv. in *d. g.* syst. p. 28. use of as aspirate in form. of act. verbs; p. 127.

ဟင်းသာအလေ *hĕng;tha ălé,* name of weight; p. 171.

ဟန် *hăn,* miscell. aff. p. 160.

ဟု *hŏŏ,* connect. aff. p. 156. used in Infinit. mood; p. 141.

ဟူ *hōō,* connect. aff. p. 157.

ဟဲ *hai,* interject. p. 166.

ဟောက် *houk,* dem. pron. p. 70.

ဟို *hō,* dem. pron. p. 70. and comp. p. 77.

ဠ *llă.*

ဠ *llă,* consonant; p. 1. class; p. 6. name; p. 7. power; p. 14. presided over by Mercury; p. 25.

ENGLISH INDEX.

A.

Abbreviations, list of; p. 23. of names of measures of distance; p. 169. of weight; p. 170. of capacity; p. 172.

Ablative, affixes used for nominat. p. 45. other uses of; p. 54 et seq.

"About," a quantity, how expr. pp. 121 and 122.

"About to," (future) how expr. p. 143.

Accents, nature of expl. p. xxxiii. applicat. of given; p. 20.

"Accidentally," aux. verb. aff. p. 154.

"According to," how expr. pp. 48, 62 and 64.

"Account" on this, how expr. p. 73.

"Account of" on, miscell. aff. p. 159.

"Accustomed to," aux. verb. aff. pp. 153 and 154.

"Across," how expr. p. 64.

Action, aux. adjuncts of; p. 128.

Active, formed from neuter; p. 127.

Adjectives, how formed; p. 79. nature of analysed; pp. xvii. and xxiv.

Adverbial form of root, expresses "quality;" p. 81. also superlat. degree; p. 87.

Adverbs, p. 163.

"Afar," how expressed; p. 60.

Affixes, classes of expl. p. 29. *Vide* causal, modal, temporal, numeral, generic, connective, verbal, assertive, auxiliary, miscellaneous, indefinite, euphonic, expletive.

"Afternoon," how expr. p. 173.

"Again," how expr. p. 118. item aux. verb. aff. p. 153.

"All," used with words of time; p. 63.

"All together," how expr. p. 117.

Allusion, point of, how shewn; p. 45.

"Almost," miscell. aff. p. 160.

Alphabet, Burman; p. 1. final remarks on; p. 21.

"Also," how expr. p. 165.

"Among," (locative) how expr. pp. 53 and 54.

"And," how expr. pp. 51 and 165.

"Anna," coin how expr. in Burmese; pp. 170. item, two and four anna pieces; p. 171.

"Another," pron. adj. p. 72. analytically referred to; p. xiii.

"Another's," how expr. p. 69.

"Anterior," how expr. p. 58.

"Apart," how expr. p. 117.

"APRIL;" p. 175.

"AQUARIUS;" p. 176.

"ARIES;" p. 175.

"Around," how expr. p. 63.

"Arrive at, obtain," idiomat. use of; p. 64.

Articles; p. xviii.

"As," miscell. aff. pp. 159 and 161.

"As far as," how expr. p. 62.

"Aside," how expr. p. 77.

"As much as," idiomat. use of; p. 63.

Aspiration, of initial letter forms active; p. 127.

Assertive affix (of time), necessary to complete meaning; p. 133. sometimes aux. p. 133 and 134.

"As to," expr. by locat. aff. p. 54.

"At," how expr. in ref. to time; pp. 46 and 53. locative; p. 53.

"AUGUST;" p. 175.

Auxiliaries, numeral; p. 119.
Auxiliary adjunct, of active verbs; p. 128. of passive ditto; pp. 128 and 129. affixes, list of; p. 153.

B.

"Because," how expr. p. 50. miscell. aff. p. 160.
"Before," how expr. (time); p. 64. (negative); p. 150.
"Begin to," aux. verb. aff. p. 155. idiomat. use of in connect. with negat. p. 151.
"Beginning," expr. p. 59.
"Besides," expr. p. 165.
"Beyond," how expr. p. 86.
BOODHISM, its tenets alluded to; pp. x., xlviii. and 89.
"Bow," Zodaic. sign; p. 176.
"BULL," Zodaic. sign; p. 175.
Burmese Language, analysed; *Introduct. passim.* written from left to right; p. 1. derived from original roots; p. 29.
"Business, affair," idiomat. use of; p. 64.
"But," rendered; pp. 76 and 165.
"By," rendered; p. 49.
"By means of," past in signif. p. xxiii. how expr. pp. 50 and 52.

C.

"Can," potent. mood, how expr. p. 140.
"CANCER;" p. 175.
"Capacity," measures of; p. 171.
"CAPRICORNUS;" p. 176.
Cases, of nouns, how expr. p. 43 et seq.
Causal affixes; term expl. p. 29. list of; p. 43 et seq. compound; p. 57. when employed with connect. aff. p. 65. express "time;" pp. xx. et seq. 144.
"Cause" to, forms act. voice; p. 127. item aux. verb. aff. p. 154.
"Certainly," miscell. pref. p. 162.
Classes, of vowels; p. 3. of consonants; pp. 5, 6.
"Collect" to, idiomat. use of, with numerals; p. 116.
Comparative, degree how expr. p. 82. idiomat. use of with verbs; p. 85.
Comparison, peculiarity concerning degrees of; p. xxv. inferior deg. of expr. p. 83. how negatived; p. 84. similar deg. of; p. 84.
Conjunctions; p. 165.
Connective aff. term expl. p. 31. when used with caus. aff. p. 65. use as relat. increm. p. 78. use with adjectives; p. 79. list of; p. 156.
"Consistent with," how expr. p. 64.
Consonants, the number of in the Burm. Lang. p. 1. name and class; p. 6. pronunc. p. 8. double; p. 15. mute conson. p. 14.
"Contiguity," how expr. p. 59.
Continued or customary action, how expr. p. 155.
"Continues to," aux. verb. aff. pp. 153 and 154.
Contrast, how marked; p. 45.
"Courses," of the Sun; p. 177.
"CRAB," Zodaic. sign; p. 175.
"Cubit," two kinds of; p. 168.

D.

"Dare to," aux. verb. aff. p. 153.
Dates, in correspondence, how expr. in Burmese; p. 174.
Dative case, objective used for it; p. 46.
"Dear!" exclam. p. 166.
Decades, of rational beings how expr. p. 98. peculiarity in compounding with noun; p. 100.
"DECEMBER; p. 176.
Dentals; p. 6.
Derivative nouns, how formed; p. 32.
"Difference," expr. p. 118.
"Difficulty," aux. verb. aff. p. 154.
"Direction of," how expr. p. 47.
Disconnective, expr. by ablative; p. 54.
"Dislike to," aux. verb. aff. p. 153.
"Distance," expr. p. 60. tables of measures of; p. 167.
"Down," how expr. p. 61.
"During," expr. by locat. aff. p. 53. item p. 63.

E.

"Each," expr. p. 123.

"Easily," aux. verb. aff. p. 154.
"Elsewhere;" p. 77.
Emphasis, how expr. p. 45. item by miscell. aff. p. 161.
"End of," to the, expr. p. 61.
Era of, Burmah; p. 177.
"Et cetera," how expr. p. 56.
Ethics of Boodhism refer. to; p. xlviii.
"Even, like" to be, expr. p. 62. emphat. miscell. aff. p. 158.
Euphonic, } aff. list of; p. 162.
Expletive, }

F.

"February;" p. 176.
Feminine, v. gender.
"First of" from, miscell. aff. p. 158.
"Fish," Zodaic. sign; p. 176.
"Fit," suitable, consistent; p. 64.
"Fit to," aux. verb. aff. p. 154.
"Five," number refer. to; pp. x. and 89.
"Fold," in connection with numbers, how expr. p. 121.
"For," dative; pp. 49 and 57
"Former," how expr. p. 64.
Fractions, how expr. p. 120.
"Friday;" p. 175.
"From," past in signif. p. xxi. expr. by an idiom; p. 51. ablat. case; pp. 54 and 56. use in connect. with "to;" p. 55.
Future tense, how rend. p. 134. has supposit. mean. p. 135. forms an imperat. p. 137. reason of doing so; p. xxxi. expresses Infinit. Mood; p. 141.

G.

"Gemini," Zodaic. sign; p. 175.
Gender; p. xix. of nouns; pp. 42 and 43.
Generic affixes, term expl. p. 31. list of; p. 102. must be used in interrogation; p. 114.
Genitive of verbals, objective used for; p. 47
"Go," verb, conjugated; p. 131.
"Goat," Zodaic. sign; p. 175.
Gutturals; p. 6.

H.

"Half," how expr. p. 97. num. aux. p. 121.
"He," pers. pron. p. 69.
"Hence," expr. p. 73.
"Here and there," expr. p. 116.
"Hey!" exclam. p. 166.
"Holloa!" exclam. p. 166.
Homonyms, list of; p. xlv. et seq.
Honorific increment; p. 65. attach. to root of comp. caus. aff. p. 66. with verbs, forms honorific mood; p. 145.
"Hour," how expr. p. 173.
"How?" expr. p. 74.
"How many," expr. p. 71.

I.

"I," pers. pron. pp. 66 and 67.
"January;" p. 176.
"If so," expr. p. 74.
Imperative mood, future in signif. p. xxxi. aff. of; p. 137. dispenses with assert. aff. p. 133.
"In," present in signif. p. xxi. (locative); pp. 52 and 53. (in ref. to *time*,) p. 53.
"In order to," future in signif. p. xxi. (dative); p. 49.
"In reference to," expr. by locat. aff. p. 54.
"Indeed," miscell. aff. p. 158.
Indefinite time, aff. of; p. 135.
Indicative mood, present in signif. p. xxxi. aff. of; p. 136.
"Inferior," how expr. p. 61.
Infinitive mood, future in signif. pp. xxi. xxii. root by itself expr. p. 125. other mode of expr. pp. 125 and 141.
Inherent vowel, v. Vowel.
Initial letter aspirated, forms act. voice; p. 127.
Injunction, how expr. pp. 138 and 152.
Instrumental, nominat. used for; p. 44. affix. pp. 50 and 52.
"Into," analysed; p. 57.
"Interior;" p. 60.
Intercalated, what months so; p. 176.
Interrogative mood, aff. of; p. 147.
"It," pers. pron. p. 69.
"Item by item," expr. p. 116.
"July;" } p. 175.
"June;" }

" Just, and no more," miscell. aff. p. 160.
" JUPITER," Burman name for, refer. to, and meaning of Pali name given; p. xxxviii. presides over certain letters; p. 25. over day of week; p. 175.

L.

Labials; p. 6.
" Law" sacred, ref. to pp. xi. and 90.
" Length," v. Distance.
" LEO;" p. 175.
" Less than," num. aux. p. 122.
" Lest," miscell. aff. p. 159.
Letters, numb. of, in Burmese; p. 1.
" LIBRA;" p. 175.
" Like, like as;" pp. 56 and 62. miscell. aff. p. 160. " little like;" miscell. aff. p. 160.
" Likely to," aux. verb. aff. p. 155.
Linguals, p. 6.
" LION," Zodaic. sign; p. 175.
" Lower," expr. p. 61.

M.

" MALE, and FEMALE" Zodaic. sign; p. 175.
" MARCH;" p. 176.
" MARS," presides over certain letters; p. 24. over day of week; p. 174.
Masculine, v. Gender.
" May," subj. mood, how expr. p. 140. in connect. with " that;" p. 142.
" MAY," month of; p. 175.
Measures nouns implying, peculiarity, concerning; pp. 88 and 102. tables of; p. 167.
" MERCURY," presides over certain letters; p. 25. over day of week; p. 174.
" Merely," expr. p. 118.
" Midnight," expr. p. 173.
" Midst," how expr. p. 59.
Miscellaneous Affixes; p. 157.
Modal aff. term expl. p. 30. v. Indicative, Imperative, Precative, Subjunctive, Potential, Optative, Infinitive, Honorific, Interrogative, Negative.
" MONDAY;" p. 174.
" MOON," presides over certain letters; p. 24. over day of week; p. 174. " waning and waxing;" pp. 173, 174.
" More than," num. aux. p. 122. miscell. aff. p. 159.
" More," aux. verb. aff. p. 154.
Multiplicand, Multiplier, } how formed; pp. 119, 120.
" Must," how expr. p. 136.
Mute consonant; p. 14.
Mutuality, how rendered; p. 47.

N.

Nasals; p. 7.
" Near," expr. pp. 59 and 60.
" Nearly," miscell. aff. p. 160.
" Necessarily," miscell. aff. p. 158.
Negative mood, sometimes dispenses with assert. aff. p. 133. aff. of; p. 149.
" Never;" with noun; p. 78. with verbs; p. 151.
" Nevertheless," rend. p. 76.
" Nine," numb. ref. to; p. 89.
Nominative how expr. p. 44.
" None," idiomat. rendered in Burmese; p. 77.
" Noon," how rend. p. 173.
" Not," v. Negative mood.
" Not at all," miscell. pref. p. 162.
" Nothing but," rend. p. 118. miscell. aff. p. 158.
" Nothing more than," miscell. aff. p. 161.
" Notwithstanding," p. 76. miscell. aff. pp. 158 and 159.
Nouns, divisions of; p. 31.
" NOVEMBER;" p. 175.
" Now and then," rend. p. 116.
Number; p. xviii. of nouns; p. 41. of verbs; pp. 130 and 131.
Numeral affix, term expl. p. 30. system of Burmese; p. 89 et seq.
Numerals; p. xxv. mode of compound, with noun; p. 98.
Numerical, mode of writing; pp. 25 and 28.

O.

Objective case, expr. p. 46.
"Obtain, arrive at," idiomat. use of p. 64. expresses "must," p. 136. use as mod. aff. Indicat. p. 137. aux. verb. aff. p. 153.
"OCTOBER;" p. 175.
"Of," how expr. (ablative); pp. 46 and 49. (possessive,); p. 48.
"Oh!" interject. p. 166.
"On," in ref. to time pp. 52 and 53. (locat.) comp. caus. aff. p. 58.
"On account of," expr. by instrument. aff. pp. 50. 52.
"On, and up to," (time); p. 63.
"One," comb. with var. roots; p. 114.
"One and half;" p. 98.
"One, and the same;" p. 123.
"One, and three quarters;" p. 98.
"One's own," expr. p. 70.
"Only," expr. p. 118. num. aux. p. 123. miscell. aff. pp. 158 and 161.
Optative mood, aff. of; p. 141.
"Or," expr. p. 73. conjunct. p. 165.
"Or else," conjunct. p. 165.
Ordinals how formed; pp. xxx and 119.
Original nouns; p. 31.
Orthography; p. 177.
"Other" an, p. 72. the "other;" pp. 72 and 114.
"Otherwise," rend. p. 73.
"Out of," expr. p. 54.
"Outer," expr. p. 59.
"Over to" (locative); p. 53.

P.

Palatals; p. 6.
Particularising; how rend. pp. 46 and 54.
Participles, their affixes; p. 143. aff. of their time; p. 144.
Passive voice, how formed; p. 129. aux. adjunct of; p. 128 and 129.
Permutation, of triphthong; p. 3. of inherent vowel; p. 4. item; p. 17 and 19. of vowel, ăŭ; p. 5. of final consonants; pp. 8, 9, 10, 11 and 17. of certain consonants; p. 16.
Persistive, miscell. aff. p. 160.
"Pice," coin how expr. in Burmese; p. 170.
"PISCES;" p. 176.
Planets, preside over the Alphabet; p. 24. over days of week; p. 174, 115.
Plural, idiom of double; pp. 34, 37, and 81. Vide also number. indef. plur. p. 41.
Possessive case; p. 48. locative aff. used for it; p. 53. forms pron. adj. p. 69. forms adject. pp. xviii and 79.
"Posterior to," how expr. p. 59.
Potential mood, its aff. p. 140.
"Power to," aux. verb. aff. p. 155.
"Presence," expr. p. 60.
"Probably," miscell. aff. p. 160.
Pronouns; p. xxiii. pron. subst. p. 66. pron. adj. p. 69. demonstr. and interrog. p. 70. et seq.
"Proportion to," expr. p. 48.
Punctuation; p. 21.
"Purpose of," miscell. aff. p. 160.

Q.

"Quarter" of a number expr. p. 97. of a quantity, num. aux. p. 121.

R.

Rational beings, decades of, how expr. p. 98.
"Ready to," aux. verb. aff. p. 154.
"Reciprocate," aux. verb. aff. p. 155.
"Regret," miscell. aff. p. 157.
Relative, how rend. p. 78.
"Remain," aux. verb. aff. p. 153.
"Repeatedly," expr. p. 118.
"Right," or "authority to," aux. verb. aff. 155.
"Roots," of the lang. what they expr. p. xiii. verbal, some relations of, expr. by other roots; p. 125. pecul. comb pp. 125 and 126. of two descript. p. 126. by themselves, imperative; p. 137. comp. how negat. p. 151.
"Royal cubit," p. 168.

S.

"SABBATH;" p. 174.
"SAGITTARIUS;" p. 176.
"Sake of;" miscell. aff. p. 161.

" Same as," expr. p. 117.
" Saturday;" p. 175.
" Saturn," pres. over certain letters; p. 24. over day of week; p. 175.
" Scales," Zodaic. sign; p. 175.
" Scorpio;" p. 175.
" Scorpion," Zodaic. sign; p. 175.
" Sea Monster," Zodaic sign; p. 176.
" Seasons," the three; p. 176.
" Self," pron. p. 67.
" September;" p. 175.
" She," pers. pron. p. 69.
" Side," expr. p. 60.
" Similar to;" p. 51.
" Similarity," expr. in kind; p. 117. in amount; p. 118.
Singular, v. Number.
" Single one," expr. p. 115.
" So," expr. p. 48.
" So, and so," expr. p. 77.
" So forth," expr. p. 56.
" So much," expr. p. 77.
" Sorrow," miscell. aff. p. 158.
" Still," miscell. aff. p. 159.
Subjunctive mood, aff. of; p. 138.
Substantive, v. Nouns. comp. subst. p. 37 et seq. subst. with two adject. p. 81. subst. form sometimes superlat. p. 88. subst. verb, v. verb.
" Such," pron. dem. p. 72.
" Such as," pron. dem. p. 72.
" Suitable," expr. p. 64.
" Sun," pres. over a letter; p. 25. over day of week; p. 174.
" Sunday;" p. 174.
" Sunrise" } p. 172.
" Sunset" } p. 172.
Superlative deg. aff of; p. 86.
Supposition, expr. pp. 135 and 139.
" Surprise," miscell. aff. p. 157.
Symbols of vowels; p. 2. 2nd symb. of 2nd vowel; p. 3. of vocal consonants; p. 15.
Symbolic, character of Burmese lang. *Introd. pass.*

T.

" Taurus," ref. to p. xxxviii. item. p. 175.
Temporal aff. term expl. p. 30. list of; p. 134.
" That," dem. pron. p. 70.
" There," var. deg. of, expr. p. 77.
" Therefore," expr. pp. 75 and 76.
" This," dem. pron. p. 70.
" Thou," pers. pron. p. 68.
" Though," miscell. aff. pp. 158, 159 and 161.
" Three," numb. ref. to; p. 89.
" Throughout," expr. p. 61.
" Thursday," p. 175.
" Thus," var. expr. pp. 36, 48, 72, 73 and 75.
" *Tickal*" name of weight; p. 170.
" Times," in connect. with numb. v. Multiplier.
" To, towards," fut. in signif. p. xxi and xxii. how expr. p. 47. dative; p. 48.
" To wit," expr. p. 75. connect. p. 156.
" Together" all, p. 117. in ref. to " time;" p. 118.
" Together with," p. 51.
" Triad," Boodhist, ref. to; p. 89.
Triphthong; p. 3.
" Try to," aux. verb. aff. p. 154.
" Tuesday;" p. 174.

U.

" Under," how expr. p. 58.
Units, peculiarity concern. in comp. with noun; p. 99.
" Unmerciful;" aux. verb. aff. p. 155.
" Until," expr. p. 62.
" Unto," (locat.) p. 53 and 64.
" Up to" expr. p. 64.
" Upper;" expr. pp. 58 and 61.

V.

" Venus," pres. over certain letters; p. 25. over day of week; p. 175.
Verb, substantive, how qualified; p. 81.
Verbal affixes; p. 133. aux. two kinds of; p. 138.
Verbs; pp. xxxi and 125.
" Virgin," Zodaic. Sign; p. 175.
" Virgo;" p. 175.

" *Viss*" name of weight; p. 170.
Vocative, case; p. 57.
Vowel, inherent, has no symbol; p. 2. permut. p. 4. how destroyed; p. 7. 2d. vow. has two symbols; p. 3.
Vowels, numb. of in the Lang. p. 1. how comb. with cons. p. 2. symbols of; p. 2. pronunciation of; pp. 4 and 5.

W.

" Watch," measure of time; p. 173.
" WATERPOT," Zodaic. sign; p. 175.
" We," pers. pron. pp. 66 and 67.
" Wednesday; p. 174.
" Weight," table of measures of; p. 169.
" Well!" exclam p. 166.
" What," interrog. pron. p. 71.
" Whatever," interrog. pron. p. 72.
" Whence?" interrog. p. 74.
" Where, (locat. not interrog.) idiomat. expr. p. 61.
" Where?" interrog. p. 74.
" Wherefore?" interrog. p. 74.
" Wherefore," not interrog. p. 75.
" Wherein?" interrog. p. 74.
" While," miscell. aff. pp. 158 159 and 161.
" Whilst," expr. by locat. aff. p. 54.
" Whoever," pron. p. 72.
" Whole," how expr. pp. 114 and 115. of a quantity; p. 122.
" Why?" interrog. p. 74.
" Why," not interrog. miscell. aff. p. 162.
" Willing to," miscell. aff. p. 159.
" With," pres. in signif. p. xxi. (preposition) expr. p. 50.
" Without," fut. in signif. p. xv. (negat.) p. 150. deficient in; p. 152.
Words, no division between, in Burmese lang. p. 1.
" Worthy to," aux. verb. aff. p. 154.
" Would," optat. mood; p. 141.
Writing numerical mode of; pp. 25 and 28.